SMALL BOAT CERTIFICATION SERIES

# Start Sailing *Right!*

## *The national standard for quality sailing instruction*

Published by the United States Sailing Association  ISBN 1-882502-48-5. Printed in the United States of America.
United States Sailing Association P.O. Box 1260, 15 Maritime Drive, Portsmouth, RI 02871-6015

# Acknowledgments

Sailors are special people. Their love of the sport and their willingness to contribute time and effort for the good of their fellow sailors is unique. That feeling of commitment and purpose was present in virtually everyone who worked on *Start Sailing Right!*

Many people have been involved in the development and refinement of both the original and revised editions of *Start Sailing Right!* Without the vision and support of US SAILING and its past Executive Director Steve Black, his successor John Bonds, and John Malatak, past officer of Health and Safety for the American Red Cross, this book would never have become a reality. They are, in a sense, the founding fathers of *Start Sailing Right!*

Supervising the project from start to finish was Timothea Larr, who also worked with the editor/designer in refining the content and organization of the book. Jim Muldoon provided valuable assistance in the drafting of agreements and contracts between US SAILING and the American Red Cross. Mike Thompson was project coordinator for the US SAILING *Start Sailing Right!* videos. The videos, in consort with the *Start Sailing Right!* textbook and on-the-water instruction with American Red Cross/US SAILING trained instructors, form the most effective learn-to-sail teaching system in the world. The primary editing of the original edition was performed by Ron Dwelle, who worked diligently to refine and polish the text.

The outstanding team of Emmett McNamara Inc., not only produced the award-winning *Start Sailing Right!* videos, but also typeset and illustrated the original print edition.

Finally, many thanks to all the students, instructors, experts and volunteers who have shared their insights and contributed to this new edition, including Mike Espino and his colleagues at the American Red Cross, Rich Brew, Lawrence Baum, Cappy Capper, Steve Colgate, Peter Durant, Tom Fisher, Guy Fleming, David Forbes, Kim Hapgood, John Kantor, Jean Kryshak, Ginny Long, Jo Mogle, Ray Treppa, Susie Trotman, Erik Twining and Walter Wheeler.

**Mark Smith**, *Editor / Designer*
A lifelong sailor, graphic designer, editor and illustrator, Mark currently works as Creative Director for North Sails as well as on independent publishing projects. Mark was editorial and art director for *Yacht Racing / Cruising* magazine (now *Sailing World*) from 1970 - 83, editor and publisher of *Sailor* Magazine from 1984 - 86, and editor and art director of *American Sailor* from 1987 - 89. His works include design and illustration for the *Annapolis Book of Seamanship*, authored by John Rousmaniere and published by Simon and Schuster. Mark lives in Rowayton, CT with his wife Tina and daughters Stephanie, Natalie and Cristina.

**Derrick Fries, Ph.D.**, *Writer*
Derrick Fries is a regular contributor to national sailing magazines and has written two books on singlehanded racing. A two-time collegiate All-American at Michigan State, he has won six world titles and 14 national titles in small boat racing. He is currently the Level One Master Instructor Trainer for US SAILING, and was a finalist for the NASA Teacher-in-Space competition. He obtained his doctorate in Educational Administration from the University of Michigan in 1993, and currently is the principal of Avondale Middle School in Rochester Hills, MI. Derrick currently resides in Clarkston, MI with his wife Katherine and son Drew.

**Burton S. Bilbrey**, *Principal Illustrator / Cartoonist*
Burt has been an automotive and marine technical illustrator for 18 years, and is currently manager of corporate and retail identity at Kmart. He lives in Eastpointe, MI with his wife Yot Mun and daughter Jasmine.

*Cover photos:* lower left: Chuck Place, upper left: Billy Black, lower right: Maria Veghte (courtesy Hobie Cat), upper right: Onne Van Der Wal.

# Foreword *by Gary Jobson*

The great thing about sailing is that there is something in it for everyone of any age. Whether it is competing for the America's Cup or just day sailing on an inland lake, the common denominator is simple — *having fun.*

Over the past few years, thanks to my television involvement with ESPN and hundreds of lectures throughout the country, I have sensed a tremendous surge of enthusiasm for our sport. Leisure time is a precious commodity in today's busy world, and sailing is a reward many people seek.

*Start Sailing Right!* is a fantastic primer for anyone with an urge to get out on the water — and a reference guide for a lifetime. It offers one practical, usable tip after another and the profuse use of large, clear diagrams and humorous illustrations makes sailing quickly understandable and puts the new sailor at ease. But sailing can also be a challenging sport. A good sailor is always aware of changing wind and weather, and develops a healthy respect for Mother Nature and the safety of everyone on board. It's called seamanship, and it's a message that comes through loud and clear in this book.

*Start Sailing Right!* goes a long way toward giving sailors a faster start, and a chance to be better, safer sailors than ever before.

Gary Jobson

*"Frank, why don't you just break down and take some lessons?"*

The UNITED STATES SAILING ASSOCIATION (US SAILING) is our country's governing body for the sport of sailing. The American Red Cross offers educational courses in many aquatic activities, including swimming and water safety, lifeguarding, and small craft safety. With *Start Sailing Right!*, these organizations have joined together to provide unprecedented support for sailors on all levels of sailing in all kinds of sailboats.

One of the primary objectives of this historic alliance is to provide an effective standard of quality instruction for all students learning to sail. The US SAILING / American Red Cross program includes the *Start Sailing Right!* textbook, a series of video tapes designed to work with the book, a program of student certification and an extensive educational and training program for instructors themselves. It is one of the most highly developed and effective national training systems for students and sailing instructors in the world.

This program is conducted at a professional level to ensure a high degree of continuity and success for its students. Our hope is that you will become not only a successful sailor, but also a safe sailor who knows how to have fun on the water.

This textbook is intended as a supplement to your first sailing lessons, rather than as a substitute for them. It is designed to work well with a wide variety of basic courses offered in different regional sailing communities. It was created to help build your enthusiasm and make your introduction to the fantastic sport of sailing a positive experience that you can carry far into the future.

**Video Links**

*Start Sailing Right!* is designed as part of a learn-to-sail system that includes the award-winning video series *Start Sailing Right!* Throughout this book, the symbol shown here ▶ VIDEO 3 will adjoin select passages, serving as a key to coordinate the video segments with the book for instructors and students.

### Video Tapes

The award-winning *Start Sailing Right!* video tapes are a valuable supplement to the *Start Sailing Right!* textbook. To help them work better together, the book is keyed to the tapes with symbols that correspond to segments in the tapes. Like the book, the *Start Sailing Right!* tapes are intended as support for an on-the-water course with an instructor or as a post-course refresher.

The three-tape instructor / student *Start Sailing Right!* tapes are available from the United States Sailing Association.

### How to Use This Textbook

*Start Sailing Right!* was created to help you become a more confident and accomplished sailor at the end of your learn-to-sail experience. Visualize it as a tool that will accelerate your learning curve and clarify your understanding of the principles of sailing.

Sailing language and terminology have traditionally been emphasized as a first step in sailing instruction. This book places more emphasis on getting on the water quickly and learning sailing skills "by doing." It makes your learning experience more exciting and immediately satisfying. To use the book most effectively, we encourage you to follow these steps:

- Be committed and enthusiastic toward learning how to sail.

- Learn to sail with a qualified sailing instructor.
- Read each chapter thoroughly.
- Examine each of the illustrations. They have been carefully designed to help you visualize concepts and procedures clearly and simply.
- Practice each sailing maneuver onshore and then on-the-water.
- Review each chapter and be sure you understand it before moving on to the next one. ☑ *Quick Reviews* are listed at the end of each chapter for this purpose.

Remember, your own learning rate may be different from other students based on a number of factors, the most important being your commitment to becoming a good sailor. Also remember — a good sailor (even a great one) never stops learning!

### Swimming

To be a safe and accomplished sailor does require one prior skill — swimming. In the interest of safety and confidence, we recommend that everybody acquire this skill before learning to sail. You should be able to swim at least 25 yards unassisted. In addition, you should be able to tread water while fully clothed for at least two minutes without assistance and without the use of a life jacket, and be able to put on an approved life jacket in water that is six feet deep or more. While learning to sail, there will be times when you will have to enter the water to practice various boathandling skills and techniques. Such things as capsize and overboard recovery are an integral part of sailing and require swimming skills by the sailor.

The American Red Cross and local YMCAs and YWCAs offer many excellent swimming courses.

### What Makes Sailing Special?

Within the past 20 years, the advent of new technologies has opened up the sport of sailing to people of all ages, incomes and abilities. Sailing offers virtually limitless choices in boat types and designs, each with its own unique characteristics. This book has been designed to standardize the learn-to-sail process for many different boat types.

Most sailors will acquire entry level skills quite rapidly. However mastering them is an experience that will be rewarding, mentally stimulating and pleasurable for a lifetime.

As you learn to sail, you will find that sailing is more than simply being pushed and pulled by the wind. For most people, sailing is meeting new friends, enjoying nature's beauty and challenge, and sharing a unique fellowship with all boaters. A tremendous camaraderie exists among sailors, particularly on the water, which makes sailing — and the people who do it — very special.

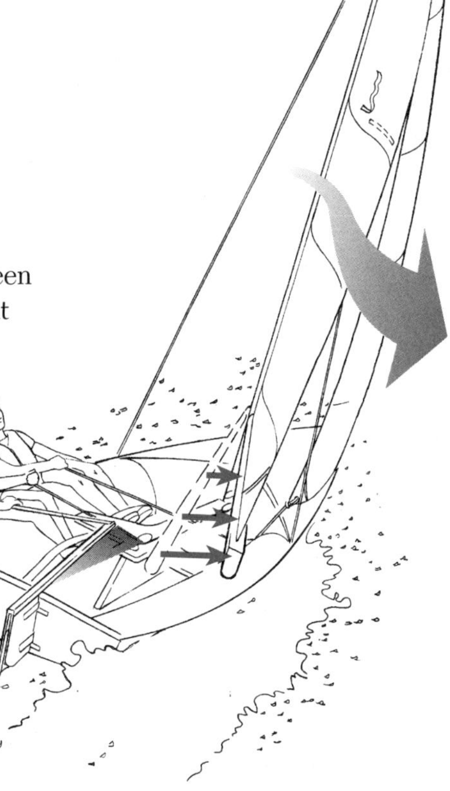

CHAPTER 1

# You as a Sailor

**KEY CONCEPTS**

- Environmental awareness
- Dressing for sailing
- Sun protection
- Physical fitness

Few hobbies offer as much freedom and choice as sailing. You can fly over the waves in a high-performance racing dinghy, unwind in a comfortable, stable daysailer or anything in between. The essential skills are the same, and improving those skills offers a lifetime of enjoyment and accomplishment.

## Environmental Awareness

All sailors get started by developing a sensitivity to the forces of wind and water and how they change. This "environmental awareness" calls for continuous observation of wind, weather, waves, current and distance from shore. By learning to sense these forces and anticipate changes in your surroundings, you will become a self-reliant sailor who can sail confidently in all kinds of conditions. The old racing sailor's axiom, *"Keep your head out of the boat!"* is good advice for all sailors.

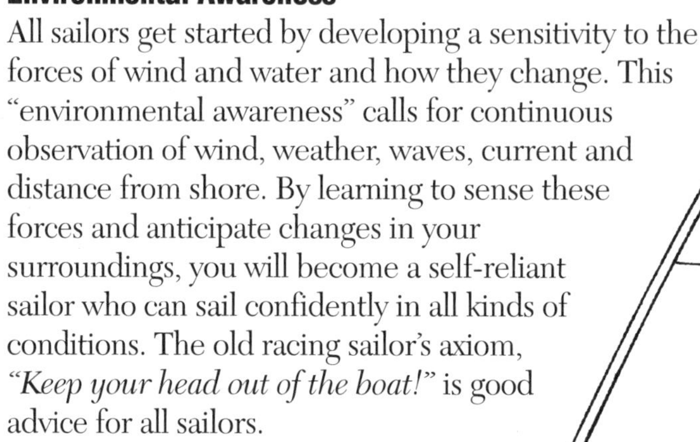

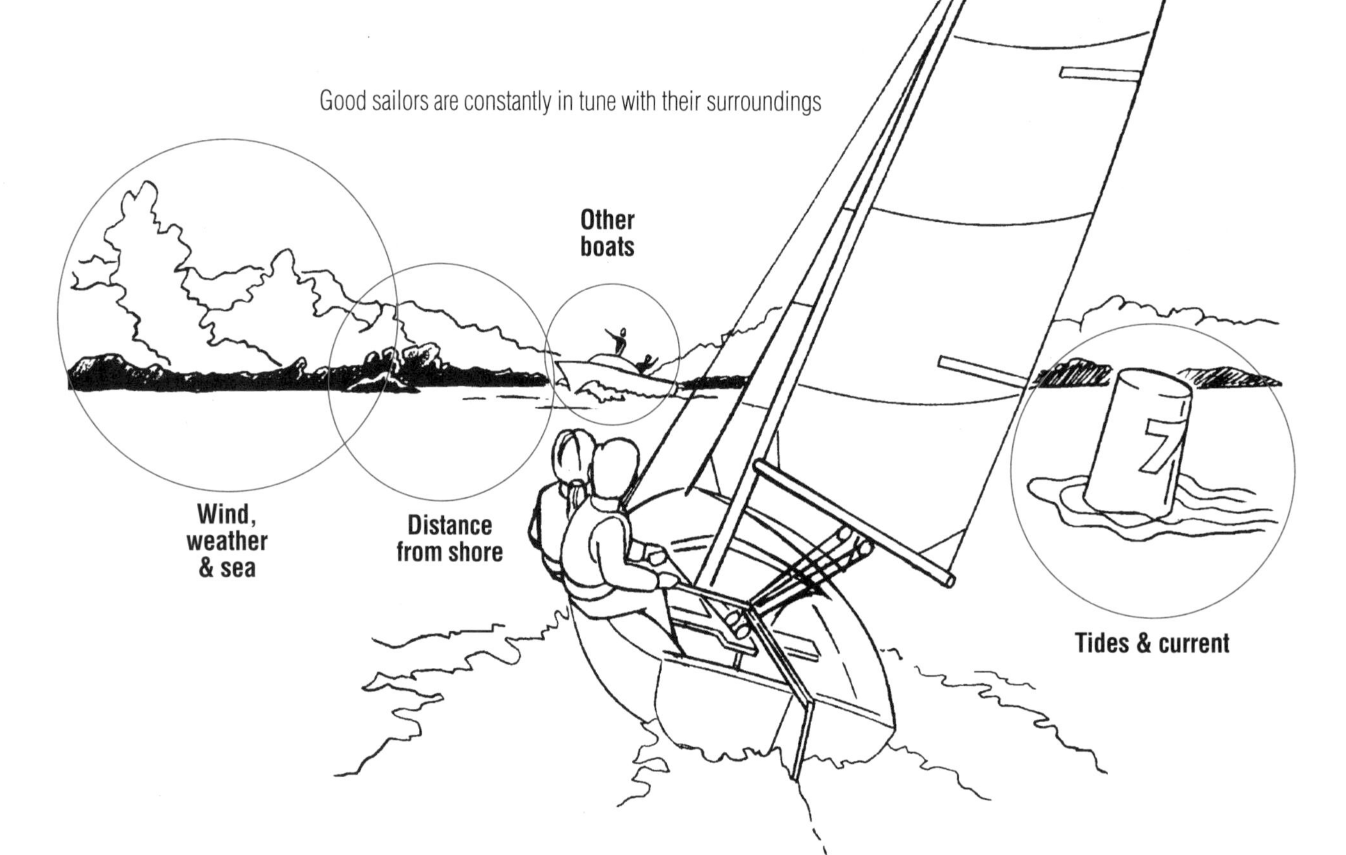


Good sailors are constantly in tune with their surroundings

## Dressing for Sailing VIDEO 1

Temperatures on the water tend to be more extreme and more changeable than ashore, so the right gear and clothing are an important part of enjoying the sport and staying comfortable. You don't need to spend a fortune on equipment, but here are a few simple guidelines for basic preparation...

- **Wear loose clothing.** Boathandling requires a lot of movement, so wear clothes that allow a full range of motion.
- **Bring extra clothing in a duffle bag** so you can add layers for warmth or change into dry clothing if you get wet.
- **On warm days, wear light, breathable clothing,** preferably in lighter colors (they're cooler). A collared shirt helps protect the back of your neck. Long sleeves will protect your arms.
- **Use sunscreen** (SPF 15 or higher) to protect skin, even on cloudy days, and reapply it frequently.
- **Wear a hat** to shield your eyes and keep sun off your head. On cool days, it minimizes heat loss through your head.
- **Wear sunglasses** with good UV (at least 90%) protection. Polarized models are great for reducing glare off the water. Wear a cord around your neck to keep them from falling overboard.
- **Nonskid shoes are a must** for traction on wet or slanted decks. Tennis shoes are OK if the tread is not worn, but boat shoes are best. Their soles are designed for wet traction and the body dries quickly. Avoid sandals or other open-toed shoes — sooner or later you'll kick something!

### *Warm Weather Checklist*

- ☐ Hat with visor
- ☐ Sunglasses with neck cord
- ☐ Lightweight, light-colored shirt
- ☐ Life jacket
- ☐ Duffle bag (see below)
- ☐ Loose fitting clothing for easy movement
- ☐ Rubber soled, non-skid shoes
- ☐ Sunscreen lotion

### *In the duffle...*

- ☐ Sunscreen lotion
- ☐ Sailing gloves
- ☐ Sweater or jacket
- ☐ Foul-weather gear
- ☐ Water bottle

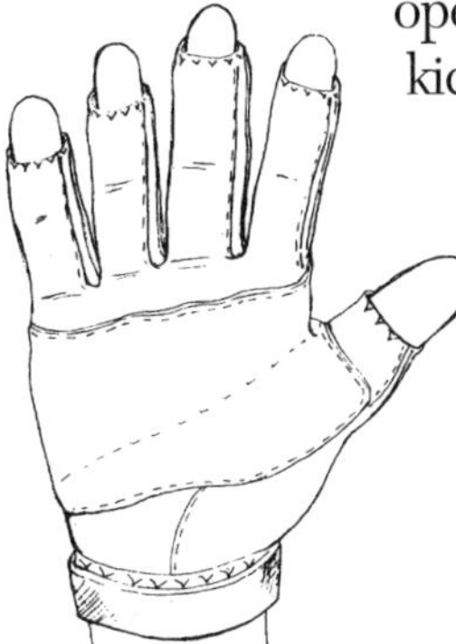

**Sailing gloves** help save tender hands and improve grip. Cutaway fingertips allow dexterity with small pieces of gear.

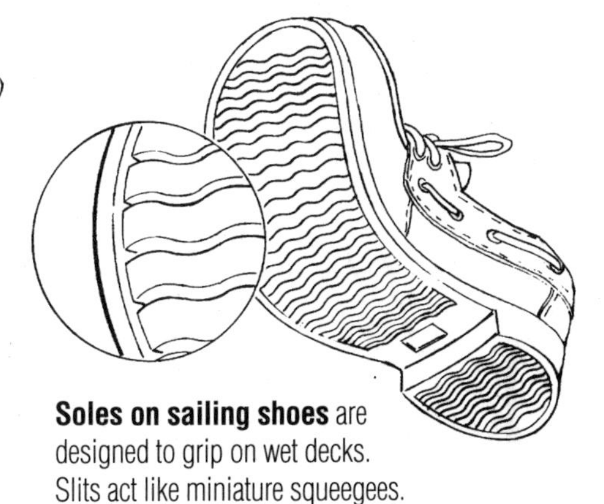

**Soles on sailing shoes** are designed to grip on wet decks. Slits act like miniature squeegees.

- **Waterproof sailing boots** are a blessing in cold weather, keeping your feet warm and dry.
- **Sailing gloves** protect your hands from chafe and improve grip, at least until your hands get toughened up. On cold days, waterproof gloves make a big difference.
- **A life jacket (PFD)** is required equipment in most states. It should fit properly and be Coast Guard approved.
- **On cool days, dress in layers.** Personal performance suffers dramatically when you get cold, so it's smart to overdress in cooler conditions. Avoid cotton fabrics and wear materials that retain warmth when wet, such as wool and polyester fleece.

### *Cold Weather Checklist*

- ☐ Wool cap
- ☐ Layered clothing (undershirt or turtleneck, sweater, jacket)
- ☐ Waterproof outer layer (foul-weather gear) with hood
- ☐ Waterproof sailing boots
- ☐ Waterproof sailing gloves
- ☐ Life jacket
- ☐ Duffle bag

## Foul-Weather Gear

Marine foul-weather gear is designed to keep you warm and dry and is available in several styles.

- Standard two-piece outfits include a waterproof jacket with hood and separate pants with suspenders.
- One-piece models keep you dryer, but don't allow you to remove a top or bottom to suit temperature and weather conditions.
- On particularly wet boats, sailors often wear wet suits similar to those used by skin divers.
- Dry suits are insulated one-piece outfits that are tightly sealed at the neck, wrists and ankles. They provide water protection and warmth.

### *Four Weather Gear Tips...*

- Zippers covered by flaps reduce seepage of wind and spray.
- Sealed seams prevent water leakage.
- Look for pockets with protective flaps and drainage holes.
- Velcro or elastic wrist and ankle closures prevent water from rushing up sleeves and legs.

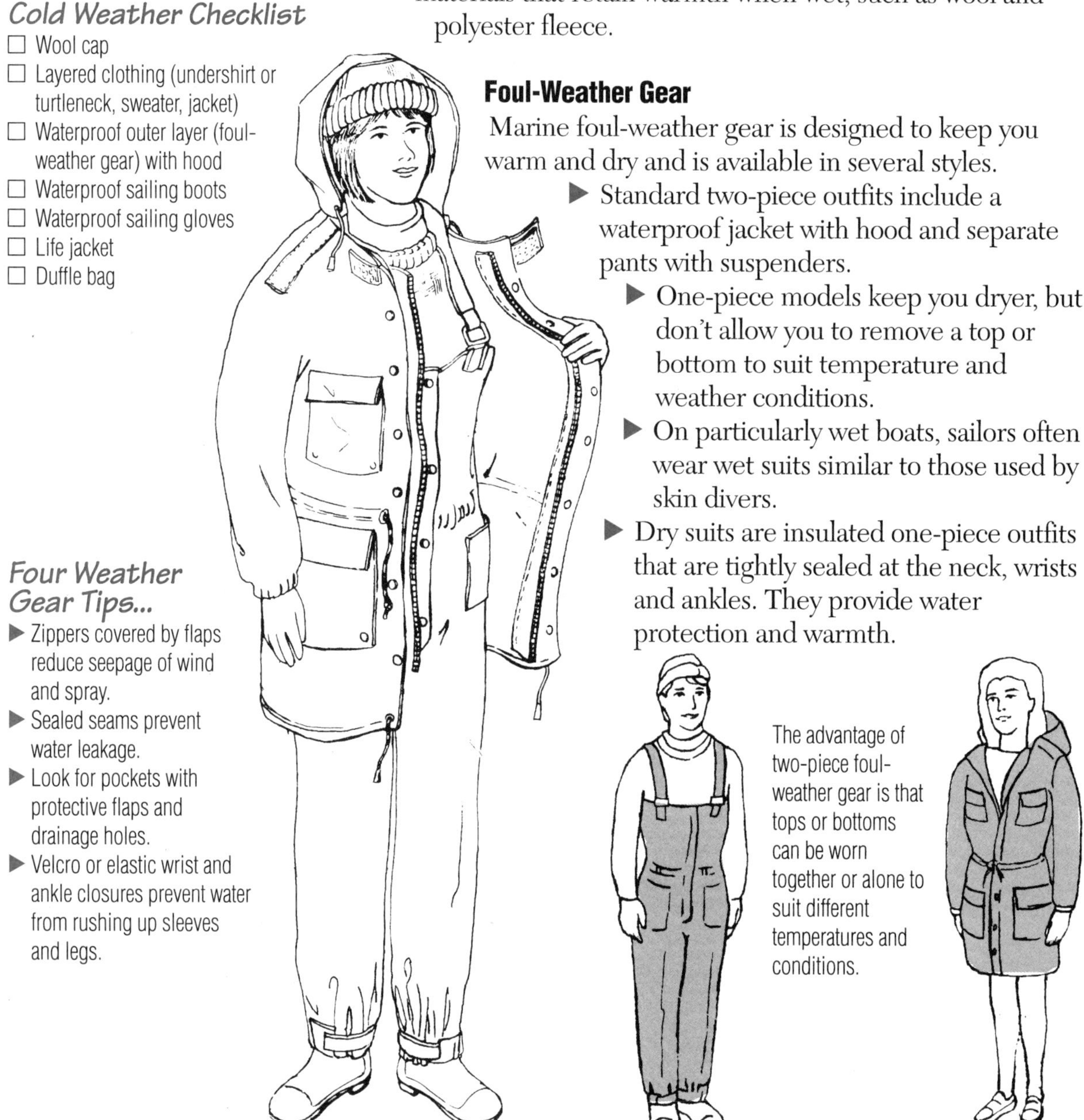

The advantage of two-piece foul-weather gear is that tops or bottoms can be worn together or alone to suit different temperatures and conditions.

## Physical Fitness

Good physical condition will add to your enjoyment of sailing. Trimming sails, hiking out, and adjusting to the constant motion of a boat can tax strength and endurance. The best form of physical preparation for sailing is aerobic (heartbeat) and anaerobic (lifting/pulling) exercise. The exercise program should be tailored to your age, physical condition and should include warm up and cool down periods. Flexibility exercises are also beneficial, as sailing requires movements in many unusual positions. Stretching before and after you sail will help minimize stiffness and discomfort.

A well balanced diet also helps on-the-water performance. Endurance and concentration are directly related to nutritional intake. An active sailor may need more than 3,000 calories a day, so don't leave yourself short on fuel. A good diet will have a balance of protein, carbohydrate, fat, vitamins, minerals, and *lots* of water. Drinking water before *and* during sailing is recommended to avoid dehydration.

### Quick Review

- The sun can "getcha" if you're not protected. Name three key clothing and/or gear items all sailors should wear for adequate protection. *(answer on p.9)*
- Describe the contents of a well-prepared sailor's duffle bag. *(answer on p.9)*
- Describe a smart foul-weather gear outfit for a sailor who will encounter a variety of conditions. *(answer on p.10)*

### Think about it...

- What are some specific environmental considerations that will affect you where you sail?
- What kind of sailing gear might you need for your sailing location and boat type?

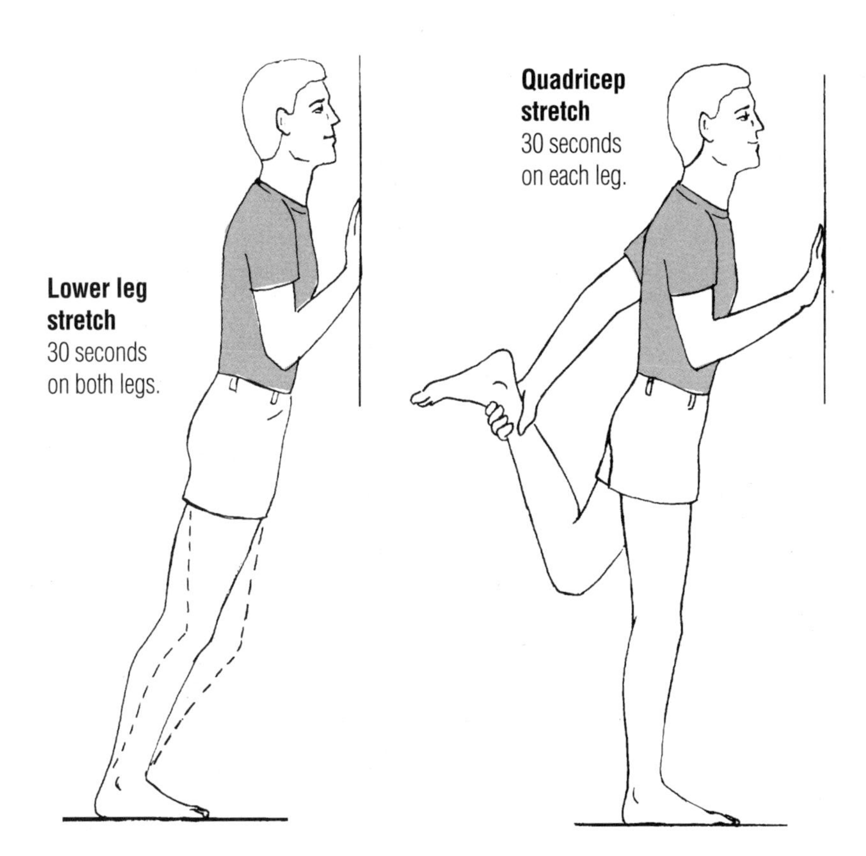


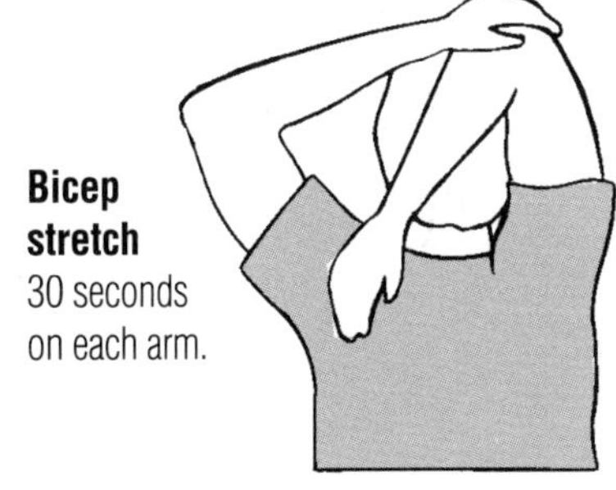


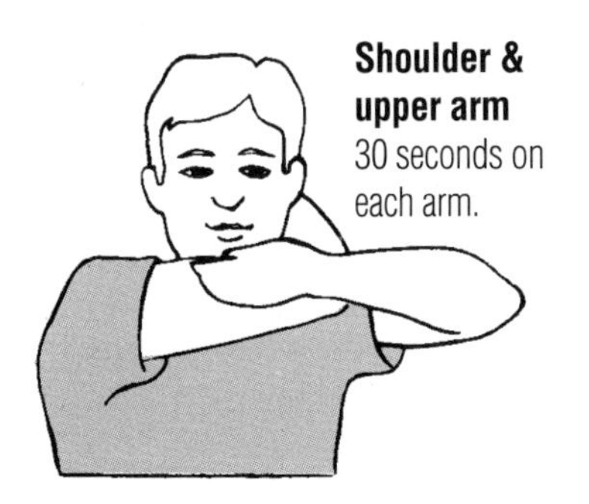


Sailing requires movements in many unusual positions. Stretching before and after you sail will help minimize the stiffness and discomfort that commonly accompanies using new muscle groups.

*NOTE: Do not engage in any of these exercises without consulting with your physician. Some of these exercises could adversely affect students who are not physically fit or have a history of back, shoulder or knee problems.*

# Safety & You

**KEY CONCEPTS**
- Sailor's code
- Life jackets (PFDs)
- Hypothermia
- Heat emergencies
- Electrical hazards
- Safety equipment
- Communication

**Type III PFD** — *Flotation aid*
This comfortable vest-style jacket is the most popular in protected waters. Remember, though, that in rough seas, it may not hold your head above the waves.

The water is not ours alone to enjoy. It is shared by other sailors, recreational powerboaters, fishermen, swimmers, waterskiers and those who earn their living in commercial transport and fishing. It is essential that we treat each other with courtesy, consideration and respect at all times. This attitude is an essential characteristic of any good sailor. Following are some of the basic points of the sailor's code of behavior:

- *Always be in total control of yourself and your boat.*
- *Always come to the aid of a boat in need of help.*
- *Observe swimming and scuba-diving areas, stay clear of fishing lines, and stay clear of commercial channels.*
- *Sailboats usually have right-of-way over powerboats. However, courtesy and safety might dictate that a small sailboat steer clear of a large powerboat in a tight harbor.*

## Life Jackets VIDEO 1

The life jacket, or PFD (Personal Flotation Device), is arguably your most important piece of marine safety equipment. It is smart to wear your PFD *at all times* around the water. After a while, it will become second nature. Be sure your PFD is Coast Guard approved, in good condition, and fits properly so it won't ride up when you're in the water. Yellow and orange are the most visible colors if you fall overboard, especially in waves.

There are five types of flotation devices:

- **Type I** (offshore) — for sailing in offshore waters where rescue could be delayed. Designed to support an *unconscious* person in a face-up tipped back position.
- **Type II** (near-shore) — for inland waters where rescue would likely occur quickly. Designed to support some, not all, *unconscious* people in face-up tipped back position. Less buoyant than Type I vests.
- **Type III** (flotation aids) — for calm inland waters. These vests or "float coats" help keep a *conscious* person in a vertical or slightly tipped back position.
- **Type IV** (throwable devices) — such as a buoyant cushion or a ring buoy can be thrown to a victim in an emergency. These devices do not take the place of wearing a life jacket.
- **Type V** — similar to Type III devices with additional piece for head support. These devices have only a small amount of buoyancy. If more is needed, some can be inflated by blowing into a valve or pulling a cord to activate a compressed air canister.

*Never underestimate the value of your life jacket around the water...it could save your life!*

### Hypothermia and Heat Emergencies VIDEO 1

Cold temperatures and/or cold water can be a threatening combination if you are not dressed properly. Hypothermia occurs when the body is subjected to prolonged cold. The most common cause of hypothermia is cold water, but cold air can also contribute. Heat emergencies can also be life threatening, so take care on hot days. Drink lots of water and integrate swimming activities when the sun is out and the breeze is still.

#### HYPOTHERMIA

**SIGNALS...**

- Shivering
- Impaired judgment
- Dizziness
- Numbness
- Change in level of consciousness
- Weakness
- Glassy stare

(Physical symptoms may vary, since age, body size, and clothing will cause individual differences.)

**TREATMENT...**

Medical assistance should be given to anyone with hypothermia. Until medical assistance arrives, these steps should be taken:

- Check breathing and pulse.
- Gently move the person to a warm place.
- Carefully remove all wet clothing. Gradually warm the person by wrapping in blankets or putting on dry clothes. Do not warm a person too quickly, such as immersing in warm water. Rapid rewarming may cause dangerous heart rhythms. Hot water bottles and chemical heat packs may be used if first wrapped in a towel or blanket before applying.
- Give warm, nonalcoholic and decaffeinated liquids to a conscious person only.

**Type I PFD** — *Offshore life jacket*

#### HEAT EXHAUSTION

**SIGNALS...**

- Cool, moist, pale skin
- Heavy sweating
- Headache
- Dizziness
- Nausea
- Weakness, exhaustion

**TREATMENT...**

Without prompt care, heat exhaustion can advance to a more serious condition — heat stroke. First aid includes:

- Move person to cool environment.
- Remove clothing soaked with perspiration and loosen any tight clothing.
- Apply cool, wet towels or sheets.
- Fan the person.
- Give person half glass (4 oz.) cool water every 15 min.

#### HEAT STROKE

**SIGNALS...**

- Red, hot, dry or moist skin
- Very high skin temperature
- Changes in level of consciousness
- Vomiting
- Rapid, weak pulse
- Rapid, shallow breathing

**TREATMENT...**

Heat stroke is life threatening. Anyone suffering from heat stroke needs to be cooled and an EMS technician should be contacted immediately. To care for heat stroke:

- Move person to cool environment.
- Apply cool, wet towels or sheets.
- If available, place ice or cold packs on the person's wrists and ankles, groin, each armpit, and neck.
- If unconscious, check breathing and pulse.

**Type II PFD** — *Near-shore buoyant vest*

## ELECTRICAL INJURY

- *Never approach a victim of an electrical injury until you are sure the power is turned off.*
- If a power line is down, *wait for the fire department and / or power company.*
- Contact a doctor or EMS (Emergency Medical Services) personnel *immediately.*
- The victim may have breathing difficulties or be in cardiac arrest. Provide care for any life threatening conditions.

### Electrical Hazards—Heads Up For Safety VIDEO 1

One danger often overlooked around sailing facilities is overhead electrical wires. A metal mast on a boat can be a conductor for electricity and cause severe shock or electrocution. When rigging and de-rigging a boat — even when sailing — sailors should check overhead. It is important that you become familiar with your sailing site and identify all electrical hazards. Also be careful when using electrical power tools around the waterfront. Electricity and water can be a dangerous mix. Other areas of danger are power cables that may be strung between docks or from the shore to islands.

Metal masts and their rigging can also act as lightning rods. When electrical storms approach, particularly thunderstorms, head for shore immediately and remove yourself from danger.

### Safety Equipment

Whenever you go sailing, you should make sure that your boat has basic safety equipment on board. The equipment may vary, depending on regional and state requirements, but a basic list usually includes:

- life jackets for everyone on board
- anchor with plenty of extra line
- paddle
- bailing device
- horn
- compass
- tools, such as knife, pliers, screwdriver, and tape
- first aid kit
- supply of water

*Check your equipment often for wear or damage!*

### First Aid for the Sailor

Although accidents seldom happen while sailing, it is always a good idea to be able to help people who may need first aid. Taking American Red Cross courses to learn first aid and CPR (Cardiopulmonary Resuscitation) skills will improve your safety as well as your ability to provide care to anyone who needs it.

*Sailing is a very safe sport.* These safety points may seem like a lot to absorb at first, but with time and experience they will become a natural part of your sailing.

## Communication

The sound of waves, wind, and sails luffing can make communication on the water difficult, particularly with your instructor. In noisy conditions, arm and hand motions — called *hand signals* — are used. The most basic signals are "safety position," "come closer," "slow down," "pull sheet in," "let sheet out," "I need assistance," and "I'm OK."

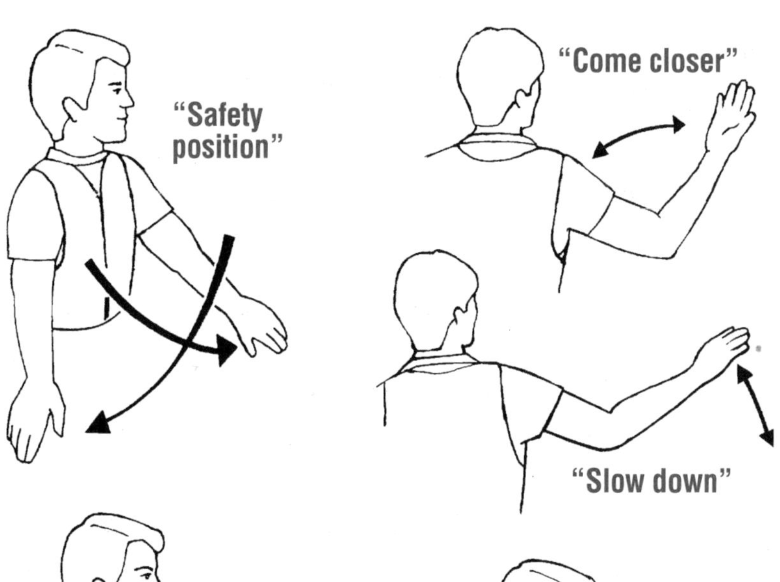

"Sheet in"

▶ TRUE or FALSE — The popular Type III vest-style life jacket provides adequate flotation for all kinds of sailing. *(answer on p.12)*

▶ Describe the early warning signs of hypothermia. *(answer on p.13)*

▶ Describe the early warning signs of heat stroke and heat exhaustion. *(answer on p.13)*

▶ Identify three electrical hazards on the waterfront. *(answer on p.14)*

▶ List the basic safety equipment you should have on a sailboat. *(answer on p.14)*

### Think about it...

▶ What other sailing and marine activities are common in your sailing area and how might they affect your sailing?

# Parts of a Sailboat

**KEY CONCEPTS**
- Monohull
- Multihull
- Centerboard
- Keel
- Rig
- Port & starboard
- Boat and sail parts

Like any sport, sailing has its own language. This new language can seem a little overwhelming at first, but as you use the new terms, they will quickly become familiar. First, let's focus on the different parts of a sailboat.

## Parts of the Hull VIDEO 2

The body of the boat is called the *hull.* There are two types of hulls: *monohulls* and *multihulls.* A monohull has a single hull. A multihull will have either two hulls, called a *catamaran,* or three hulls, called a *trimaran.* Multihulls generally sail faster than monohulls.

The front end of the hull is the *bow,* and is usually pointed. The back end, called the *stern,* is wider and has a flat, vertical surface called the *transom.* Sailboats less than 10 feet long sometimes have a squared-off bow. These are called *prams.* Two popular prams, the Optimist and the Sabot, are often used as learn-to-sail boats for young people.

When a boat floats, it will displace a volume of water equal to the weight of the boat, so the boat's weight is often called its *displacement.* The line where the water meets the hull is called the *waterline,* which is sometimes marked by a stripe.

To prevent being pushed sideways by the wind, most boats have an underwater fin, either a *centerboard,* a *daggerboard,* or a *keel.* A centerboard can be pivoted up and down. Some sailboats have a *daggerboard,* similar to a centerboard but designed to move up

**A monohull** has a single hull.

**A multihull** has either two hulls (a *catamaran* as shown) or three hulls (a *trimaran*).

and down vertically rather than by pivoting. If the centerboard is attached at the side of the boat instead of the center, it is called a *leeboard.*

A keel is fixed underneath the boat, and is different from a centerboard because it also provides *ballast* (weight), which helps keep the boat upright by counteracting the wind pressure on the sails. On a centerboard or daggerboard boat, the weight of the sailors is used as movable ballast to stabilize the boat. Daggerboards, centerboards, and keels all act to prevent the boat from slipping sideways through the water.

The *rudder* is used to steer the boat, and is controlled by a *tiller* and a *tiller extension* which is held by the helmsman (the person steering the boat). To steer, you push or pull the tiller in the opposite direction you want the boat to go.

**A pram** is a small sailboat known for its square, flat bow.

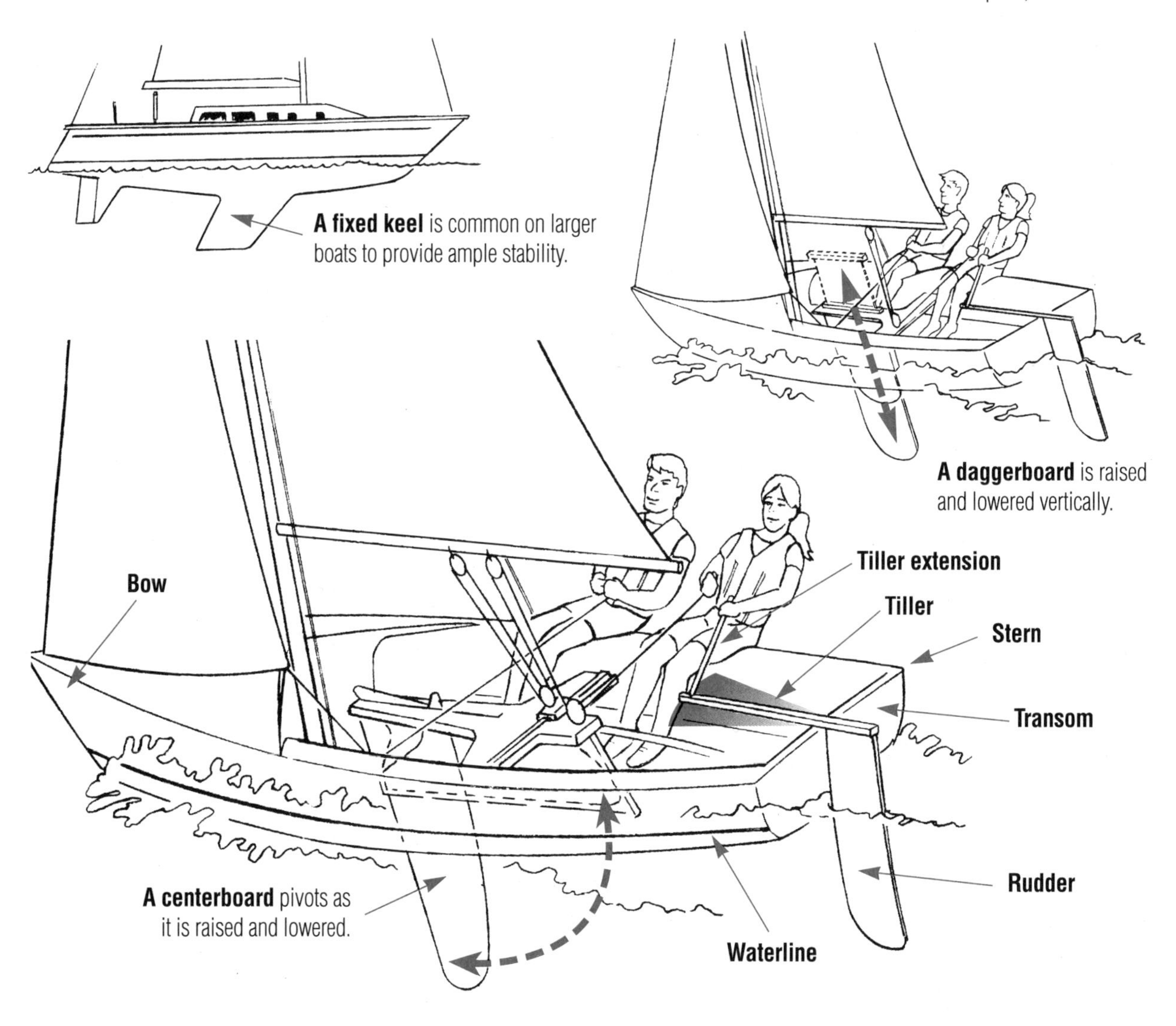


**A fixed keel** is common on larger boats to provide ample stability.

**A daggerboard** is raised and lowered vertically.

**A centerboard** pivots as it is raised and lowered.

## Parts of the Rig VIDEO 2

Above the hull is the *rig*, consisting of *sails*, *mast*, and *rigging*. The mast holds up the sails to the wind. Boats with a single mast have either one sail called a *mainsail*, or two sails, a mainsail and a smaller forward sail, called a *jib*. A boat with only a mainsail is *cat-rigged* (not to be confused with a catamaran). A boat with both a mainsail and jib is called a *sloop*. Typical examples are shown. Other kinds of rigs are shown in the APPENDIX.

The mast on many smaller boats is strong enough to stand upright by itself without additional support. Other boats need supporting wires to keep the mast standing. These supporting wires are called *standing rigging*. The wires connecting the

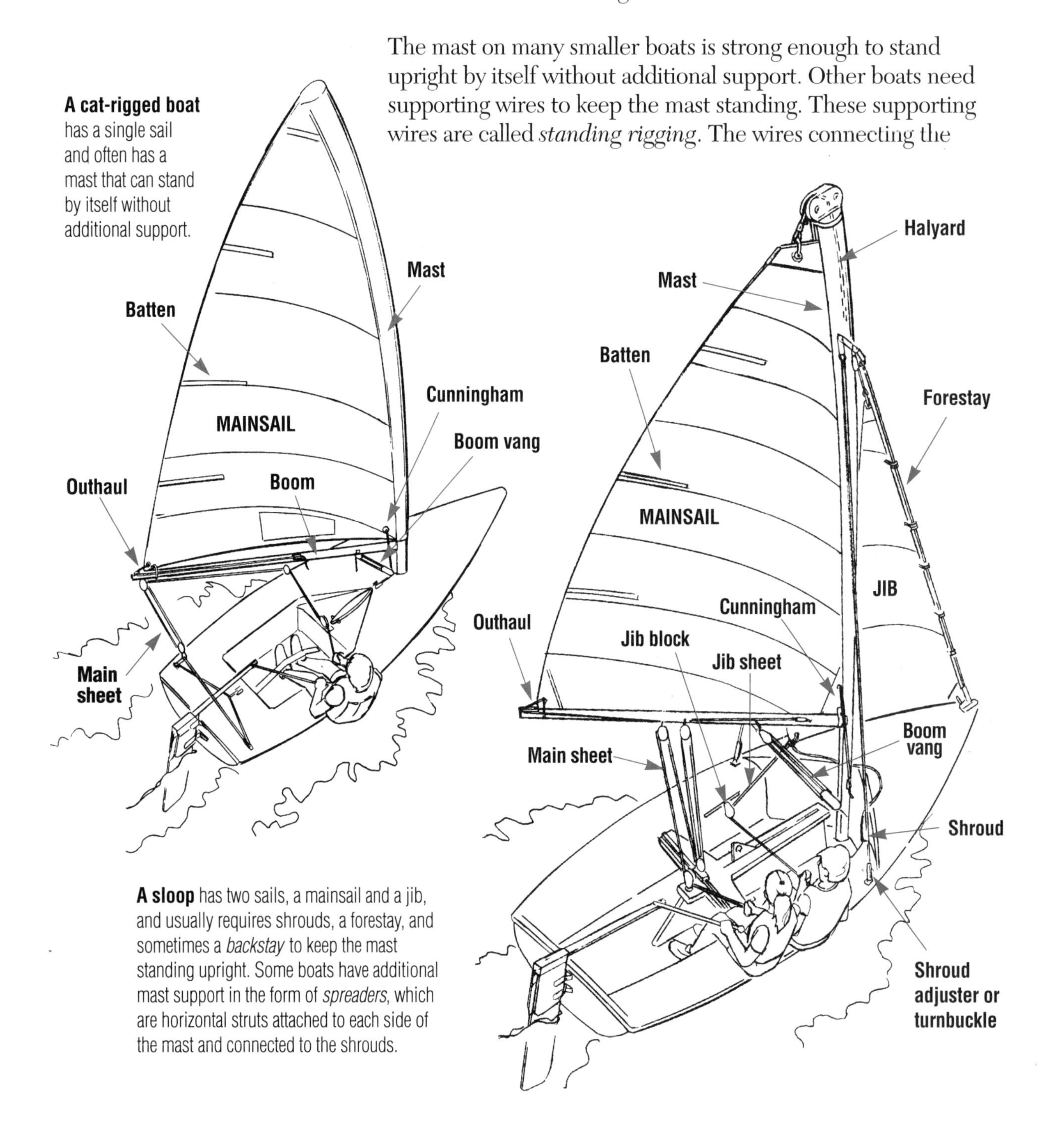


**A cat-rigged boat** has a single sail and often has a mast that can stand by itself without additional support.

**A sloop** has two sails, a mainsail and a jib, and usually requires shrouds, a forestay, and sometimes a *backstay* to keep the mast standing upright. Some boats have additional mast support in the form of *spreaders*, which are horizontal struts attached to each side of the mast and connected to the shrouds.

mast to the sides of the hull are *shrouds*, the wire connecting the front of the mast to the bow is the *forestay*, and the wire connecting the top of the mast to the stern is the *backstay*.

Control lines used to adjust the sails are *running rigging*. Typical control lines are *main sheet*, *jib sheet*, *outhaul*, *halyard*, *cunningham*, and *boom vang*, shown in the preceding illustration. We will explain their functions a bit later.

**Starboard and Port (Right and Left)**

VIDEO 2

PORT
LEFT
RED

STARBOARD
RIGHT
GREEN

The left side of a boat is called the *port* side, and the right side is called *starboard*. Colors are used to help identify port and starboard — red signifying port and green signifying starboard. An easy way to remember these: port, left, and red are short words. Starboard, right and green are longer words. Some beginning sailors find it helpful to put green tape in a visible location on the deck on the starboard side, and red tape on the port side.

## Quick Review

- What is the difference between a monohull and a catamaran? *(answer on p.16)*
- What is the primary function of a centerboard? *(answer on p.16)*
- What is the difference between a keel and a centerboard? *(answer on p.17)*
- On a rig with two sails, what is the smaller forward sail called? What is the larger sail called? *(answer on p.18)*
- What color signifies the port (left) side of a boat? What color signifies the starboard (right) side of a boat? *(answer on p.19)*

## Think about it...

- On a centerboard boat, where crew weight is used as movable ballast to provide stability to the boat, how would a crew increase stability as the wind gets stronger?

A **winch** helps you pull in and hold a sheet. The friction of wrapping a sheet around the winch drum reduces the pull needed to hold the sheet in. A winch handle can be inserted into the top of the winch to provide additional power for pulling in the sheet.

A **cam cleat** has jaws with "teeth" that are spring loaded so they press and grip a line snugly. To release the line, pull and lift. Cam cleats can be difficult to release under heavy load.

A rope (line) is often secured to a *cleat*. The most common is a **horn cleat**, which is secure and easy (but slow) to release under heavy load. A line that will be left unattended, such as a docking line, should be secured with a *cleat hitch* (shown).

A **clam cleat** is very easy to use...simply pull the line through it and let go. To release the line, pull and lift it out (this can be difficult under heavy load).

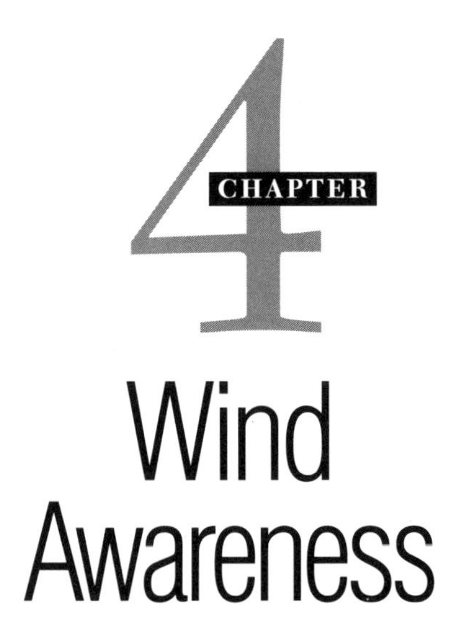


# Wind Awareness

**KEY CONCEPTS**

- Wind direction
- Puffs and lulls
- Actual wind and apparent wind

AWARENESS RULE #1: *The wind is always changing!* Sometimes changes in wind can be so small that you'll hardly notice. Other times you may have to make major adjustments in the course you are steering or the trim of your sails. Part of the fun in sailing is learning to anticipate and react to changes in wind.

## Wind Direction VIDEO 9+12

To sail you need to know the direction of the wind. How can you tell which direction it's blowing from? Turn in a circle and feel the wind on your face, hands, and neck. Look out on the water and notice the waves or ripples on the surface. The wind is usually blowing perpendicular — at right angles — to the ripples. Look around you onshore for flags, smoke, trees, telltales, and flapping sails. NOTE: Don't use flags on other boats that are moving fast. Their flags do not show the true wind direction (more on that later).

**Wind Clues**

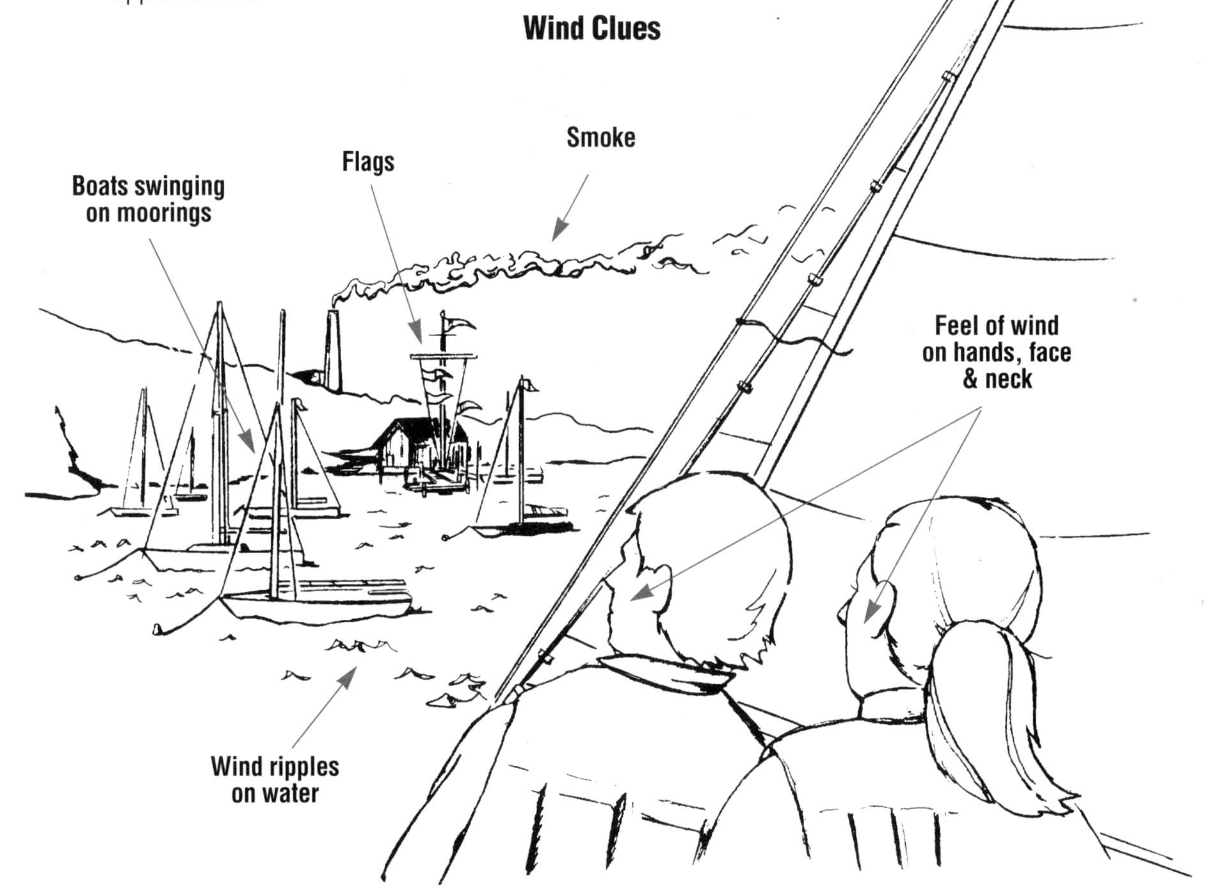

The direction the wind is blowing *from* (not blowing *to*) is the designated direction of the wind. This direction can be described geographically — North, East, South, or West — or by the degree numbers on a compass — 0°, 90°, 180°, 270°, etc. If the wind is blowing *from* the East, you would say, *"We are sailing in an Easterly wind,"* or *"The wind is at 90 degrees."* If you have a compass on your boat, you can determine the wind direction by pointing your boat into the wind and reading the number on the compass.

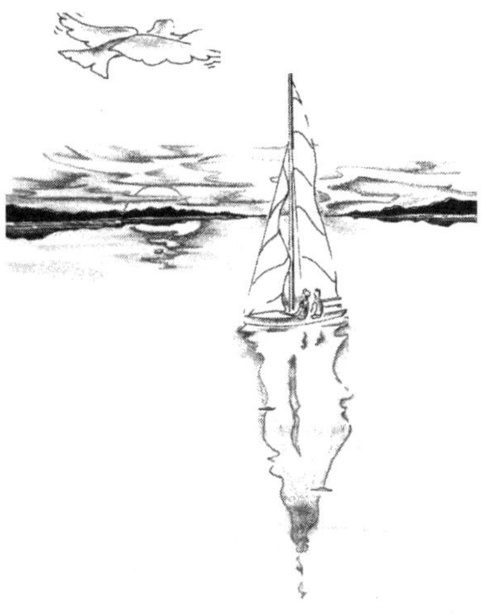

*"What do you mean, you THINK you left the bathtub running?"*

**The face of a compass** is divided into 360 degrees, with North, South, East, West and other major directions (*points*) usually identified with prominent numbers or letters.

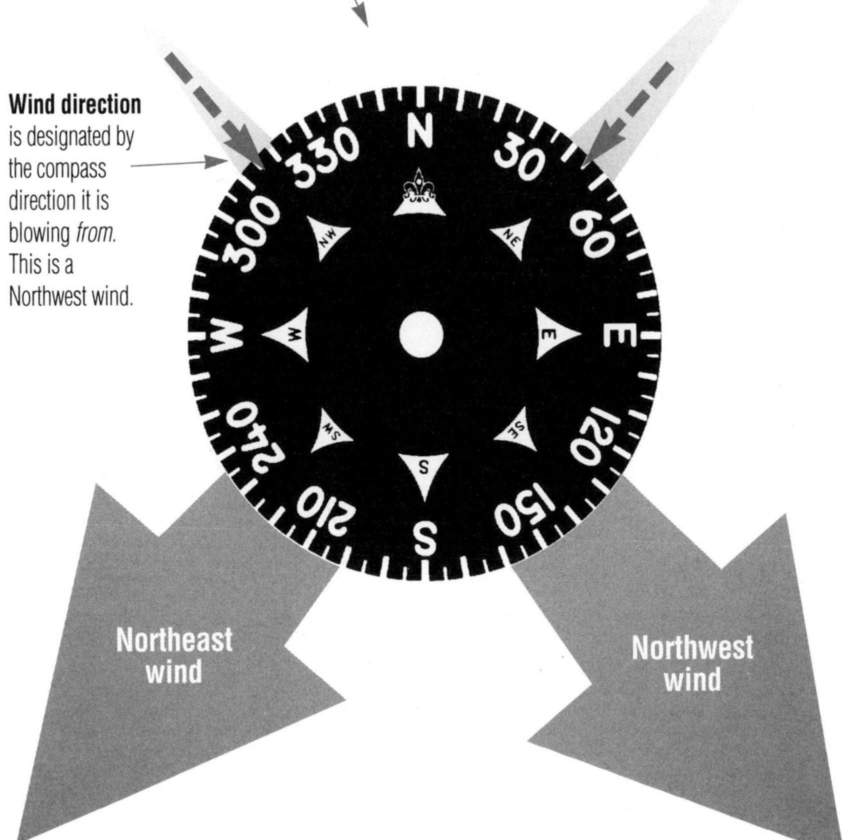


A wind blowing *from* the Northeast *to* the Southwest is called a Northeast wind, or a "Northeaster."

A wind blowing *from* the Northwest *to* the Southeast is called a Northwest wind, or a "Northwester."

## Puffs and Lulls

Abrupt changes (of short duration) in wind speed are usually called *puffs* or *lulls*. A puff is an increase in speed for a short duration, and a lull is a similar decrease in speed. A lull is sometimes called a "hole" in the wind. You will sail in and out of many puffs and lulls.

A puff usually makes the water surface look darker. A lull is a little more difficult to see, but it's usually lighter in color than the surrounding water. Always watch the water for puffs and lulls. In describing the speed or strength of the wind, the nautical term *knots* is frequently used. One knot = 1.15 mph. 10 knots = 11.5 mph, etc.

## The Wind the Boat Sails In

To understand the interaction between a sailboat and the wind, it is helpful to know how the movement of the boat can effect the wind that boat sails in. If your boat is not moving, you will feel the same wind speed and direction you would if you were standing onshore. But when the boat moves, the wind will feel a

A **puff** usually makes the water look darker, allowing you to see it approaching.

little stronger or lighter, depending on your sailing direction. Sailing downwind with the wind coming from behind the boat, you will feel almost no wind. If you turn and sail toward the wind, the wind will feel much stronger. In multihulls, which sail much faster than monohulls, this wind effect is much more dramatic.

You can compare this effect to riding on a bicycle. If you are riding on a bicycle at 20 mph, you will feel a strong wind from directly ahead, even if the actual wind is 0 mph. If the actual wind was blowing 20 mph from behind you, you would feel no wind. If the actual wind was blowing 10 mph from ahead of you, you would feel 30 mph of wind. If the actual wind was blowing at right angles to you, the wind you feel would be a mixture of the actual wind and the "wind" made by the forward motion of your bicycle. A term often used to describe the wind you "feel" when moving is *apparent wind*.

## Quick Review

- Name three things onshore that can help you identify wind direction. *(answer on p.20)*
- Is a Northerly wind coming *from* the North or blowing *to* the North? *(answer on p.21)*
- Does a puff make the water darker or lighter? *(answer on p.22)*
- When you are sailing, are you feeling the actual wind or apparent wind? *(answer on p.23)*

## Think about it...

- When the wind is coming from behind, why does the breeze feel weaker than when you are sailing toward the wind?

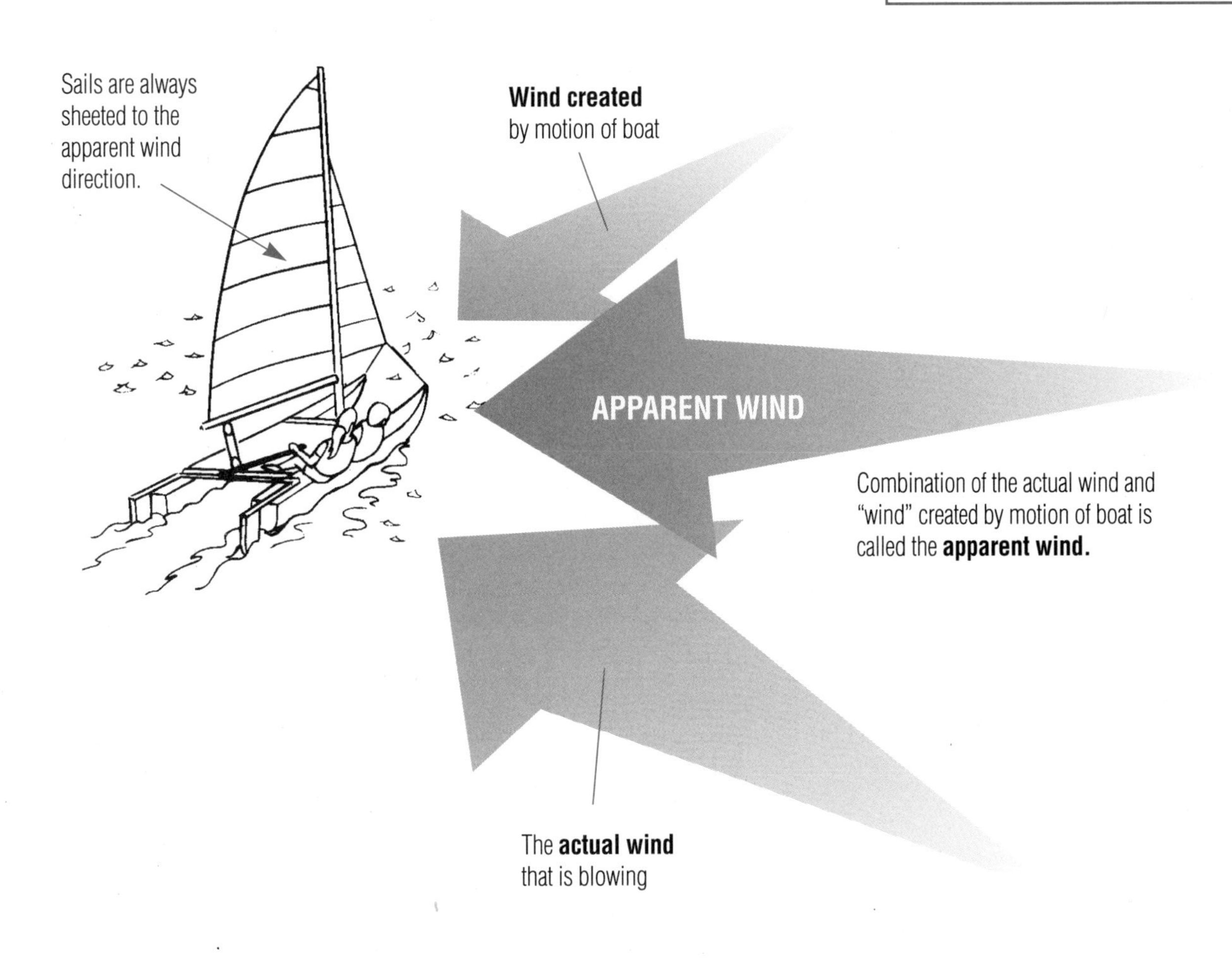

# How Sails Work

**KEY CONCEPTS**
- Push-pull principle
- Lift
- Windward & leeward
- Controlling sail power
- Constant angle to the wind
- Sail telltales

Most beginning sailors are surprised to learn that there are two ways wind and sails interact to propel a boat. In one mode, sails "bend" the wind to create lift which actually *pulls* the boat forward. In another mode, the sails simply block the wind and *push* the boat forward. Remember these two principles...*push* and *pull*.

## Push and Pull VIDEO 4

Modern sails are designed to form a curved shape when they are hit by the wind. This curved shape generates *lift* by "bending" the wind as it flows across both sides of the sail's surface. This lift is your boat's power, and it *pulls* the boat forward and sideways. The centerboard or keel keeps the boat from slipping sideways, so most of the sail's lift is translated into forward motion.

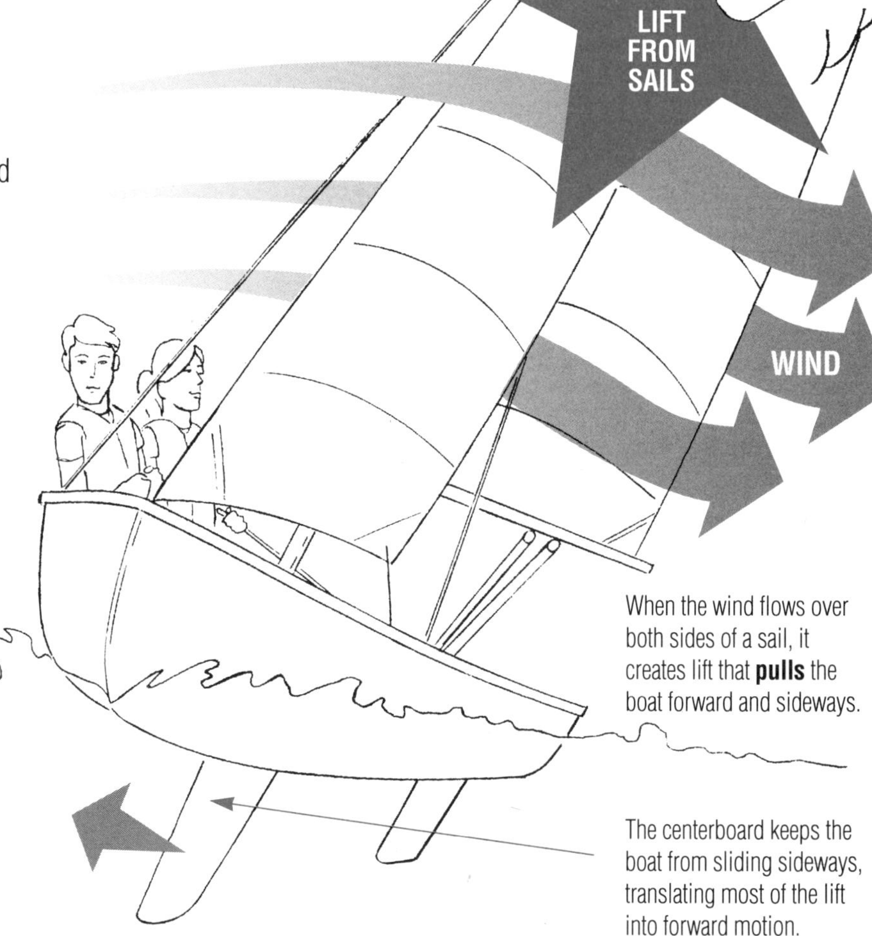


When the wind flows over both sides of a sail, it creates lift that **pulls** the boat forward and sideways.

The centerboard keeps the boat from sliding sideways, translating most of the lift into forward motion.

Other times the sail simply blocks the wind, which *pushes* the boat forward. This is typically the case when you are sailing with the wind coming from directly behind.

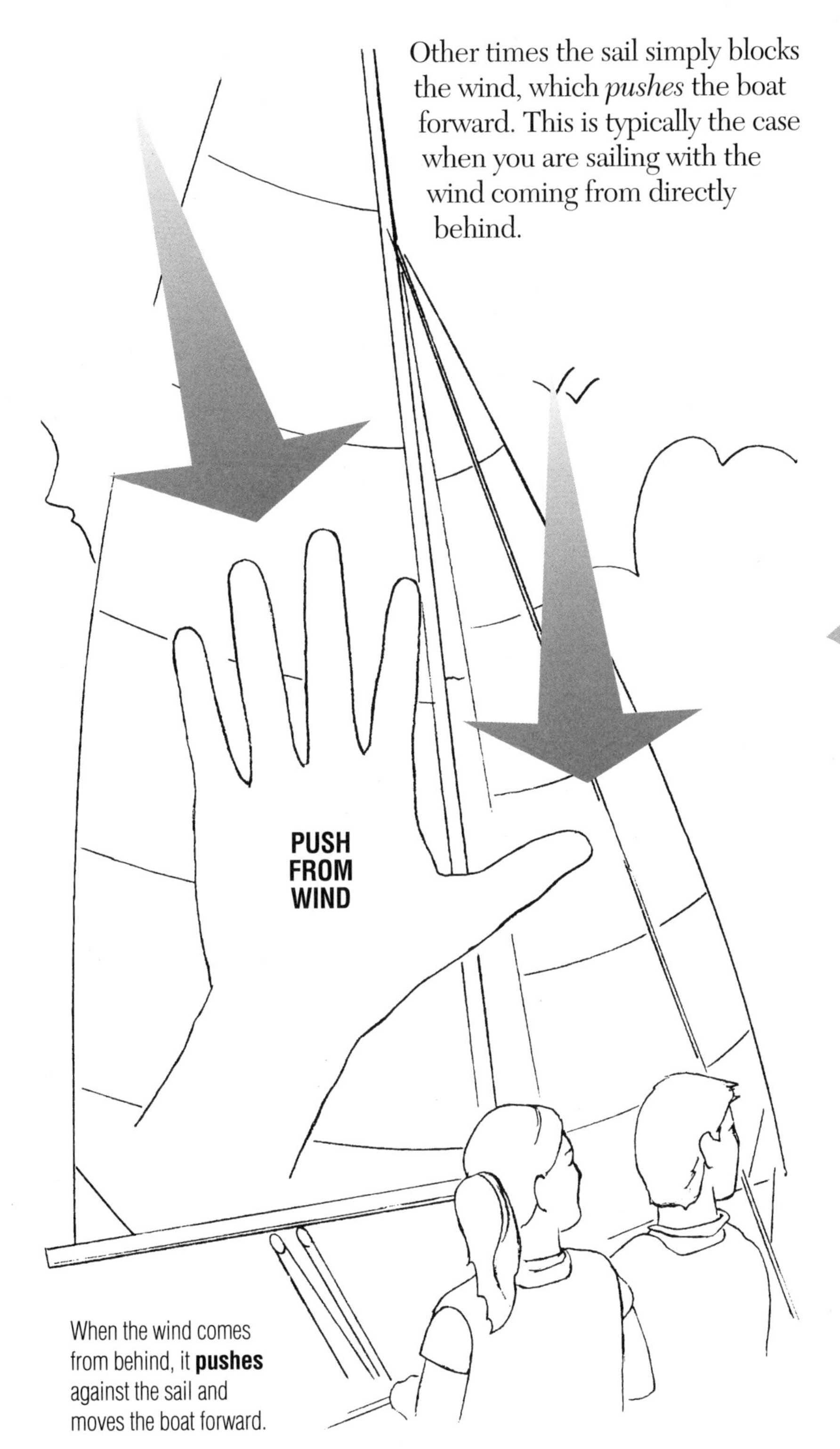


When the wind comes from behind, it **pushes** against the sail and moves the boat forward.

**Windward and Leeward**

To help describe this push-pull principle better, we need to introduce two key sailing terms...*windward* and *leeward*. Windward refers to the direction that is toward the wind source. Leeward is the direction away from the wind source. The windward side of a boat is the side the wind blows over first. Leeward is the side it blows over last. Windward and leeward can describe the sides of a boat: *"Please move to the windward side,"* or relative position: *"Let's sail to leeward of that boat."*

## Controlling Sail Power VIDEO 8

The amount of power (pull) your sails produce — and hence your speed — can be controlled by altering the air flow over the sails. Maximum power is obtained when the air flows smoothly across both the windward *and* leeward side of the sail. If the air flow is turbulent, the sail will develop less power and your boat will slow down.

When the sail is flapping in the wind like a flag, it develops no power at all. This is called *luffing.* Luffing is a normal part of sailing and can be used to reduce boat speed or to stop the boat. A luffing sail can make a lot of noise in a fresh breeze, but don't be alarmed...it's a natural part of sailing.

For maximum power, you need to adjust the sail so that it has the optimum angle to the wind. Adjusting the angle of the sails to the wind can be done two ways.

1. **Using the sheets** to change the angle of the sails relative to the wind. This is called *sail trim.*
2. **Changing the direction of the boat**, which changes the angle of wind relative to the sails.

Pulling in or letting out the main sheet or jib sheet is called *sheeting.* Pulling in the sails is called *sheeting in.* Letting the

### Depowering Your Sails

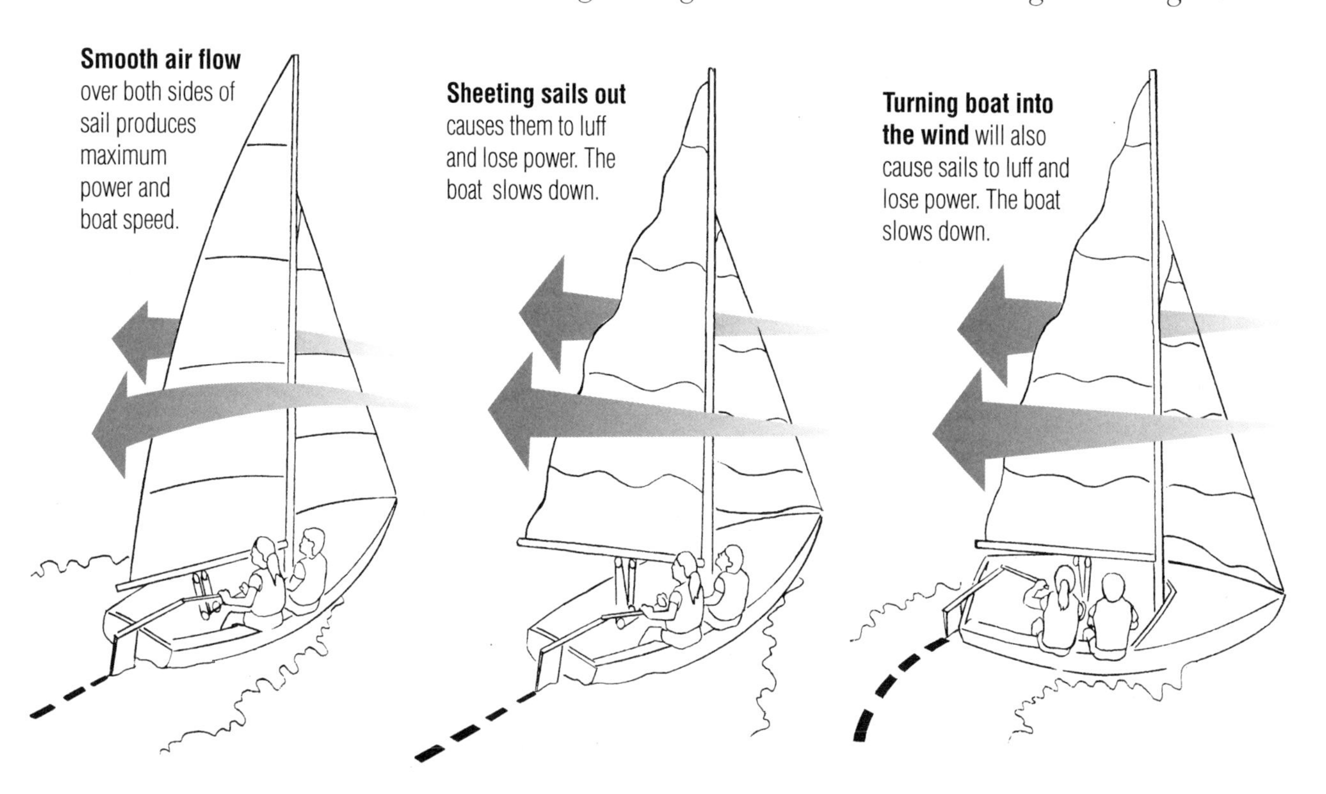

sails out is called *sheeting out*. Sailors sometimes refer to sheeting in as *trimming* and to sheeting out as *easing*. When sheeting for maximum speed, the sail will keep a *constant angle to the wind*. This constant angle is controlled by steering and sheeting the sails.

## Using Sail Telltales

VIDEO 8

*Telltales* are often used to "show" the invisible wind flow over the sails. They are made of yarn, thread, or any other lightweight material that blows easily in the wind. They are normally placed on the forward one-third of the jib and near the center of the mainsail. Some sailors place a telltale on the *leech* (back edge) of the sail to show the air flow as it leaves the sail's surface.

Telltales show whether the air flow along the sails is smooth or turbulent. When a telltale is flowing parallel to the water, the wind flow is smooth. When the telltales bounce around and flutter erratically, the air flow is turbulent. While telltales are very helpful, don't get too wrapped up in them. Remember to "keep your head out of the boat," constantly observing changes in the wind direction and strength by looking at the water around you and checking how other boats are doing.

### Quick Review

▶ Describe the difference between the "push" and "pull" mode when sailing. *(answer on p.24-25)*

▶ Define the terms *windward* and *leeward*. *(answer on p.25)*

▶ Describe two ways to depower your sails and slow your boat down. *(answer on p.26)*

▶ Describe how telltales work. *(answer on p.27)*

### Try it out...

▶ While sailing with the tiller centered, ease and trim your sails and notice how the boat decelerates and accelerates. Next, sail with the sails sheeted properly and steer slowly toward the wind and then away from the wind, noticing how the boat decelerates and accelerates. This exercise demonstrates how you can control your boat speed by adjusting your sail trim or by steering.

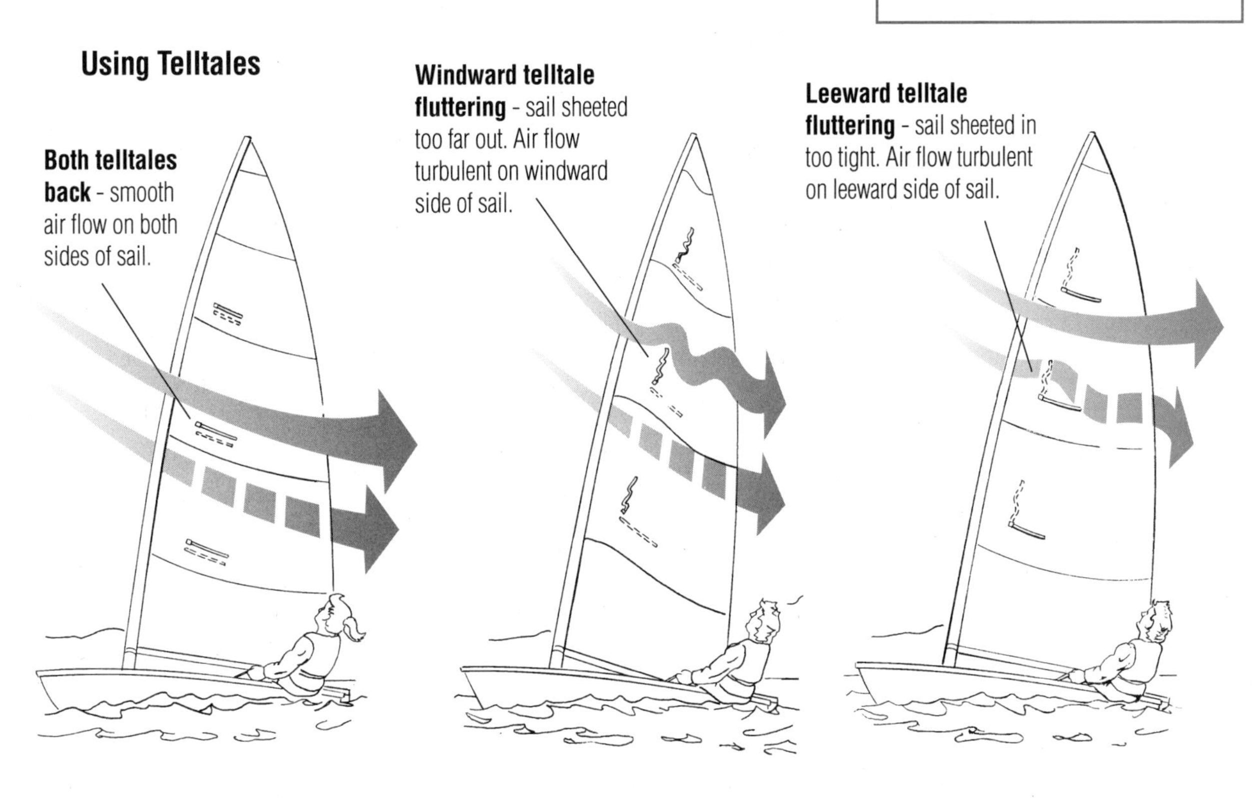

# Rigging the Boat

**KEY CONCEPTS**
- Rigging the hull
- Rigging the mainsail
- Rigging the jib
- Raising and lowering the sails
- Handling/folding sails
- Lifting boats

*"Rule # 1: Check the drain plug before launching."*

Before you can go sailing, the sailboat must be *rigged*. Rigging and unrigging each boat will be a little different, but there are a few things that all have in common.

- Always try to start with the boat pointed into the wind. This will keep the sails from blowing over the side and prevents the sails from filling with wind before you are ready to start sailing.
- If necessary, remove accumulated water from the boat and close any drain plugs.

## Rigging the Hull

Once the boat is in the water, begin by lowering the centerboard all the way down or inserting the daggerboard all the way into its slot. Next, attach the rudder, tiller and tiller extension to the boat.

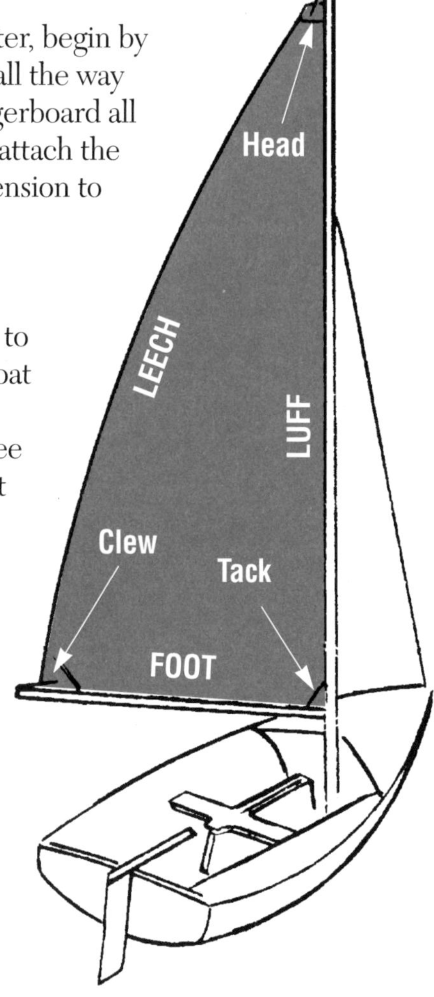


## Rigging the Mainsail

To ease handling, it is best to take the sails aboard the boat while they are in their sail bags. The mainsail has three corners, and it is important to keep track of all three corners as you take the mainsail out of the bag. Try not to let the sail get twisted as you unfold and rig it. The best way to do this is to find the top corner (*head*) and run your hand down the front edge of the sail (*luff*), to make sure the sail is not twisted.

Some mainsails may have *cunningham* and *boom vang* controls (more on their function later). At this point, you only need to know how to rig them. There are several different ways, and your instructor will show you the best way for your boat.

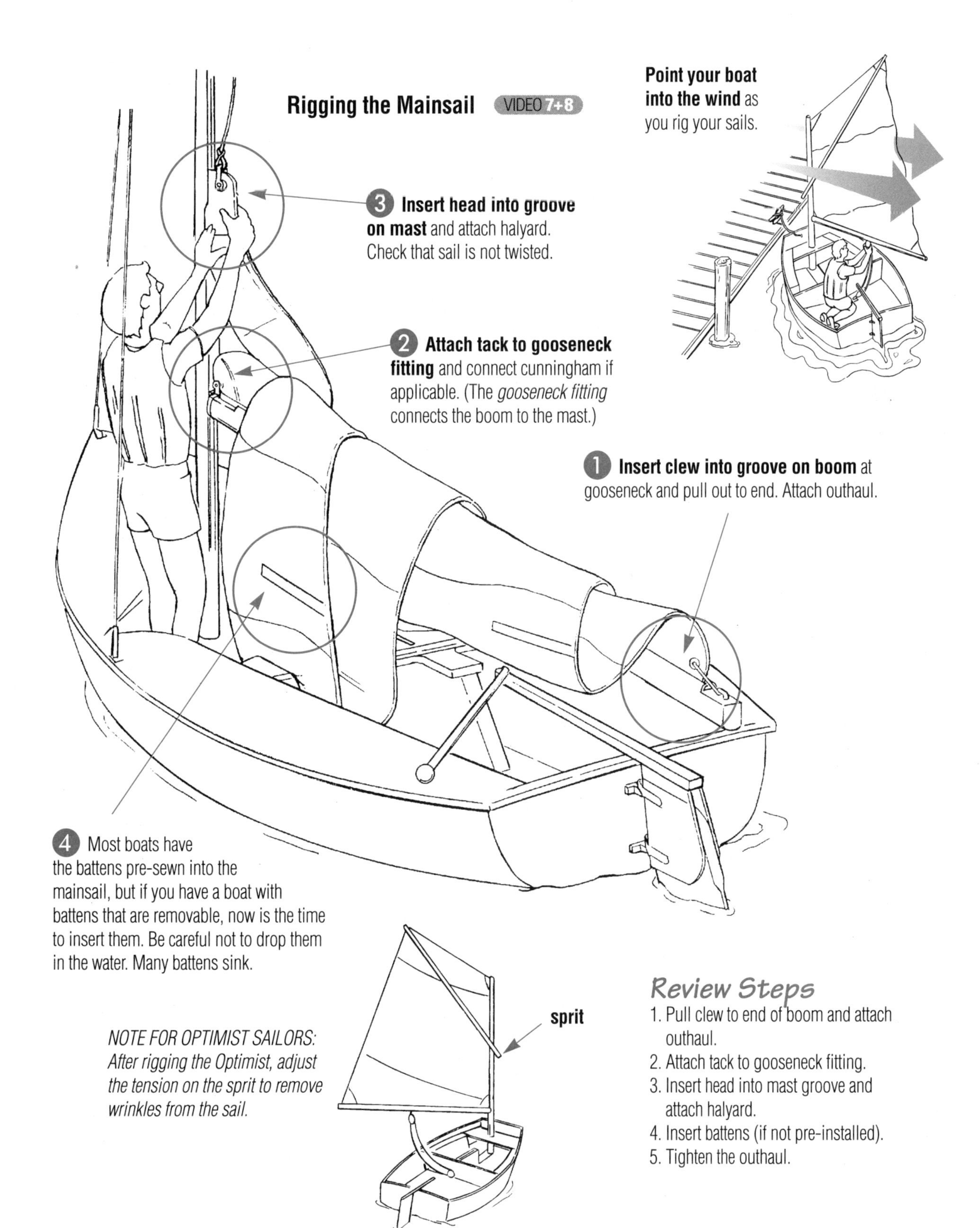
Rigging the Mainsail
VIDEO 7+8
Point your boat into the wind as you rig your sails.
3 Insert head into groove on mast and attach halyard. Check that sail is not twisted.
2 Attach tack to gooseneck fitting and connect cunningham if applicable. (The gooseneck fitting connects the boom to the mast.)
1 Insert clew into groove on boom at gooseneck and pull out to end. Attach outhaul.
4 Most boats have the battens pre-sewn into the mainsail, but if you have a boat with battens that are removable, now is the time to insert them. Be careful not to drop them in the water. Many battens sink.
sprit
NOTE FOR OPTIMIST SAILORS: After rigging the Optimist, adjust the tension on the sprit to remove wrinkles from the sail.
Review Steps
1. Pull clew to end of boom and attach outhaul.
2. Attach tack to gooseneck fitting.
3. Insert head into mast groove and attach halyard.
4. Insert battens (if not pre-installed).
5. Tighten the outhaul.

## Rigging the Jib VIDEO 7+8

Rigging the jib varies somewhat for different boats. Some jibs have fasteners or clips on the *luff* (front edge) of the sail. Attach them to the *forestay* (the wire connecting the mast to the boat's bow), starting with the fastener at the bottom of the luff first and continuing up to the top.

## Raising the Sails VIDEO 8

Once the jib and main are rigged, you are ready to raise the sails. But before you hoist, double check to make sure...

1. the main sheet and jib sheets are not cleated and will run freely,
2. the outhaul control line has been adjusted and cleated,
3. the cunningham or downhaul and the boom vang are not cleated,
4. the centerboard or daggerboard is in the down position,
5. the tiller and rudder are secured and working properly,
6. the boat is pointed into the wind.

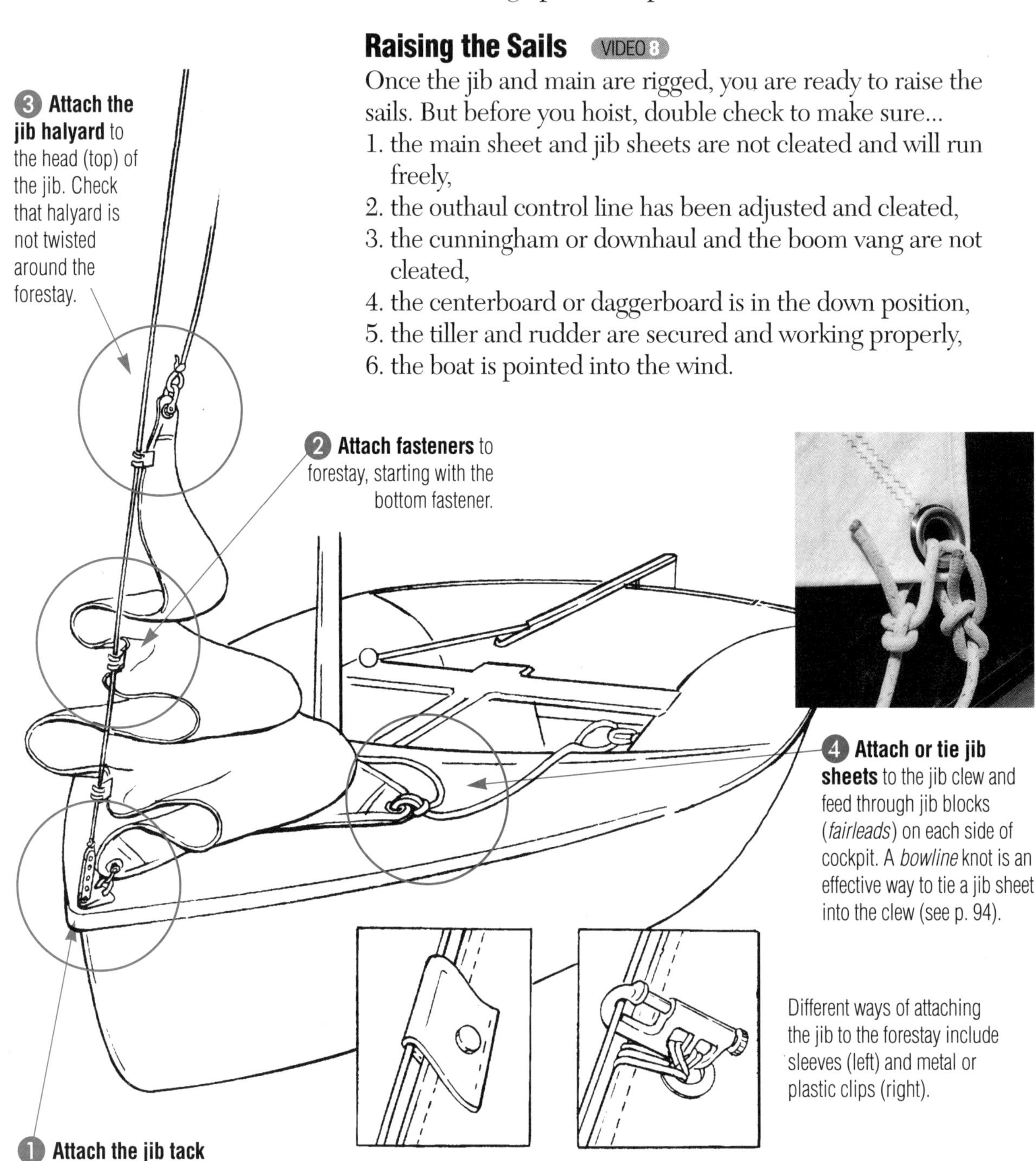


Different ways of attaching the jib to the forestay include sleeves (left) and metal or plastic clips (right).

Raise the jib by pulling on the halyard, cleating it when the sail is up and the halyard feels good and tight. Raise the mainsail by hoisting the halyard hand-over-hand while the crew feeds the sail into the mast groove to prevent jamming.

If the mainsail has a downhaul or cunningham control line, or a boom vang, now is the time to tighten and cleat them. Which sail you raise first depends on where your boat is. If your boat is attached to a mooring, you usually raise the mainsail first because it helps to keep the boat pointed into the wind until you have the jib up and are ready to leave the mooring. If your boat is tied to a dock or you are sailing off a beach, often the jib will be raised first. Your instructor will help you decide what best suits your situation.

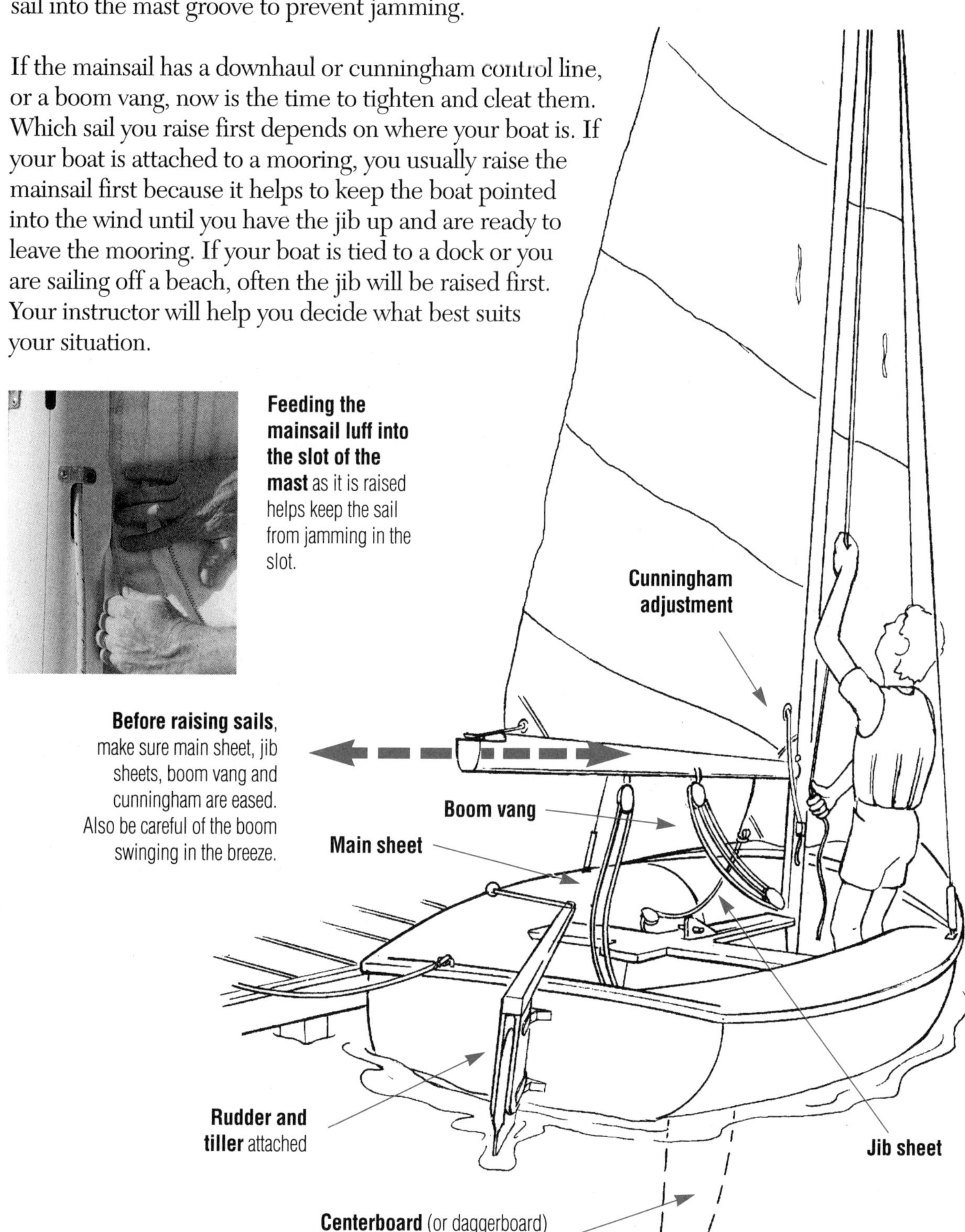


**Feeding the mainsail luff into the slot of the mast** as it is raised helps keep the sail from jamming in the slot.

**Before raising sails**, make sure main sheet, jib sheets, boom vang and cunningham are eased. Also be careful of the boom swinging in the breeze.

## Lowering the Sails

Lowering the main before lowering the jib helps to stabilize the boat and stops the boom from swinging in the wind, but when picking up a mooring it is best to lower the jib first. With the sails down, you can de-rig the hull, removing the rudder, other hardware and mast and boom if necessary.

## Folding the Sails VIDEO 7

Folding sails makes them easier to store and helps them last longer. If you have been sailing in salt water, try to rinse and dry your sails before folding. If a lawn is available, this makes drying and folding faster and easier.

Fold your sail in a zig-zag pattern, like a road map, with folds lying parallel to the *foot* (bottom) of the sail. Once the folding is complete, you can then fold or roll the sail starting at the luff and moving to the clew. Wrapping the jib sheets around the outside of the folded jib will secure it. If you are using one sailbag for both the mainsail and the jib, put the larger mainsail into the sailbag first.

If the battens are sewn into the sail, the same folding method can be used, except that during the zig-zag you should make the folds larger at the back (*leech*) of the sail than at the front side (*luff*) when you start. This way the leech and battens will line up.

Before folding, rinse and dry sails (if they have gotten wet), and stretch them out on a lawn.

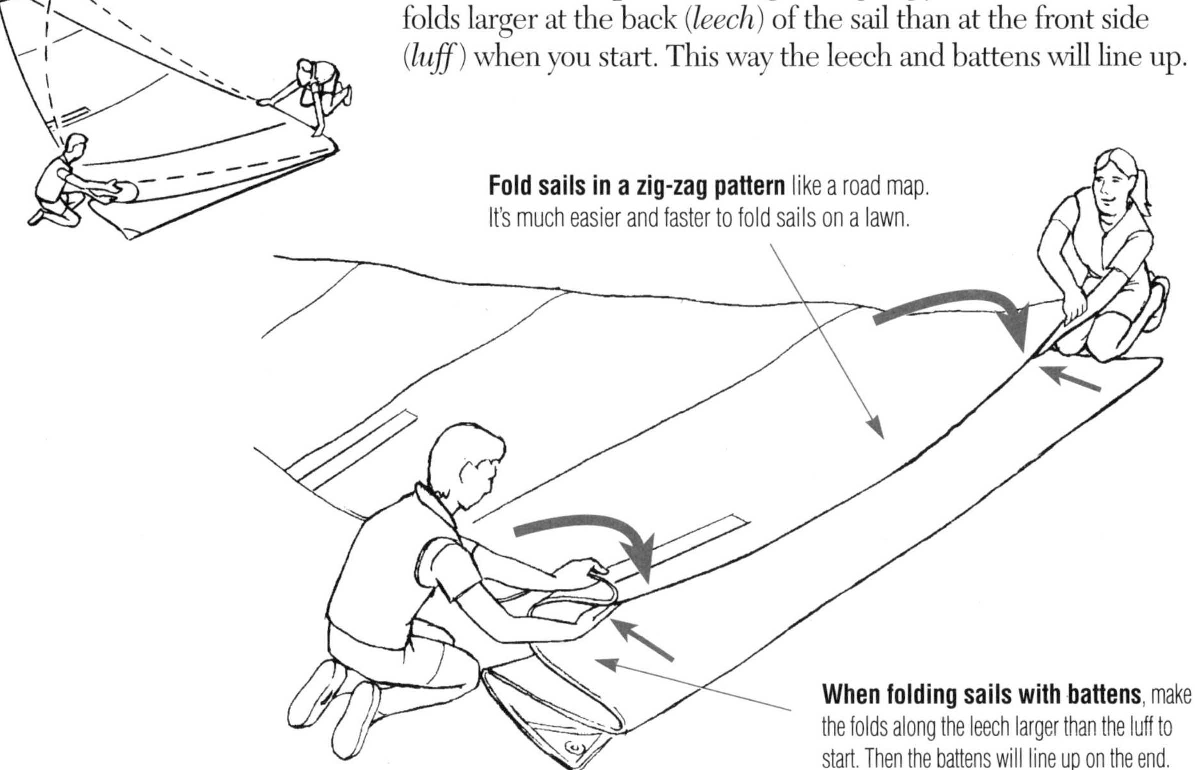

**Fold sails in a zig-zag pattern** like a road map. It's much easier and faster to fold sails on a lawn.

**When folding sails with battens,** make the folds along the leech larger than the luff to start. Then the battens will line up on the end.

On small sailboats that have only a mainsail, the sail is often rolled around the mast, which is then removed from the boat and stored inside on a rack. On larger sailboats, the main is often stowed (*furled*) on the boom, then protected from sun and weather with a sail cover.

## Storage, Maintenance and Lifting

VIDEO 1

▶ Like the sails, the boat too should be rinsed off with fresh water to remove dirt and salt. Rinsing is particularly important for fittings and blocks. If the boat is kept on a trailer, try to tilt it so that rinsing and rain water will drain. Boat covers are often used to keep boats clean, dry and protected from sun damage.
▶ When storing a boat on a trailer or dock, leaving the mast in the boat increases the chance of the boat moving in high winds. It's smart to tie a safety line over the hull to prevent moving.
▶ If you have to lift a boat, *don't use your back!* Lift with your legs — keeping your back straight — to reduce the chance of injury. Lifting a boat is a team effort. Don't do it alone.

A sailing center will usually have special areas for storing boats and trailers, and a building for storing equipment, such as sails, masts and booms, rudders and tillers, daggerboards, life jackets and so forth. This equipment is often stored on moveable racks which can be rolled to the boats when they are rigged on land or at the dock.

Sailing centers have developed special storage techniques which allow sailors to get on and off the water quicker.

### Quick Review

▶ In what direction should your boat be pointed when rigging the sails? *(answer on p.28-29)*
▶ What important steps should be taken before you start to raise your sails? *(answer on p.30)*
▶ If you are rigging your boat at a dock, should you raise the jib or mainsail first? *(answer on p.31)*
▶ If you are rigging your boat at a mooring, should you raise your jib or mainsail first? *(answer on p.31)*
▶ In what order should you lower your sails when picking up a mooring? *(answer on p.32)*

### Think about it...

▶ Why does it matter what sail is raised first when rigging a boat at a dock or at a mooring?

# Your First Sail

**KEY CONCEPTS**

- Getting into a boat
- Helmsman and crew
- Steering with the tiller
- Steering with weight
- Steering with sails
- Boat balance
- Safety position
- Starting and stopping
- Tacking

During your first sail you will discover the magic feeling of harnessing the wind to move your boat over the water. Your instructor will show you how to use the wind and your sails to start, to stop and to steer the boat. You will begin to see how the wind direction affects the way the boat is sailed, and you'll get a chance to steer and adjust the sails. *Relax and enjoy!*

## Boarding a Boat VIDEO 9

When you enter or leave a boat, step into or out of the boat's center to keep it from tipping too much. Make sure that you have a firm grip on some part of the boat when you are boarding. If another person is already in the boat, he or she should also be near the center. The centerboard should be lowered to make the boat more stable. For your first sail, you can keep the centerboard lowered the entire time.

## Taking Your Position VIDEO 10

The person who steers the boat, controls the main sheet, and helps balance the boat is the *helmsman*. The helmsman should always sit opposite the boom, facing the sail, at the front end of the tiller. This position gives a better view of the sails and of the approaching wind and waves. Using a *tiller extension* will allow the helmsman to sit farther outboard. The helmsman should make sure everyone on board is wearing a life jacket and following safe procedures.

The *crew* helps balance the boat, adjust sails and look out for other boats and obstacles. The crew should sit even with the centerboard so the boat will float with neither the bow nor the stern too low in the water. A good crew moves around the boat as smoothly as possible.

**Step into or from the center of a boat** to keep it from tipping too much.

If the boat has a jib, the crew trims it. The crew also adjusts the *boom vang*, *outhaul*, and *cunningham* for the mainsail if necessary.

If you are sailing a singlehanded boat, you are responsible for all sail controls, centerboard, and boat balance. This may seem like a lot to do, but it soon becomes second nature.

## SAFETY TIP

▶ Whether you are a beginner or expert, it's smart to hold the main sheet in your hand *uncleated* at all times. This will give you a better feel for how the sail is working, as well as allow you to respond faster to changes in wind strength and direction.

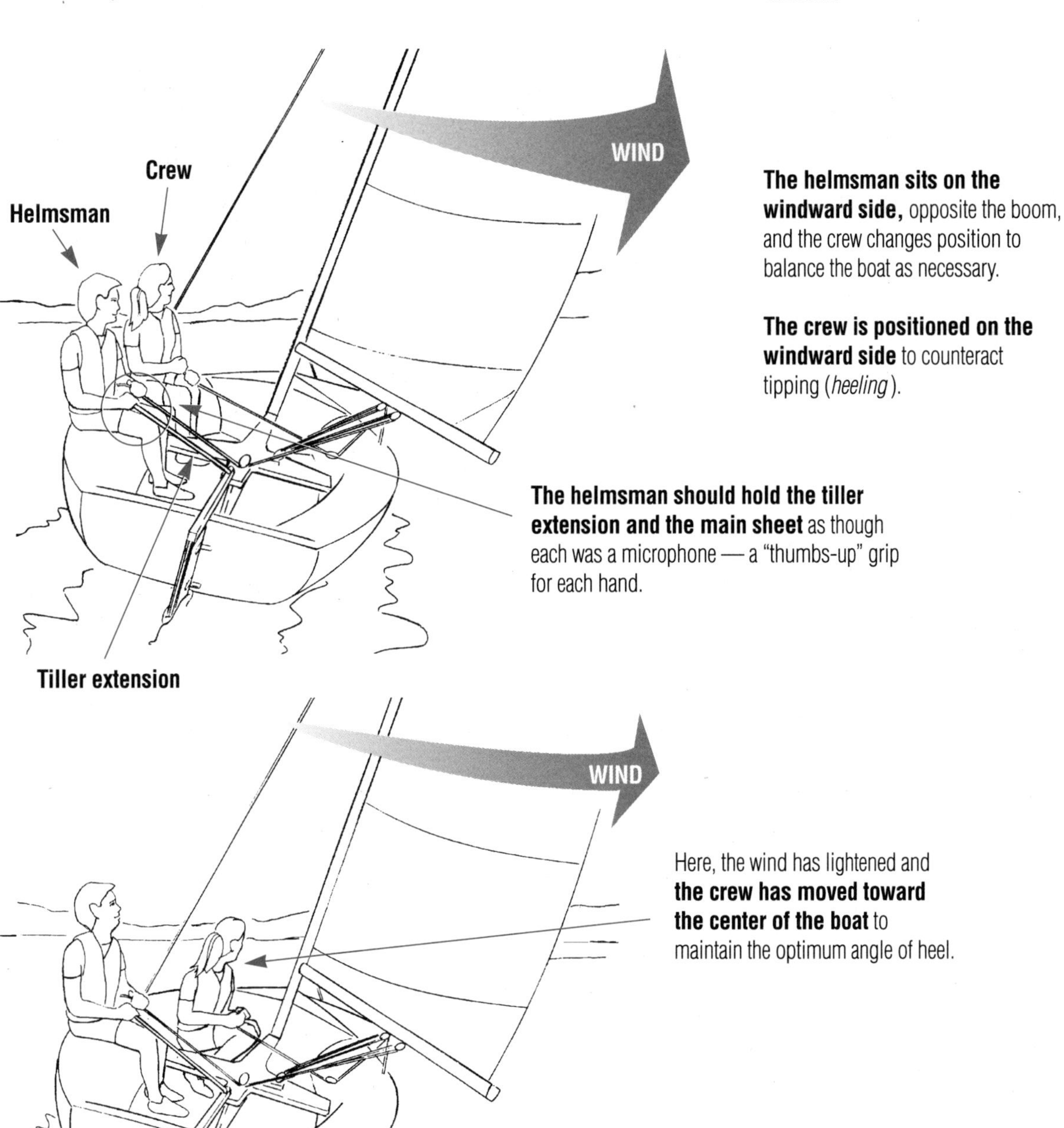


**The helmsman sits on the windward side,** opposite the boom, and the crew changes position to balance the boat as necessary.

**The crew is positioned on the windward side** to counteract tipping (*heeling*).

**The helmsman should hold the tiller extension and the main sheet** as though each was a microphone — a "thumbs-up" grip for each hand.

Here, the wind has lightened and **the crew has moved toward the center of the boat** to maintain the optimum angle of heel.

## Steering with the Tiller VIDEO 4+10

To steer, you simply push or pull the tiller in the opposite direction you want the boat to go. To turn left (*port*), you move the tiller to the right. To turn right (*starboard*), you move the tiller to the left.

Turning toward the wind is sometimes called *heading up*. Turning away from the wind is sometimes called *heading down* or *falling off*.

When steering, the helmsman's hands should be close together and his or her head should be turned forward to constantly check the sails, the approaching waves and wind on the water in front of the boat. Don't forget to check under the boom to leeward for boats approaching from that side.

You may want to learn to steer using just the tiller, but a tiller extension allows the helmsman to sit further outboard.

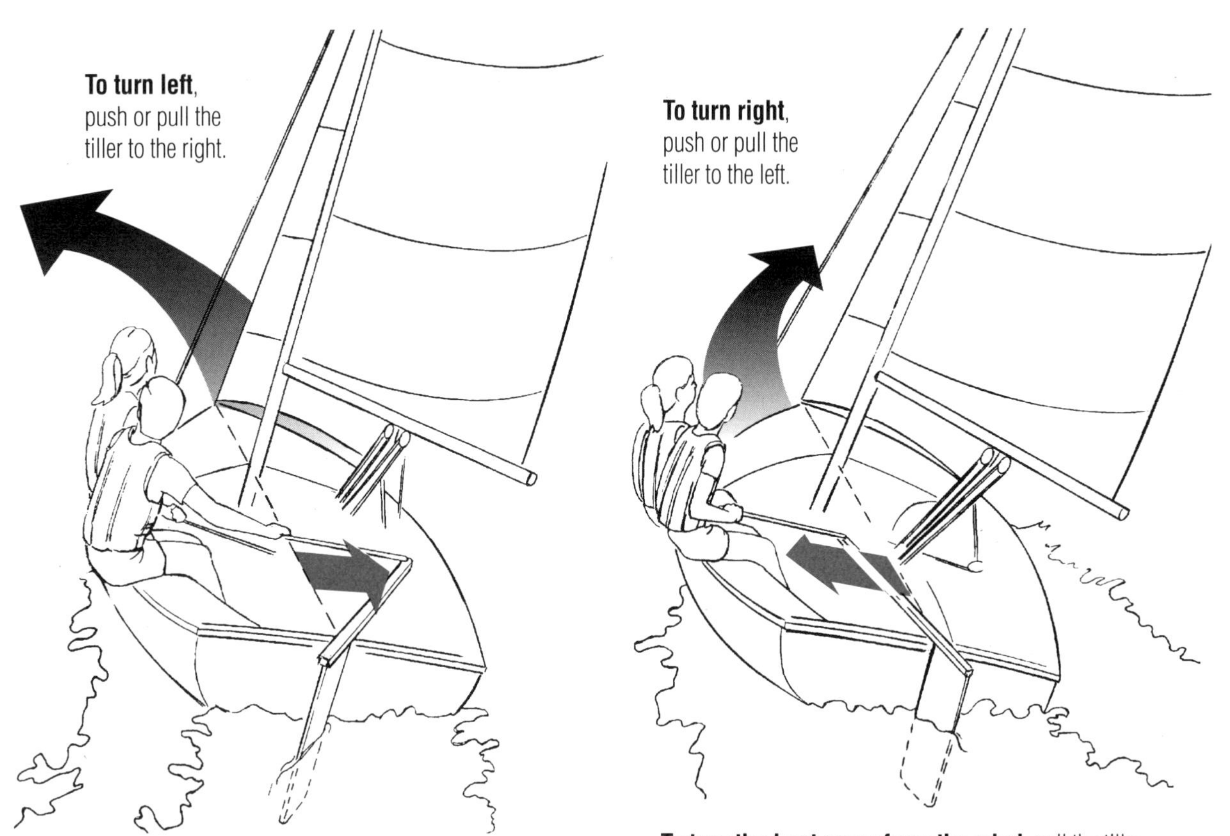


**To turn the boat toward the wind**, push the tiller toward the sail. Turning toward the wind is sometimes called *heading up*.

**To turn the boat away from the wind**, pull the tiller away from the sail. Turning away from the wind is sometimes called *heading down* or *falling off*.

## Steering with Body Weight

Your boat can also be steered using only sails and your body weight. At this stage you won't do this very often, but it's good to know how the boat's angle (*heel*) and sail trim can affect the balance of your boat.

Try sailing with the rudder fixed on the centerline, turning the boat by leaning (*heeling*) it first to windward and then to leeward (see illustration below).

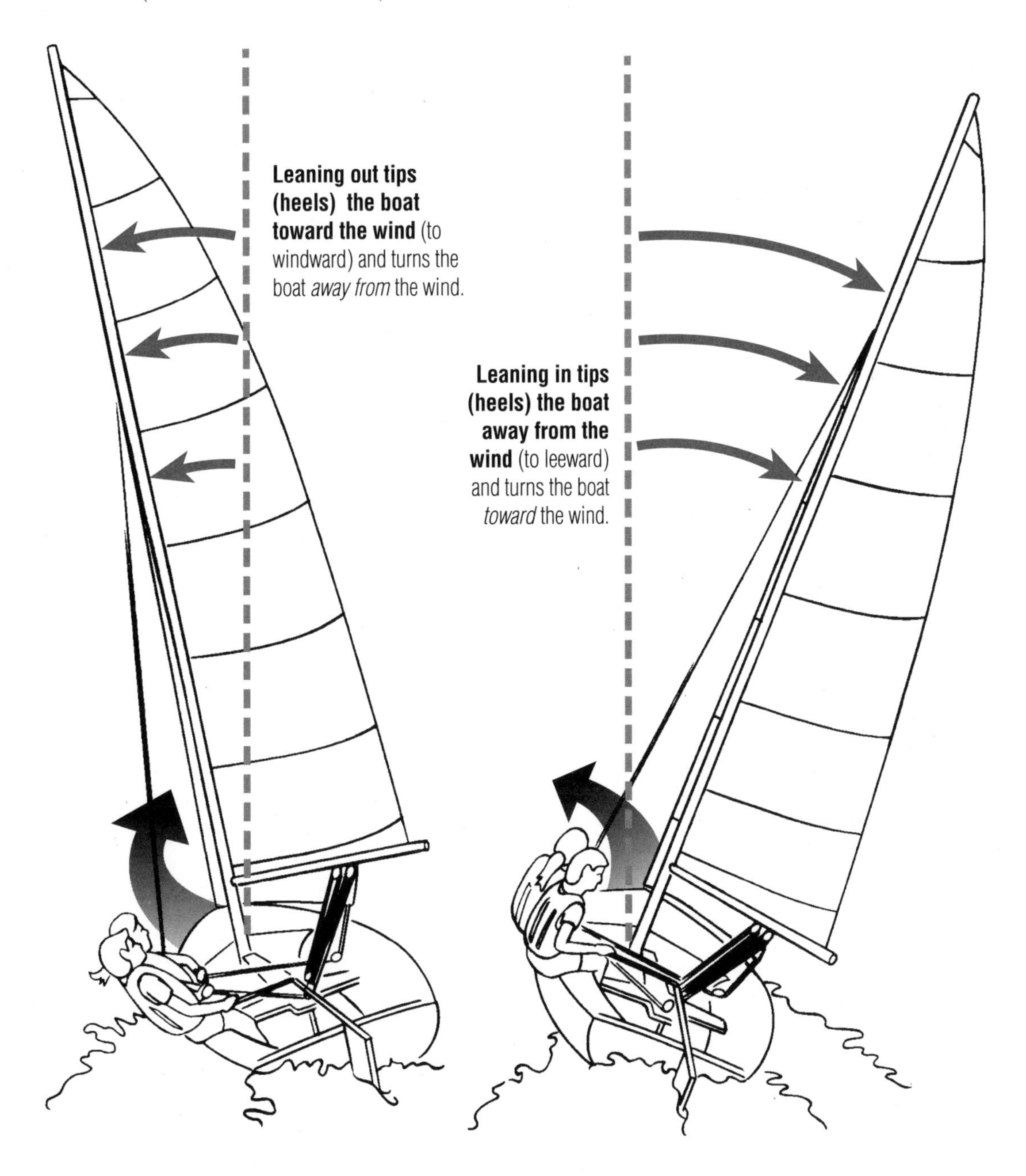

## Steering with Sails

You can also use the sail trim to turn the boat. Easing out the jib (while the mainsail is trimmed) will make the boat turn toward the wind. Easing out the mainsail (while the jib is trimmed) will make the boat turn away from the wind. For this reason, you will notice that it can be difficult to steer the boat away from the wind if the mainsail is not eased, especially in medium or heavy winds.

*"I think they're starting to get the hang of it!"*

**Sheeting out the mainsail** will make the boat turn *away from* the wind.

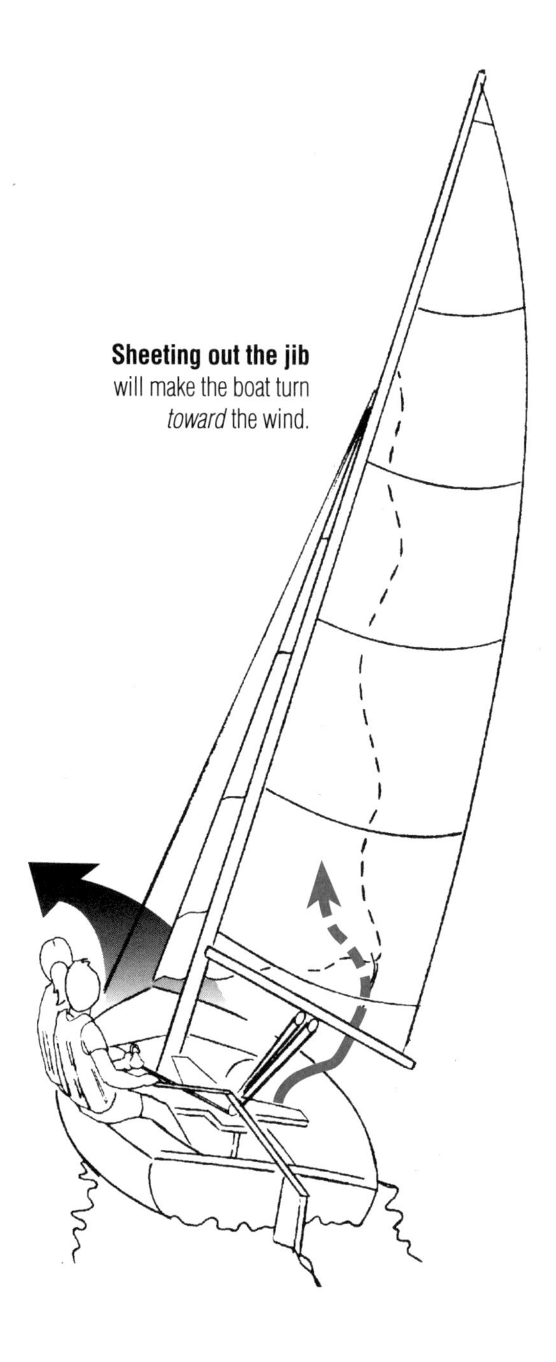

**Sheeting out the jib** will make the boat turn *toward* the wind.

## Balance

You can steer a boat with its sails instead of its rudder because of a principle called *balance*. A sailboat is a collection of forces in motion, not all of which are headed in the same direction. There are forces exerted by the mainsail and the jib, both of which pull the boat forward and sideways. There are opposing forces exerted by the water on the centerboard and rudder.

When all of these forces are *in balance*, the boat will sail forward in a straight line. If they are not, the boat will want to turn. This is why you are able to steer the boat by trimming in or easing either the mainsail or jib. By doing so, you are consciously throwing the boat *out of balance*.

As your sailing skills improve, you will use the principle of balance more and more to get the best performance out of your boat and execute more advanced maneuvers. For now, just understanding balance will help explain why certain things are happening on your boat.

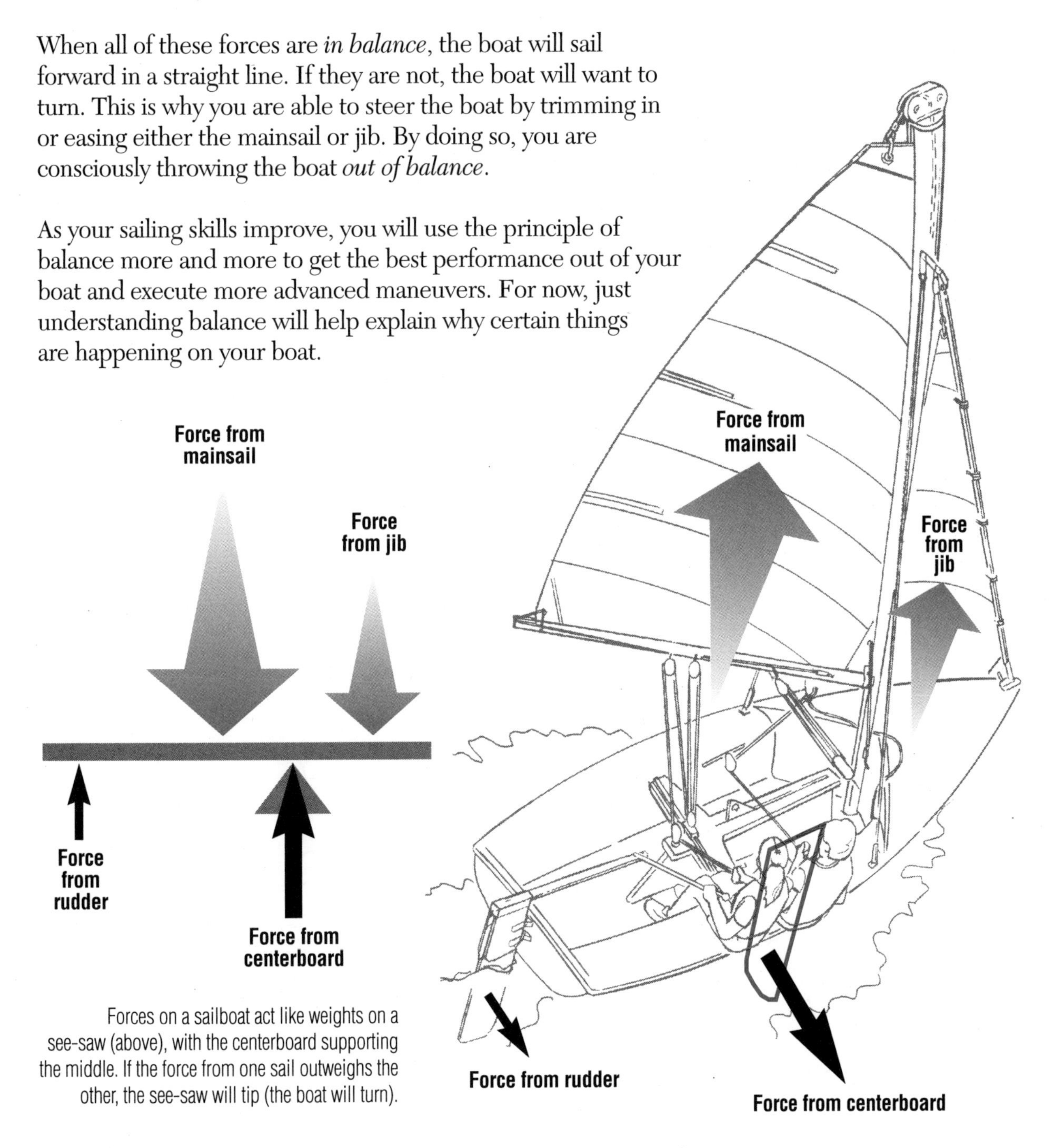


Forces on a sailboat act like weights on a see-saw (above), with the centerboard supporting the middle. If the force from one sail outweighs the other, the see-saw will tip (the boat will turn).

## Safety Position VIDEO 9+10

During your first sail, you will probably sail most of the time across the wind with it coming over the side of the boat (called *reaching*). This is the easiest point of sail for a beginner, and you will be able to try different methods of turning the boat, stopping and starting it, and using the telltales on the sail.

With the wind coming over the side of the boat, let the sheets out until they flap in the wind like a flag and the boat slows down to a stop. You are now in the *safety position*. Sheet in your sails and you're on your way. Let them out again, and you'll stop. Try this several times until you get the hang of it.

### Multihull Tip...

**Safety Position**

1. Release jib and main sheets, leaving sails luffing.
2. Push tiller to turn boat into the wind.
3. Continue to hold tiller hard over for as long as you wish to keep boat in Safety Position.

*NOTE: In stronger winds (with more waves), the mast may rotate sharply from side to side. Easing the downhaul will calm things down.*

## Starting and Stopping Your Boat VIDEO 9+10

The first step in developing sound sailing skills is learning how to start and stop your boat. Starting is really very easy. Your centerboard must be down and the tiller should be centered. Now sheet in the sails just enough to allow the air to start

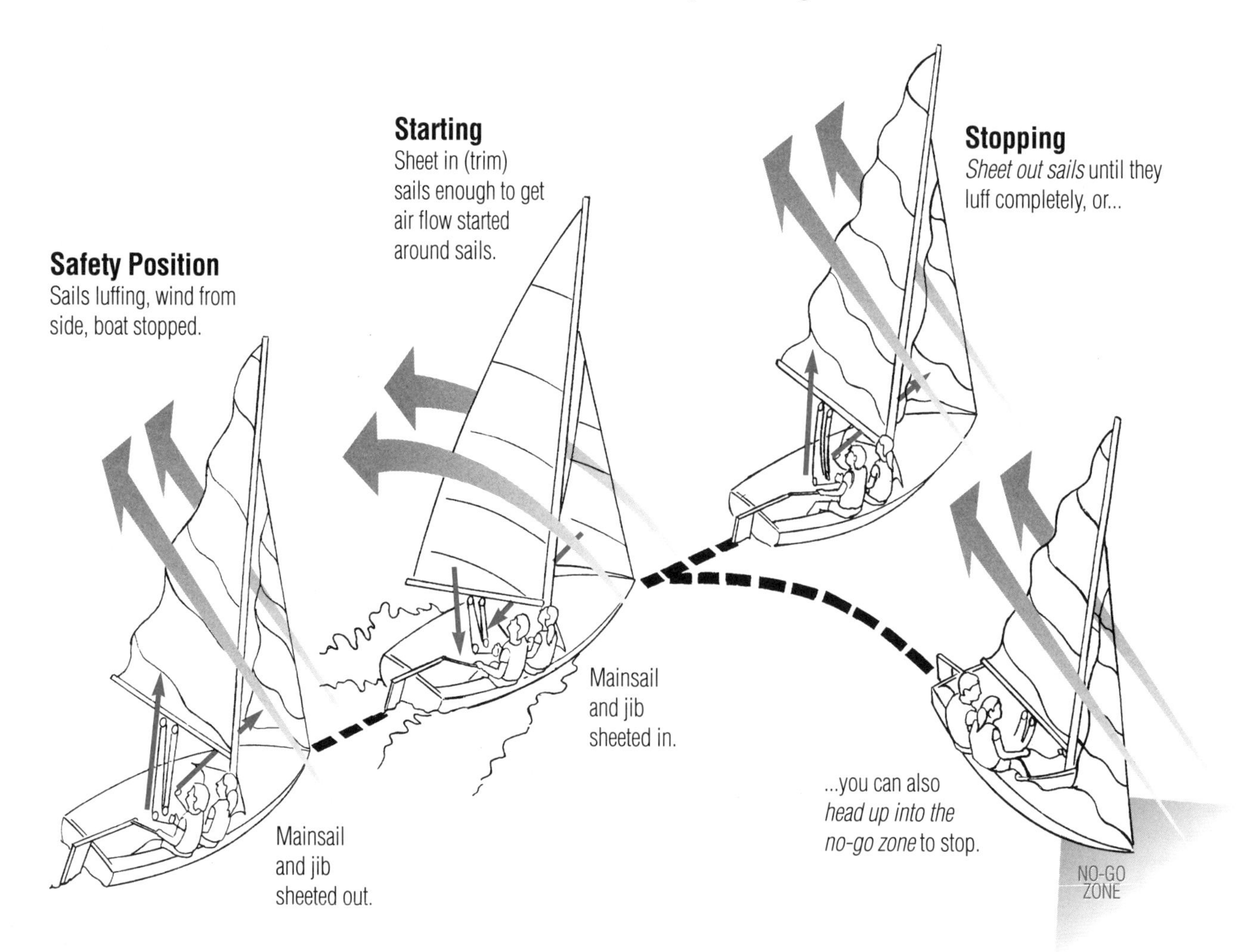

flowing evenly on both sides of the sails. If you are sheeting properly, the telltales on the windward and leeward sides of the sail will flow back smoothly. Steer straight ahead and *you are now sailing!*

Stopping is just as easy as starting, and there are two ways to do it. One is to simply ease the sails out until they luff and lose power. Letting the sails luff completely will put you in the safety position. Once in the safety position you can make crew changes, adjust equipment, or just stop and rest. A second way is to head up, turning the boat directly into the wind (the *no-go zone*). This is the preferred way to stop at a dock.

## Tacking from Reach to Reach VIDEO 10

One of the first maneuvers you will practice on the water is to switch from sailing in one direction across the wind to the other by turning your boat through the *no-go zone*. You will start with the wind blowing across one side of the boat (*reaching*), and end up with it blowing across the opposite side. Any time you switch the wind from one side of the boat to the other by sailing through the *no-go zone*, you are *tacking*. The *reach-to-reach tack* is the easiest and safest for a beginner.

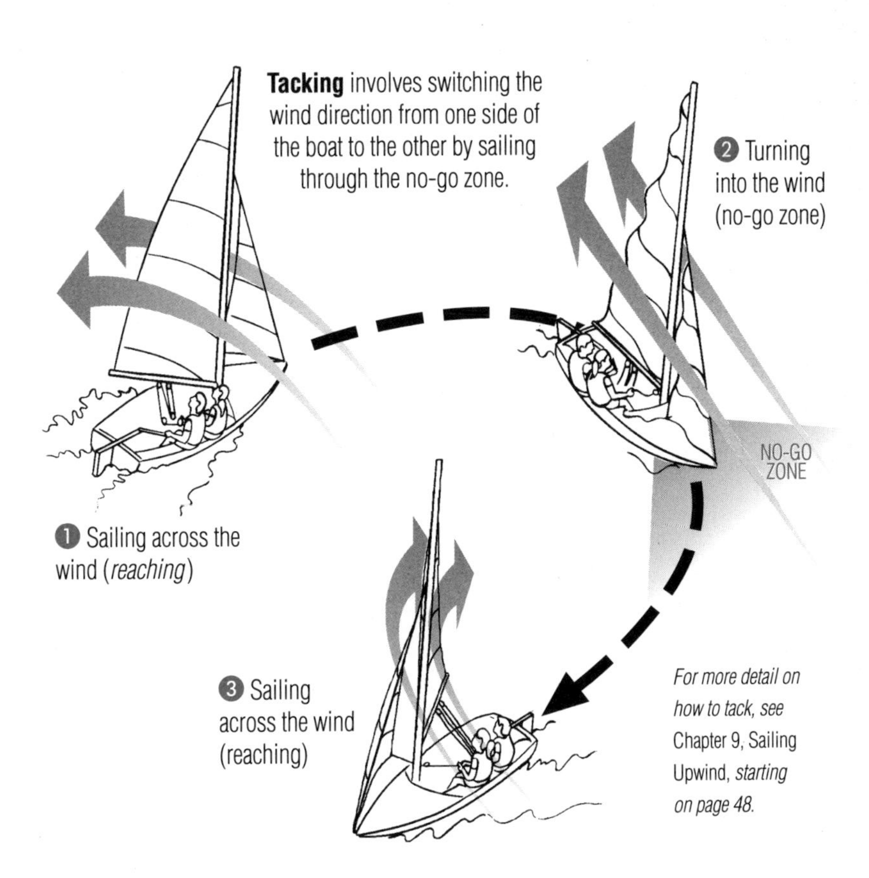


*For more detail on how to tack, see* Chapter 9, Sailing Upwind, *starting on page 48.*

### Multihull Tip...

**Stopping the Boat Quickly**

1. Push tiller to turn boat into the wind.
2. Ease the sheets so the sails are luffing.
3. Push the boom forward until the wind is pushing against the back of the sail. You can also do the same with the jib.
4. When the boat stops, go into the Safety Position.

*NOTE: In stronger winds (with more waves), the mast may rotate sharply from side to side. Easing the downhaul will calm things down.*

### Quick Review

▶ Describe the essential roles of the helmsman and the crew. *(answer on p.34-35)*

▶ To turn your boat *toward* the wind, which way should you push or pull the tiller? *(answer on p.36)*

▶ If your boat is heeling to leeward a lot, which way will it want to turn? *(answer on p.37)*

▶ If you wanted to turn away from the wind quickly, which sail would you ease? *(answer on p.38)*

▶ Describe two ways to stop your boat. *(answer on p.40-41)*

### Think about it...

▶ How did the safety position get its name?

▶ What would be the best way to make a safe landing at a dock?

# Sailing Directions

**KEY CONCEPTS**
- Basic sailing directions
- Heading
- Using the mainsail & jib together

The sails are the sailboat's engine. They convert wind energy into lift that powers your sailboat to where you want to go. As you change direction under sail, you cause the direction of the wind to change relative to your boat. When wind direction changes, your sails need to be adjusted to keep working their best. It's a good idea to hold the sheets in your hand (rather than cleating them) while you are learning these adjustments so you can develop a feel for what the wind is doing to the sails.

**BASIC SAILING DIRECTIONS**

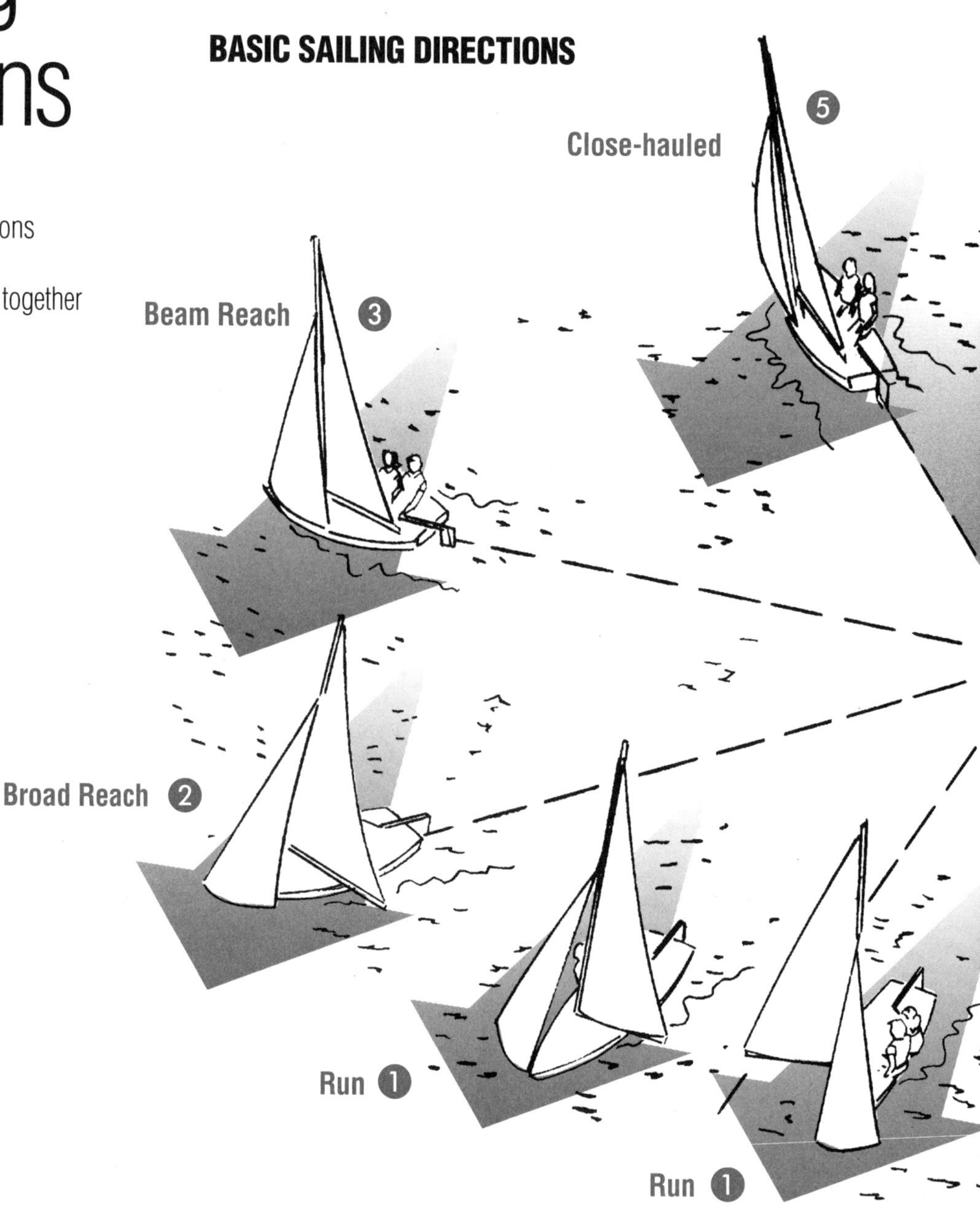

## Basic Sailing Directions (Points of Sail) VIDEO 11

Changes in a boat's direction relative to the wind are described in terms of angles or sectors within a 360 degree circle. There are six basic sailing directions:

1. *run* — wind from directly behind
2. *broad reach* — wind from rear quarter
3. *beam reach* — wind from side
4. *close reach* — wind from just forward of side
5. *close-hauled* — wind from forward and to the side
6. *no-go zone* — wind from directly ahead

A boat cannot sail directly into the wind. The sails will flap and the boat will slow down and stop. As a matter of fact, very few boats can sail closer than 45 degrees to the wind. This area from directly into the wind to approximately 45 degrees either side of the wind is called the **no-go zone**.

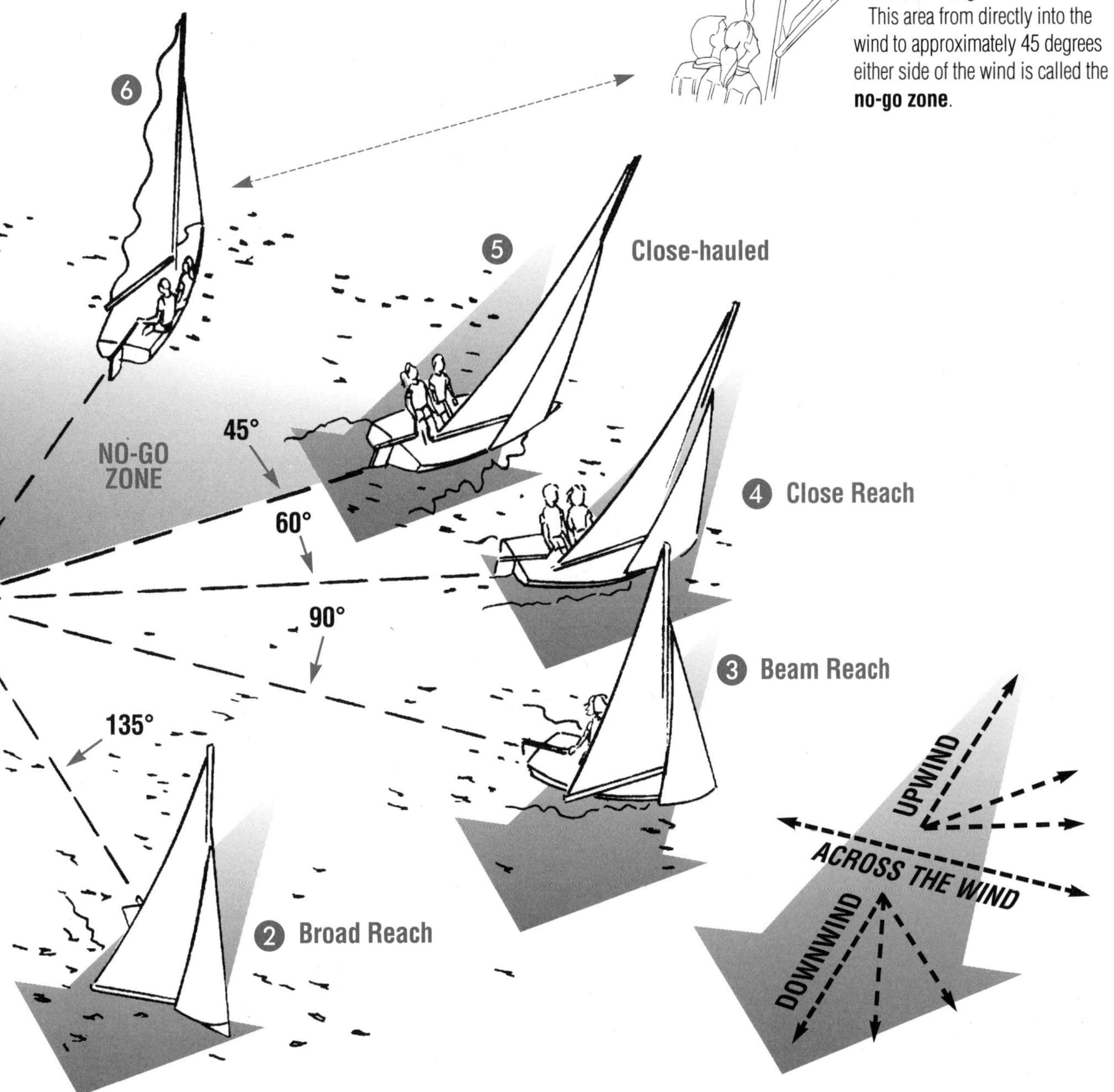

NO-GO ZONE
Close Reach
Beam Reach
Run
Broad Reach

VIDEO 11

## Run (Dead Downwind)

When sailing downwind on a run, the wind is coming from directly behind the boat. Your sails should be eased out all-the-way, working in the push mode. You will sense a decrease in wind speed because you are moving with the the wind. Downwind, you can trim the jib on the opposite side from the mainsail to catch more wind. This is called sailing *wing-and-wing.*

## Broad Reach

VIDEO 11

By turning the boat closer toward the wind so that it's blowing over the rear corner of the boat — approximately 135 degrees back from the bow — the boat is now on a *broad reach*. Usually the boat will sail a little faster, and the sails will have to be sheeted in slightly. You will begin to feel a little more wind on your skin and face. Your sails are starting to shift from the push mode to the pull mode. On a broad reach, it's not possible to trim your sails wing-and-wing.

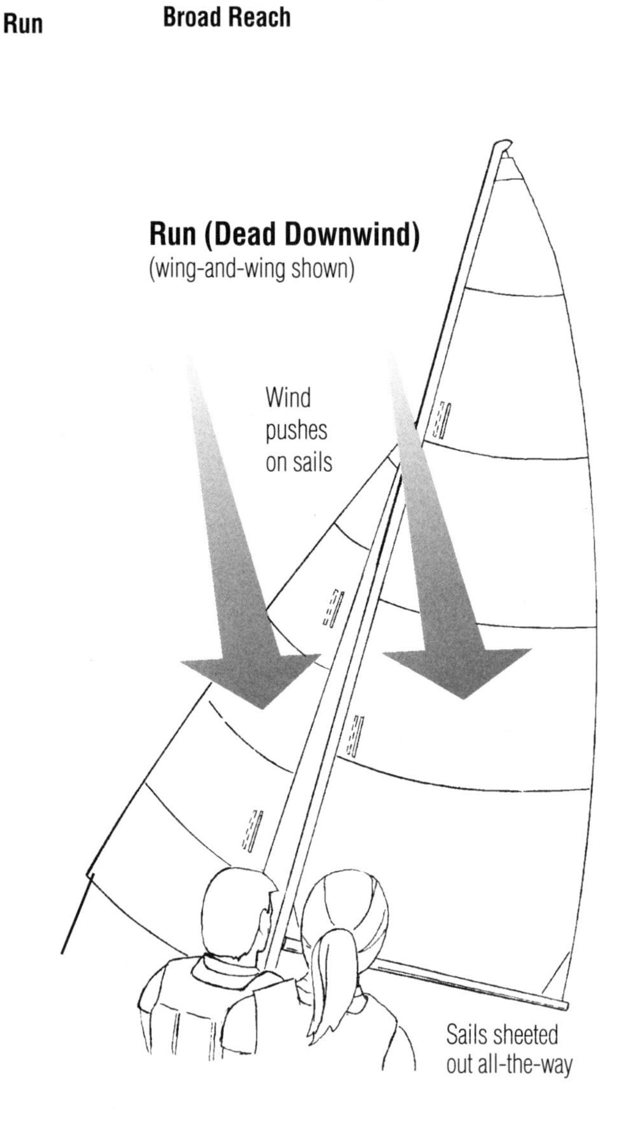

## Beam Reach VIDEO 11

A *beam reach* means the wind is coming directly over the side of the boat. This means that the angle to the wind is approximately 90 degrees back from the bow. For most boats this is the fastest point of sail. Your sails are now operating in the pull mode and should be trimmed in approximately halfway. Some lightweight dinghies may even rise up on top of the water and accelerate rapidly. This is called *planing*, and normally requires the breeze to be at least medium strength and the sails to be trimmed properly. Planing is one of the most exhilarating thrills in sailing.

## Close Reach VIDEO 11

If you head up closer to the wind so that it is a bit forward of the side — approximately 60 degrees from the bow — it is called a *close reach*. You are now starting to head toward the wind, and you will feel an increase of breeze on your skin as the forward motion of the boat adds to the actual wind. You will need to sheet in the sails more, and the boat will want to tip (*heel*) more than when beam reaching or sailing downwind. This is normal.

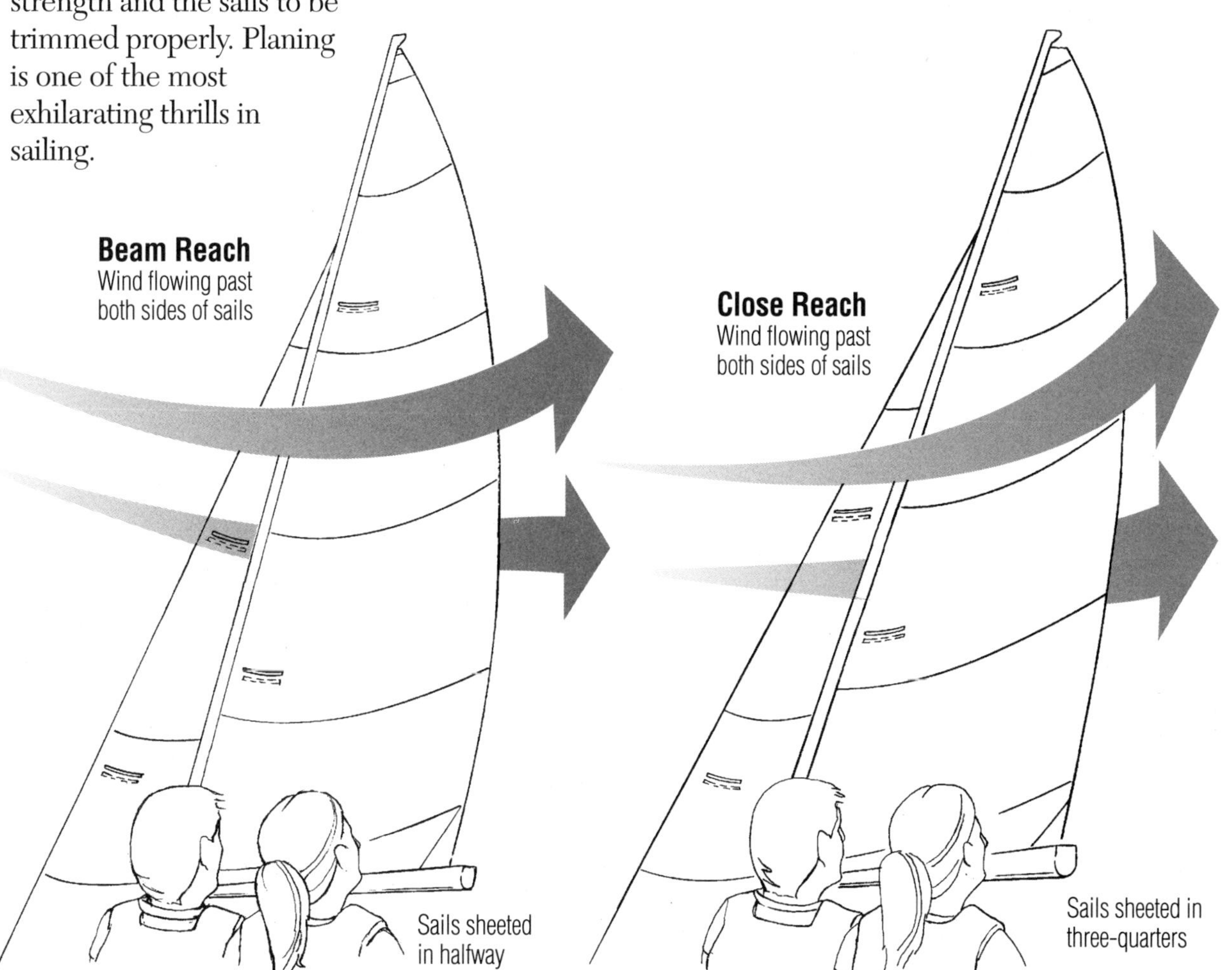

VIDEO 4+10

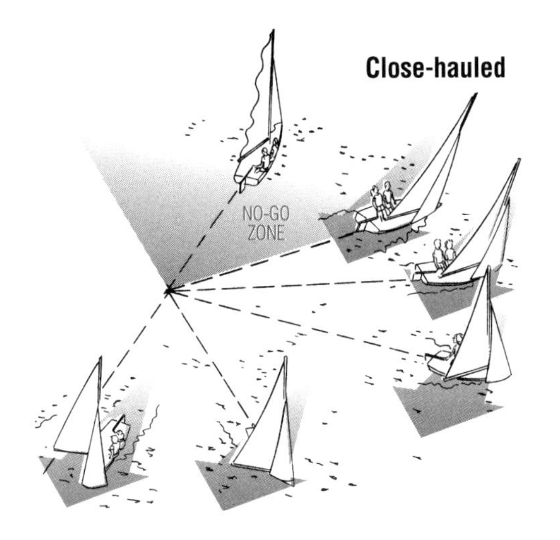


## Close-hauled (Upwind)

With the sails sheeted in all the way and the boat sailing approximately 45 degrees to the wind, you are sailing *close-hauled* or *upwind*. The sails are operating totally in the pull mode. Often, beginning sailors don't sheet in the sails enough, sometimes because of fear of heeling too much (to counteract heeling, move your weight outboard). With help from your instructor, you will see how important it is to pull the sails in all-the-way in order to sail upwind.

## No-Go Zone

VIDEO 4

A boat cannot sail directly into the wind. The sails will flap and the boat will slow down and stop. As a matter of fact, very few boats can sail closer than 45 degrees to the wind. This area from directly into the wind to approximately 45 degrees on either side is called the *no-go zone*. Steering into the no-go zone is an excellent way to slow down your boat or stop it — a maneuver often used in docking or approaching a mooring.

### "In the groove..."

When sailing upwind, steering is very important. If you steer too close to the wind, the sails will luff or flap and lose power. If you steer too far away from the wind, the boat will gain speed (you are now sailing on a close reach), but will not make good progress toward the wind. You will soon develop a knack for steering the boat upwind at just the right angle. Sailors call this sailing "in the groove" (see p. 72-73).

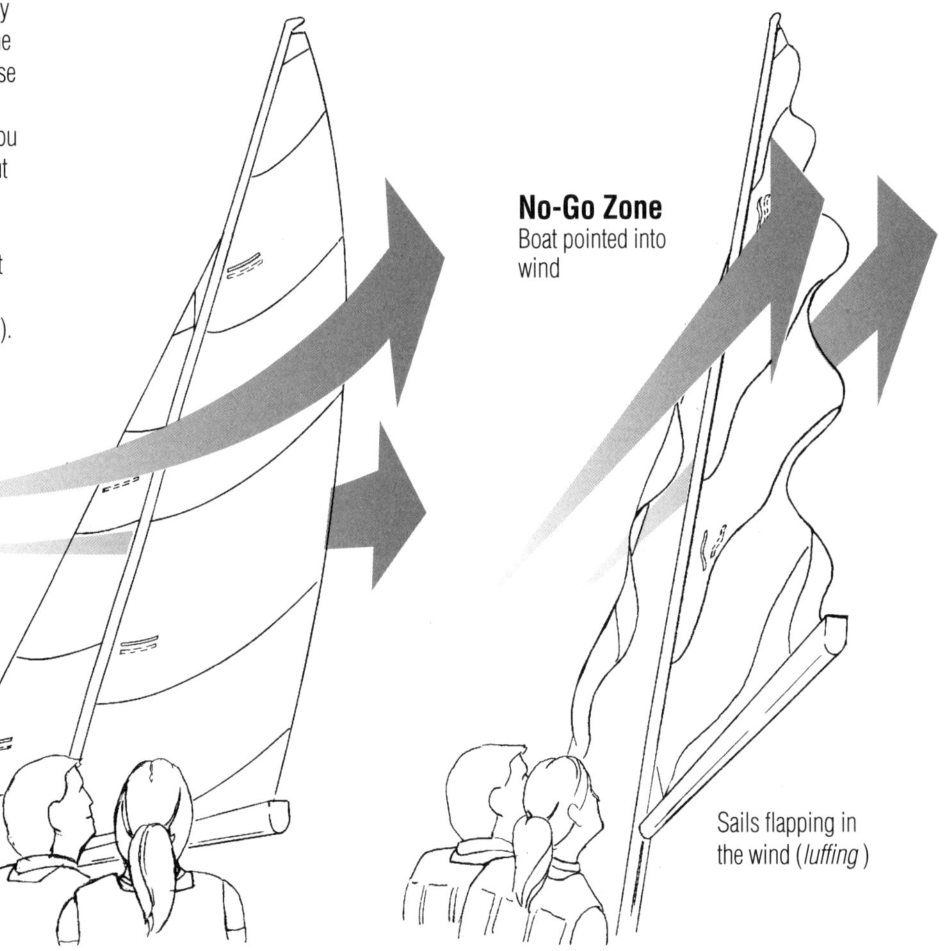

## Heading

The direction your bow points is referred to as your *heading*. Your heading determines your sail trim. Whenever you change to a new direction, you should change the trim of your sails.

## Using the Mainsail and Jib Together

VIDEO 13

When sailing on a boat with both a mainsail and jib, you should try to sheet the two sails in and out simultaneously. If you are going from a beam reach to a broad reach, let out (*ease*) the main and jib together. If you are going to head up from a close reach to close-hauled, sheet in (*trim*) the main and jib together. If the sails are not adjusted in harmony, they can affect each other's wind flow and reduce performance. When the helmsman decides to change direction, it is important that he or she lets the crew know whether it is time to ease or trim the jib by saying, "We are going to sail on a beam reach," or "We are changing course to a close reach." This helps the crew to prepare for changes in sail trim and crew position. Good communication makes for better sailing!

### Quick Review

- ▶ Describe the six basic points of sail. *(answer on p.42-43)*
- ▶ On what points of sail do your sails operate in the "push" mode? *(answer on p.44)*
- ▶ For most boats, what is the fastest point of sail? *(answer on p.45)*
- ▶ How close can most boats effectively steer toward the wind before the sails begin to luff and lose power? *(answer on p.43 & 46)*

### Think about it...

- ▶ Why is the beam reach the fastest point of sail for most boats?
- ▶ How can the no-go zone be used as a valuable tool in sailing?
- ▶ Why is sailing close-hauled the most difficult point of sail to learn?

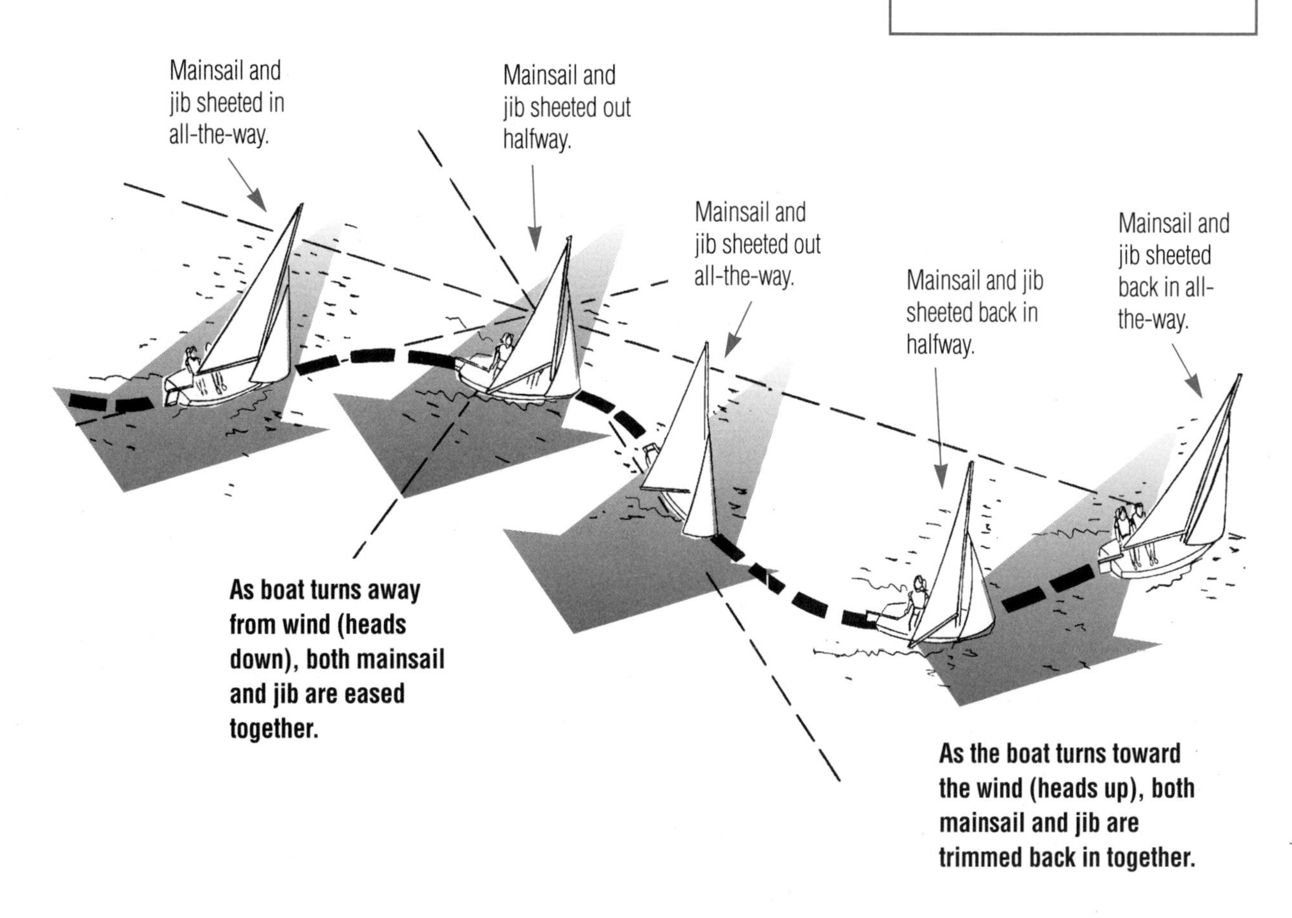

# Sailing Upwind

**KEY CONCEPTS**

- Sailing upwind
  - Tacking
  - In irons
- Communication
- Tacking sequence
- Tacking problems

Learning to sail a boat upwind is one of the most rewarding experiences in sailing. It involves coordinating both steering and sail trim as you react to changes in wind strength and direction. As you learn, you will develop a sense of how all these elements work together. Experienced sailors often call this "sailing by the seat of your pants."

Sailing upwind requires proper body position, just the right angle of heel, and steering at a specific angle toward the wind. In the illustration below, notice the helmsman and crew sit facing the center of the boat with the helmsman steering from the "high" (*windward* ) side, opposite the boom. Ideally, the boat should have a small amount of heel to leeward. In lighter wind, the crew may have to move inside the boat to maintain a bit of heal.

When sailing upwind, sails are trimmed in all-the-way and wind is about 45° from the bow.

NO-GO ZONE

**Use telltales** to help steer a course with wind about 45° from the bow.

**Centerboard** down all-the-way

## Tacking Upwind

VIDEO 10

As we explained in the last chapter, a sailboat cannot sail directly into the wind, but can sail approximately 45° from the wind. So how do you reach a destination that is toward the wind? By sailing a course at 45° from the wind with the wind on one side of the boat, and then on the other, you can sail a "zig-zag" course that makes progress upwind.

This zig-zag course requires *tacking*. Tacking is changing the direction the wind hits your boat from one side to the other by turning the bow toward the wind and through the no-go zone.

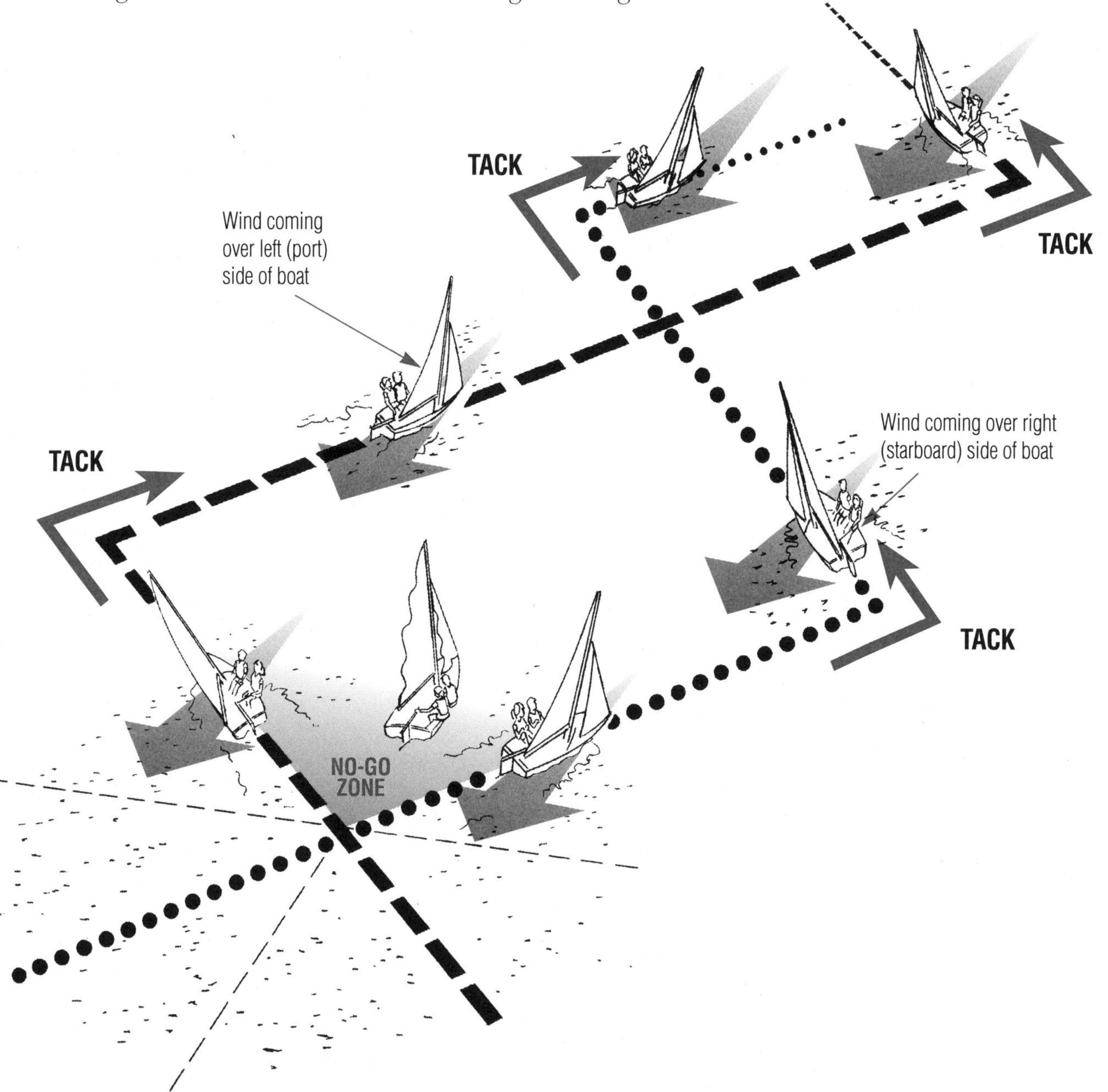

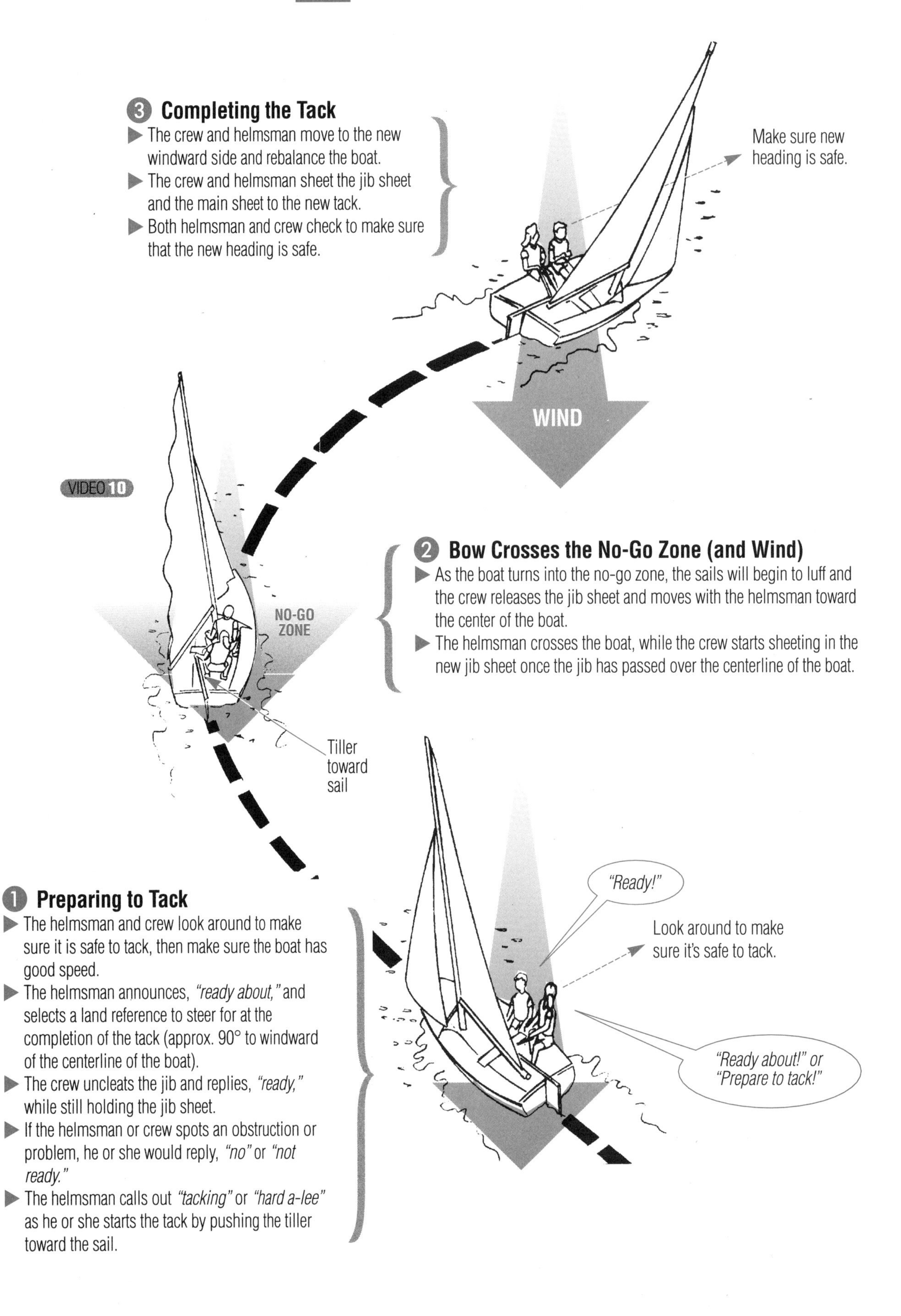


### ❶ Preparing to Tack

- ▶ The helmsman and crew look around to make sure it is safe to tack, then make sure the boat has good speed.
- ▶ The helmsman announces, *"ready about,"* and selects a land reference to steer for at the completion of the tack (approx. 90° to windward of the centerline of the boat).
- ▶ The crew uncleats the jib and replies, *"ready,"* while still holding the jib sheet.
- ▶ If the helmsman or crew spots an obstruction or problem, he or she would reply, *"no"* or *"not ready."*
- ▶ The helmsman calls out *"tacking"* or *"hard a-lee"* as he or she starts the tack by pushing the tiller toward the sail.

### ❷ Bow Crosses the No-Go Zone (and Wind)

- ▶ As the boat turns into the no-go zone, the sails will begin to luff and the crew releases the jib sheet and moves with the helmsman toward the center of the boat.
- ▶ The helmsman crosses the boat, while the crew starts sheeting in the new jib sheet once the jib has passed over the centerline of the boat.

### ❸ Completing the Tack

- ▶ The crew and helmsman move to the new windward side and rebalance the boat.
- ▶ The crew and helmsman sheet the jib sheet and the main sheet to the new tack.
- ▶ Both helmsman and crew check to make sure that the new heading is safe.

## Communication VIDEO 10

A good tack requires good communication between helmsman and crew. Since the helmsman is steering and in command, he or she should give the voice commands. The helmsman starts the maneuver by announcing *"prepare to tack!"* or *"ready about!"* This means the crew should get ready to uncleat the jib and to move from one side of the boat to the other.

Once the crew is ready, he or she responds by saying *"ready!"* When the helmsman starts to turn the boat, he or she will say *"tacking!"* or *"hard a-lee!"* which indicates that the tiller is being pushed hard to leeward. The crew now knows the tack is beginning.

### A Good Idea...

It's a good idea to practice tacking with land drills first before trying it on the water. In medium to light winds, a normal tack should take about five to seven seconds.

## The Crew's Role

In tacking, the crew plays a vital role. He or she must help with boat balance and tack the jib while keeping a lookout. Spotting land references and checking to make sure the way is clear, the crew provides important feedback to the helmsman. When first learning to sail, most helmsmen have their focus inside the boat, coordinating the main sheet and tiller. The crew can act as the helmsman's second pair of eyes until the tack is completed.

*"Whatever happened to the shortest distance between two points being a straight line?"*

## Tacking Problems

It is common to make mistakes when you are learning to tack. Some of the common mistakes are listed here, but with help from land drill practice and your instructor, it will not take long before you are tacking with confidence.

| Tacking Problems... | Solutions... |
|---|---|
| *The boat stops turning while in the no-go zone.* | Start your tack by pushing the tiller more quickly toward the sail (do not shove it over abruptly, however). Be sure to begin a tack when the boat is moving with good speed. |
| *You forget to change jib sheets and the jib ends up sheeted on the wrong side.* | As you change position, release the old jib sheet and trim the new one. |
| *The boat is turned too far through the wind and the tack ends with the boat sailing on a reach rather than close-hauled.* | Before tacking, choose a landmark approximately 90° to windward (see illustration) to help establish your new course heading. As you finish your tack, aim your boat at this landmark. |

1 Push tiller and boom in direction you want the bow to turn. While drifting backward, pull jib to the opposite side.

2 When the boat has turned out of the no-go zone, sheet in the jib and center the tiller.

3 Sheet in the mainsail and resume sailing.

## Getting Out of Irons

Before you start a tack, you'll need to be sailing fast enough to pass through the no-go zone without stopping. If you stay in the no-go zone too long, the boat will stop and then start drifting backward. This condition is called *getting in irons*, and is common for beginning sailors (it occasionally happens to experienced sailors, too!). The easiest way to get out of irons is to push both the tiller and the boom in the same direction you want to turn as your boat moves backward (see illustration). If the boat has a jib, the crew should pull it to the side opposite from the boom.

## Crossing the Boat While Tacking VIDEO 10

During a tack, the helmsman crosses from one side of the boat to the other while switching both the tiller and main sheet from one hand to the other. A smooth hand exchange is key to a

**Crossing the boat while tacking**

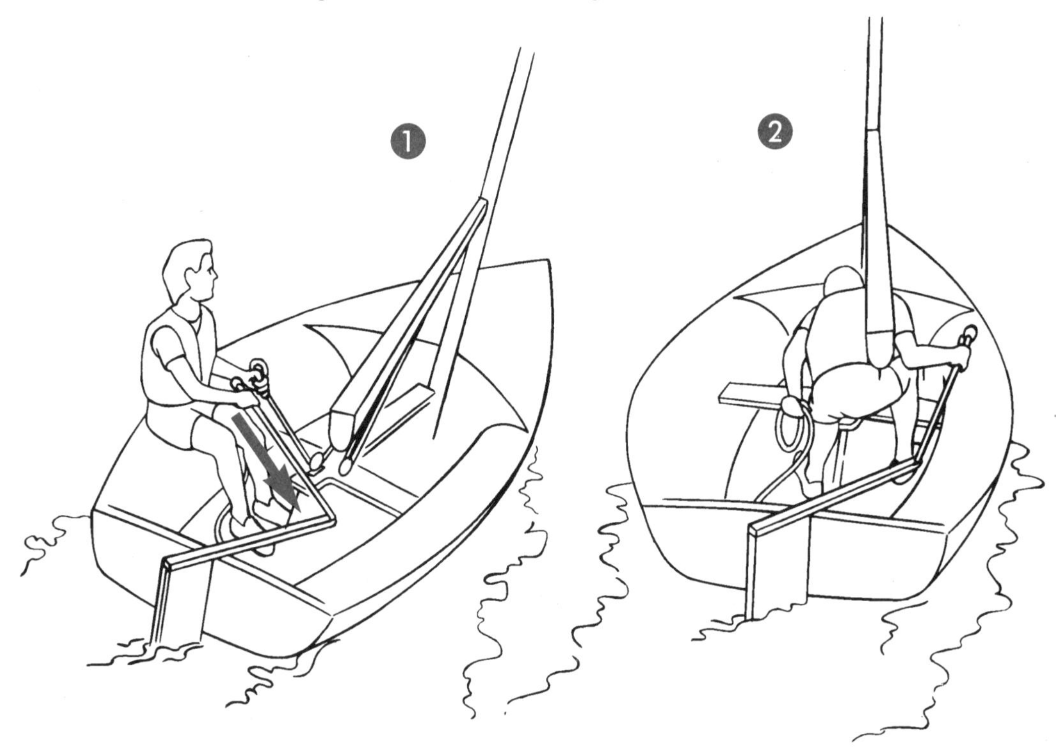


**Start tack** by pushing tiller extension (or tiller) firmly toward the sail.

Hold tiller over and **cross the boat** while facing forward. Take the sheet with you as you duck under boom. Watch for sails to luff (flap).

smooth tack, so practice it first on land (see Appendix for land drill) until you can do it smoothly and automatically.

As you cross the boat while facing forward, switch hands by pivoting and reaching your sheet hand (still holding the sheet) behind your back to grab the tiller or tiller extension. When your sheet hand has the extension, then your other hand lets go of the tiller or tiller extension. One hand now holds both sheet and extension. After you are on the new side, your free hand grabs the main sheet in front of your body.

The timing of your hand switch will vary a bit depending on whether a tiller or tiller extension is used. (See Appendix for a land drill to practice tacking with a tiller.)

Many expert dinghy sailors prefer to switch hands *after* the tack to give them better control of boat balance and trim.

## Four Key Points for Successful Tacks...

1. Keep tiller pushed over in its turning position throughout the tack.
2. Face forward and look ahead as you cross the boat.
3. Duck as you go under the boom.
4. Hold onto sheet and tiller, but switch hands that hold them (neither sheet nor tiller ever escapes your control while switching hands).

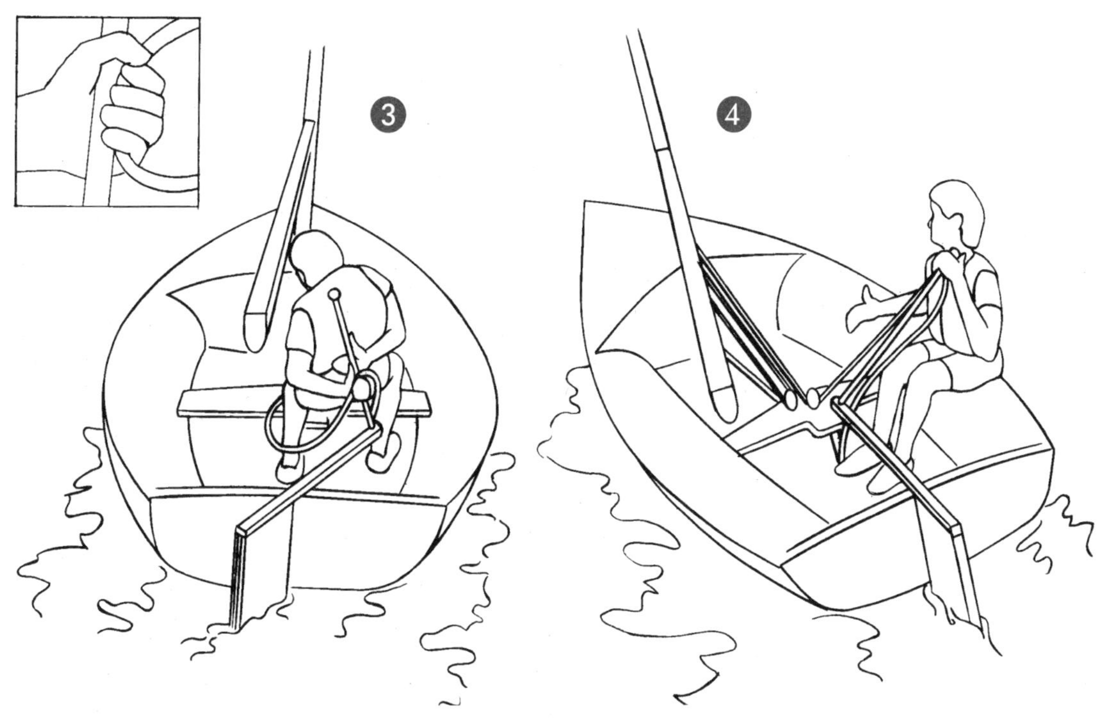


**Reach sheet hand behind back** and grab tiller extension, trapping the main sheet and the extension in one hand (see inset illustration above). Other (right) hand releases tiller extension.

Watch for sail to fill, then **finish tack** by pushing tiller back to the center. Reach for sheet with empty front hand so tiller hand can release it.

## Tacking a Multihull

Tacking a multihull is similar in concept to tacking a monohull, but because multihulls are wide and light, they do not steer through a tack as easily as monohulls. A few adjustments in technique will keep your tacks smooth.

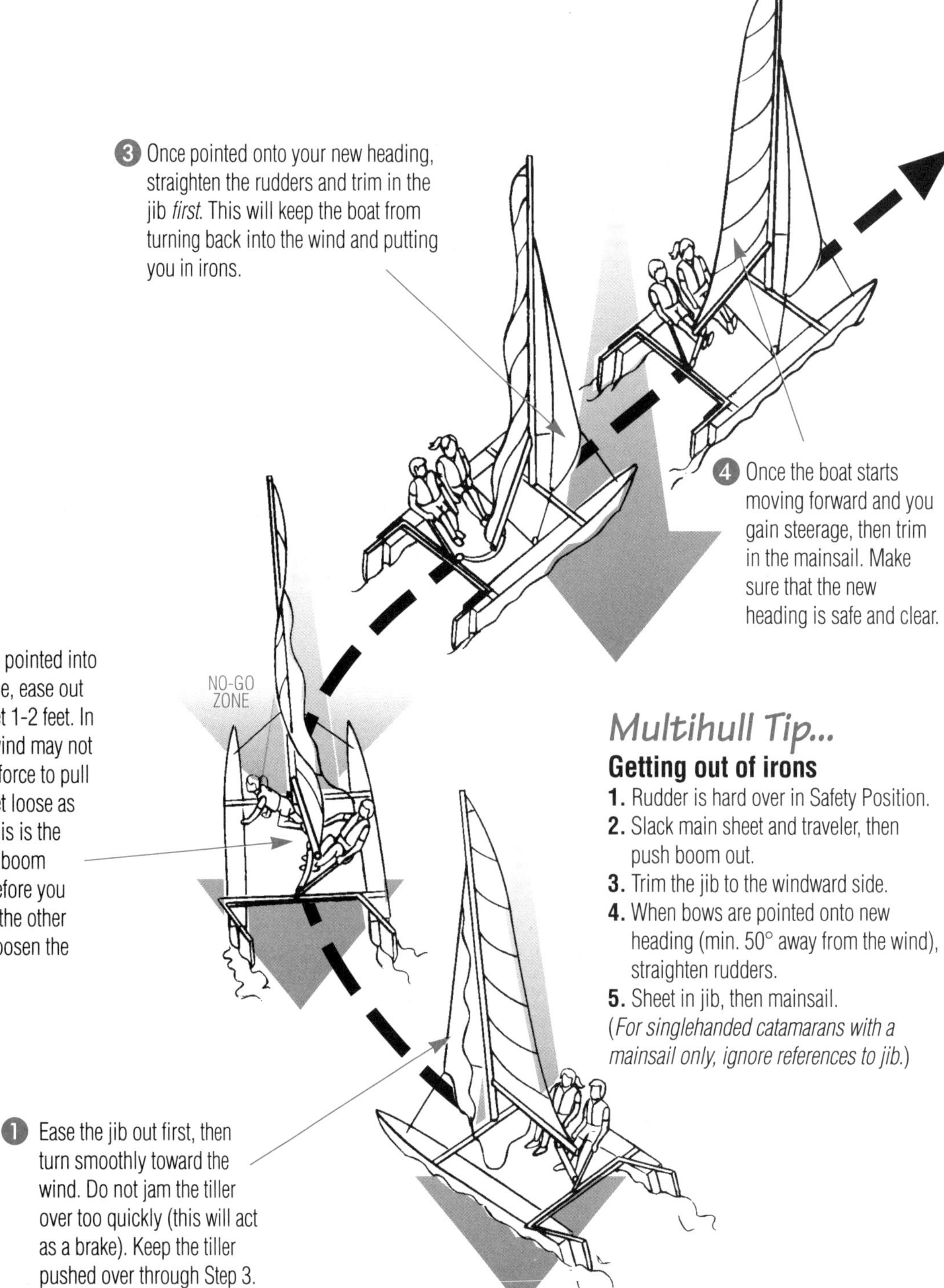


### Multihull Tip...

**Getting out of irons**

1. Rudder is hard over in Safety Position.
2. Slack main sheet and traveler, then push boom out.
3. Trim the jib to the windward side.
4. When bows are pointed onto new heading (min. 50° away from the wind), straighten rudders.
5. Sheet in jib, then mainsail.

(*For singlehanded catamarans with a mainsail only, ignore references to jib.*)

## The Dime Tack (Getting Out of Irons)

The *dime tack* (as in "turn on a dime") is a useful maneuver when a multihull is stationary, moving very slowly, or stalled in the middle of a tack (*in irons*). It is also an effective method for turning the boat around quickly if a crew member falls overboard.

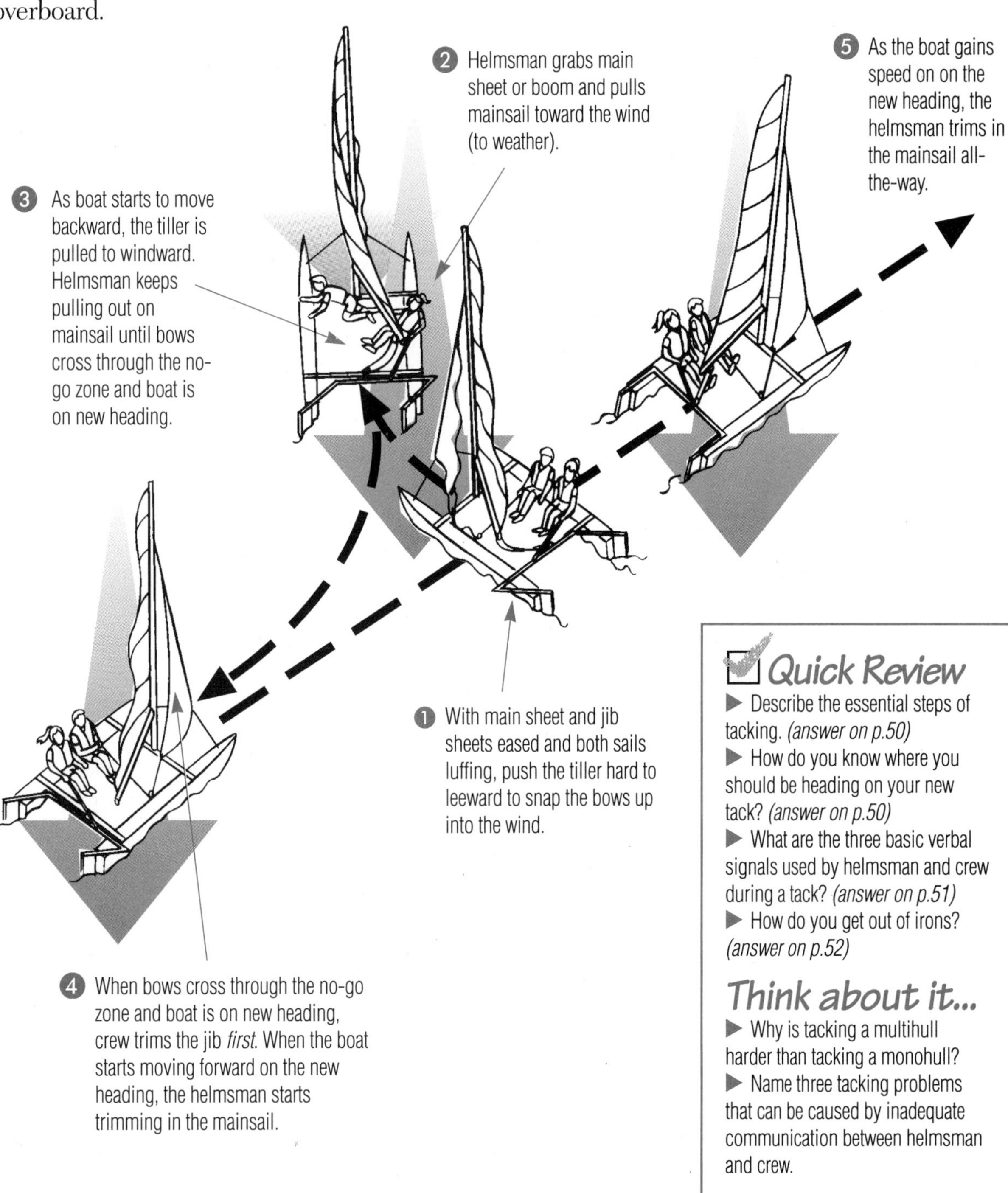


### Quick Review

- Describe the essential steps of tacking. *(answer on p.50)*
- How do you know where you should be heading on your new tack? *(answer on p.50)*
- What are the three basic verbal signals used by helmsman and crew during a tack? *(answer on p.51)*
- How do you get out of irons? *(answer on p.52)*

### Think about it...

- Why is tacking a multihull harder than tacking a monohull?
- Name three tacking problems that can be caused by inadequate communication between helmsman and crew.

# CHAPTER 10 Sailing Downwind

**KEY CONCEPTS**

- Sailing downwind
- Sailing by the lee
- Jibing
- Types of jibes

Sailing downwind, or *running* with the wind coming over the stern, is often the sailor's favorite sailing direction because it's so easy.

When sailing on a run, the boat is in the *push* mode, and the sails are sheeted out all-the-way to expose as much sail area as possible to the wind's pushing force. Because the wind is pushing on only one side of the sail, the sail telltales do not work in their normal way. Since you are traveling at nearly the same speed as the wind, the feel of the wind on your face and body will be greatly reduced.

## Downwind Maneuvers VIDEO 11

When sailing upwind (toward the wind), steering to change the wind orientation from one side of the boat to the other is called a *tack*. When sailing downwind (away from the wind), steering to change the wind orientation from one side to another is called a *jibe*. During a tack, you push the tiller *toward* the sails to turn the boat *toward* the wind, and the bow (front) of the boat crosses the wind. In a

WIND

**Sails sheeted out all-the-way** (operating in the push mode).

**Telltales hang limp.**

**Centerboard or daggerboard raised** 3/4 of the way up.

jibe, the tiller is pulled *away from* the sails to turn the boat *away from* the wind, and the wind swings across the stern (back) of the boat. Both tacking and jibing require moving the sails across the boat from one side to the other.

A jibe requires a clear sense of the wind direction. By knowing the wind's direction, you can time your jibe just right, smoothly swinging the sails from one side of the boat to the other. If your timing is off, the sails and the boom can snap across the boat unexpectedly. This is called an *accidental jibe*.

One of the most common causes of accidental jibes is *sailing by the lee*. When you sail dead downwind, the wind is coming directly over the stern — down the centerline of the boat. If you sail by the lee, the wind moves toward the side of the boat that the sails are on. When this happens, the wind can push on the wrong side of the sail and snap the mainsail across the boat. One of the signs that you are by the lee is that the jib will hang limp and start to cross the boat. You can also watch the wind indicator at the top of the mast (sometimes called a *masthead fly*), the telltales on the windward shroud, and the ripples on the water as indicators of the wind direction.

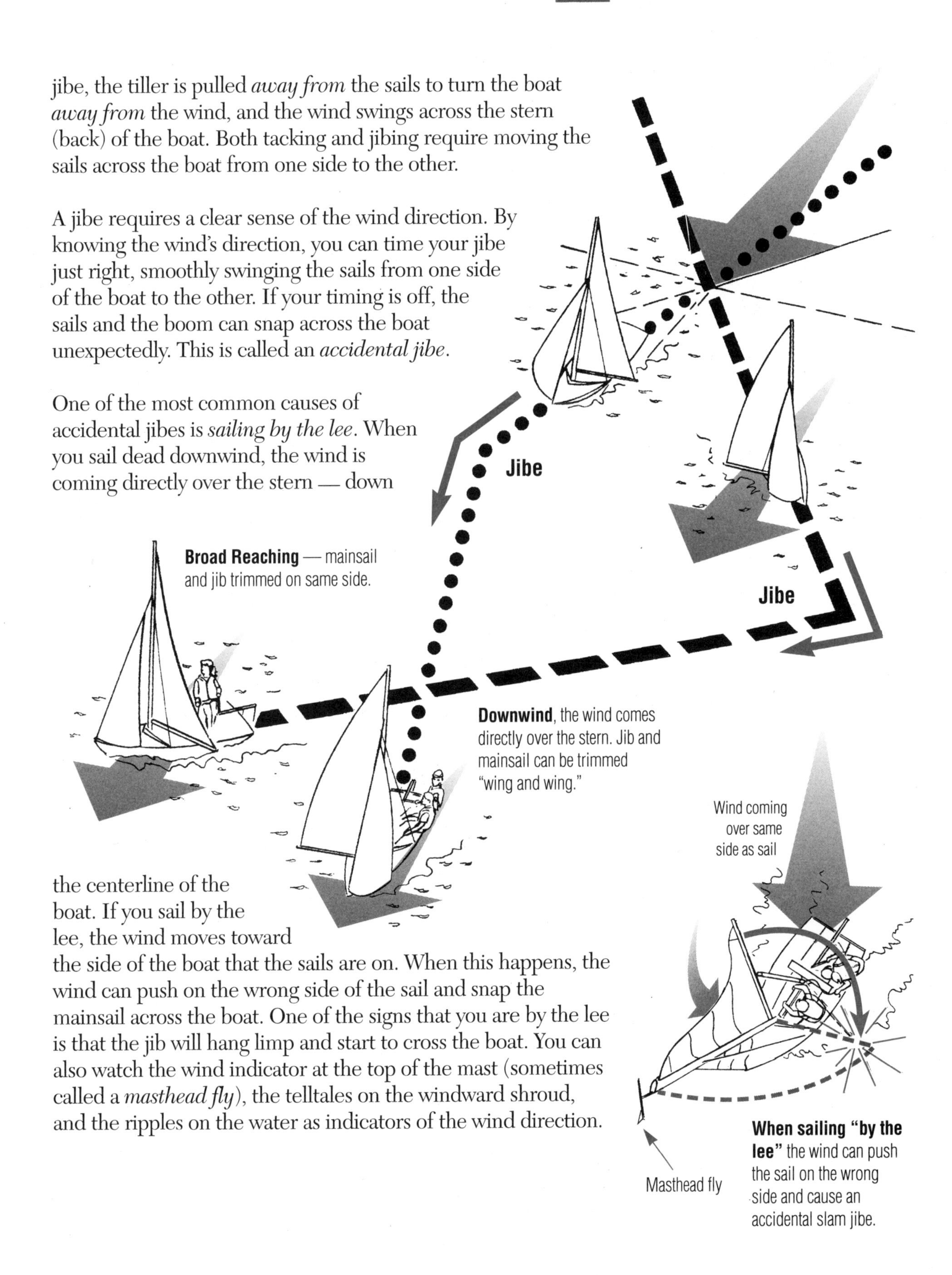

## Jibing Smoothly VIDEO 11

When jibing, the mainsail will want to snap across the back of the boat and then suddenly fill with wind when it reaches the other side. In stronger winds, this sudden force can cause the boat to heel and spin, or even capsize. The best way to counteract this — and make your jibe smooth and safe — is with a *controlled jibe.* The key to a controlled jibe is how you handle the mainsail during the jibe. It should be slowly sheeted in as you start the jibe, then centered as the stern crosses the wind. Finally it is eased out "under control."

If you steer straight through the jibe without controlling the mainsail, it will suddenly swing across uncontrolled. This is called a *C-jibe* or a *slam jibe*. Slam jibes are no problem in lighter winds, but in stronger winds they can cause loss of control and strain rigging and gear.

Remember, if the air is too strong for a safe jibe, you can steer around into the wind and tack the boat instead.

### Tips for Easier Jibing

1. Practice the land drills first until you perfect the hand and tiller exchanges.
2. Before the jibe, try to locate the wind direction by wind sensing or looking at the masthead fly or the telltale on the windward shroud.
3. Lower the centerboard halfway.
4. Make sure all the sheets are free and clear of any entanglements.
5. Turn the boat very slowly while jibing.
6. Keep an eye on the new course sailed.
7. Make sure the crew and helmsman talk through the maneuver.
8. Practice at first in smooth seas and light winds.

## Crew and Helmsman Responsibilities VIDEO 11

In addition to handling the jib, the crew helps balance the boat and serves as lookout for the helmsman. The crew also may have to help the helmsman jibe the boom. The helmsman should always call out *"prepare to jibe!"* and *"jibe-ho!"* at the proper times.

Of all the sailing maneuvers, the jibe has the greatest potential for error. But if you combine wind awareness, smooth steering and a little practice, your jibes will soon be safe and confident.

**5 Completing the Jibe**

- The helmsman adjusts the boom to the new heading.
- The crew trims the jib sheet.
- The helmsman and crew check to see that the new heading is correct and reorient themselves to the new wind direction.

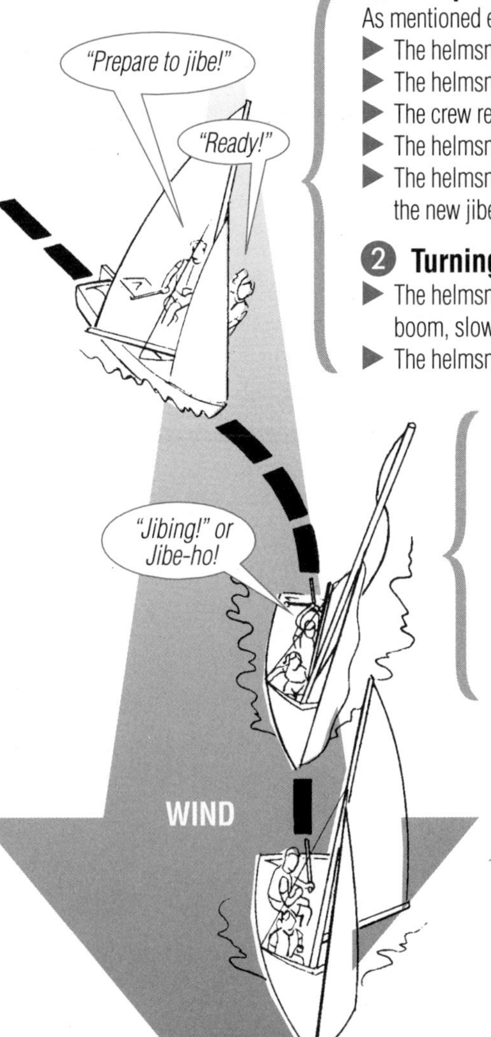


### ❶ Preparing for a Controlled Jibe

As mentioned earlier, timing is key to a smooth jibe.

- ▶ The helmsman and crew check to see that it is safe to jibe.
- ▶ The helmsman announces, *"prepare to jibe!"*
- ▶ The crew responds, *"ready to jibe!"* if all is ready.
- ▶ The helmsman determines the exact location of the wind.
- ▶ The helmsman picks a land reference to steer toward on the new jibe.

### ❷ Turning Away From the Wind

- ▶ The helmsman moves the tiller gradually away from the boom, slowly turning the boat. The crew lets the jib luff.
- ▶ The helmsman slowly starts to pull in the main sheet.

### ❸ Stern Crosses Through Wind

- ▶ Grabbing all the main sheet, the helmsman brings the boom to the centerline and says, *"jibe-ho!"*
- ▶ The helmsman lets the boom cross the centerline and eases out the main sheet. As the boom crosses the centerline, the helmsman briefly centers the tiller.

### ❹ Turning Toward Wind

- ▶ The helmsman switches the main sheet and the tiller to opposite hands and then resumes steering gradually through the jibe. Helmsman and crew reposition themselves on the new windward side opposite the boom.

## Quick Review

▶ Define a jibe. *(answer on p.56-57)*

▶ What direction do you push or pull the tiller to begin a jibe? *(answer on p.57 & 59)*

▶ Define an accidental jibe and two signals that it is about to happen. *(answer on p.57)*

▶ Define a slam jibe and a C-jibe. *(answer on p.58)*

▶ What part of the rig should you be particularly aware of during a jibe? *(answer on p.58)*

▶ Describe the essential communication between helmsman and crew during a jibe. *(answer on p.59)*

## Think about it...

▶ Why does the wind seem to have less velocity when you are sailing downwind?

▶ What are three ways of preventing an accidental jibe.

▶ If you are unsure or nervous about jibing, what are your options?

### Hand Exchange While Jibing

❶ Just before you grab the main sheet to throw the boom across the boat, transfer the sheet from your sheet hand to your tiller hand. Grab the main sheet between the boom and the cockpit with your sheet hand, and pull the boom across the boat.

❷ As the boom crosses the boat, step across the boat facing forward, pass your old sheet hand behind your back and grab the tiller extension or tiller. Release the tiller from your other hand.

❸ Adjust the main sheet to the new heading.

CHAPTER 11

# Capsize Recovery

**KEY CONCEPTS**

- Windward and leeward capsizes
- Capsize safety rules
- Scoop recovery method
- Multihull recovery method
- Traditional recovery method
- Walkover recovery method
- Turning turtle
- Entering and exiting

As you learn to sail, or become more experienced and start sailing in stronger winds, there's a chance your boat may capsize. It is nothing to be afraid of — it's a natural part of small boat sailing. Even the most experienced sailors capsize. Your instructor will show you the safest and quickest ways to recover from a capsize, and once you have mastered the recovery techniques, you may even find that it's fun.

Most centerboard boats are self-rescuing, which allows you to right the boat and quickly begin sailing again. Self-rescuing boats have built-in buoyancy which keeps the boat from swamping and makes capsize recovery easier. (Make sure the drain plugs in air tanks or flotation bags are securely fastened before you go sailing.)

There are three ways a boat will capsize. The most common way is for the boat to roll over to leeward, away from the wind. The sails will lie on the water downwind from the boat. The second way, the boat rolls over to windward, toward the wind. This happens less frequently, but when it does, it usually happens quicker. The third way, mostly occurring in multihulls, is called a *pitchpole*, when the bows dig into the water and the boat rolls over in a forward direction.

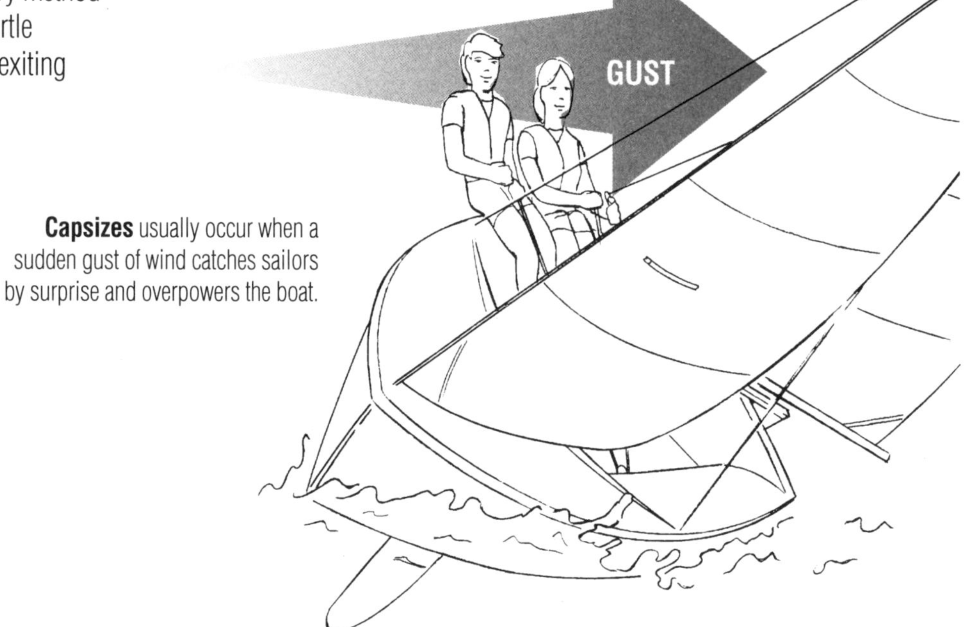


**Capsizes** usually occur when a sudden gust of wind catches sailors by surprise and overpowers the boat.

## Causes of Capsize VIDEO 5

There are a number of reasons why sailboats capsize:

- A sudden gust of wind or change in wind direction catches sailors by surprise and overpowers the boat.
- A poorly executed jibe unbalances the boat and makes it heel or roll too much.
- A broken tiller or hiking strap puts the boat out of control.
- Letting go of the tiller or main sheet makes the boat suddenly turn or change its angle of heel.

There are ways to avoid capsizing. Most important is to sail with the main sheet uncleated, so that you are ready to release it quickly to depower the mainsail if a sudden gust hits. It's also important to keep the boat balanced by adjusting your weight and sail trim. If a boat heels too much, you will lose control. Avoid sudden and unexpected changes in sail trim and weight position that will unbalance the boat, and remember to watch for puffs and gusts so that you are prepared to react.

### The Capsize Safety Rules

If you do capsize, there is one important rule that you should always remember: STAY WITH THE BOAT! Even if you don't think you can turn the boat upright, ***do not try to swim to shore!*** The shore is always further than it looks. If the boat cannot be righted, climb up onto the hull. You will be more comfortable, and rescuers will be able to see you better. Stay with the boat and you will be rescued sooner. When swimming around a capsized boat, you should ***avoid swimming underneath the hull or sails!*** It is easy to get confused or lose your orientation.

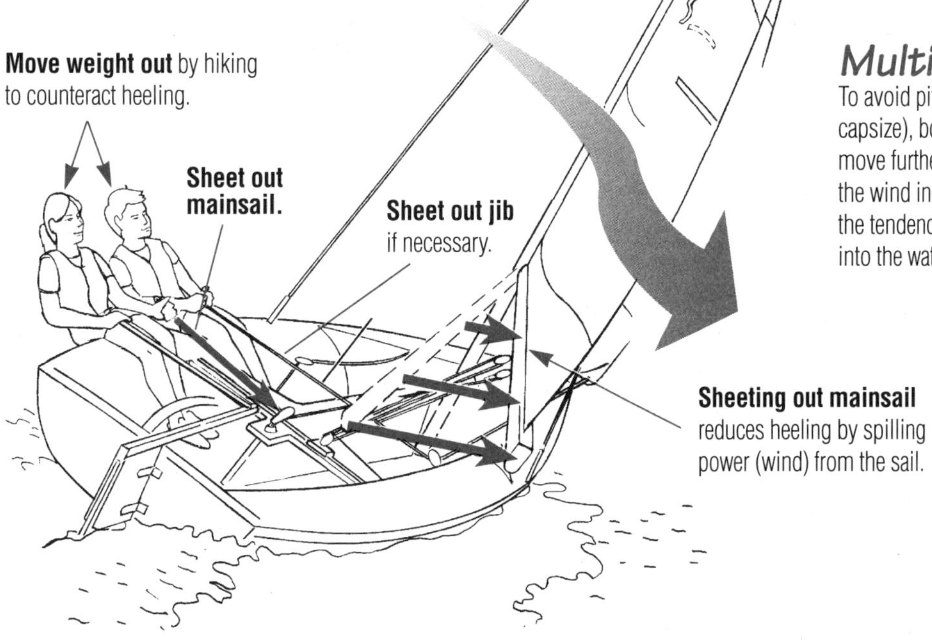


### Multihull Tip...

To avoid pitchpoling (a forward capsize), both skipper and crew should move further back toward the stern as the wind increases. This will counteract the tendency of the boat to dig its bows into the water at higher speeds.

## Scoop Recovery Method VIDEO 5

The *scoop capsize recovery* is the best righting method for boats that are sailed by two or more people. As the boat rights, a person is "scooped" into the boat, and this person can then balance the boat when it is back upright and place it in the safety position. This person can also help the other person into the boat. It's important that the sailors keep in constant touch with each other during the capsize recovery.

❶ **A** supports mast at gooseneck to prevent boat from turtling while **B** moves to centerboard, keeping in constant contact with boat.

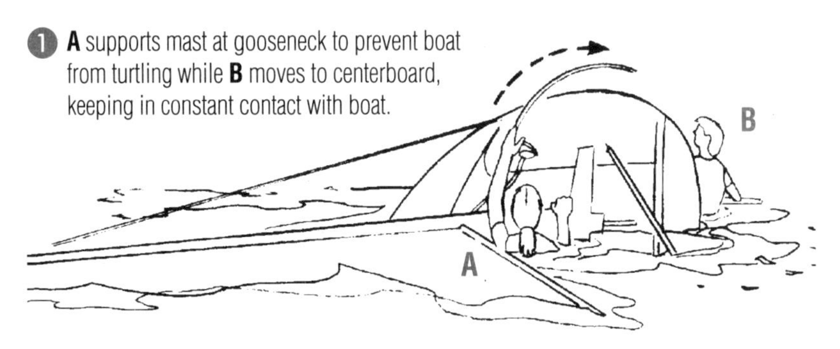


❷ **A** frees the main sheet and throws a jib sheet over the side of the boat. **B** climbs on centerboard, using jib sheet as a safety and righting line.

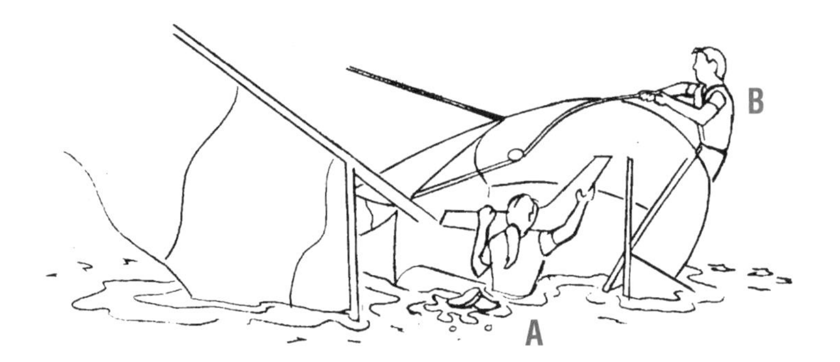


❸ **B** leans out on centerboard while **A** holds onto stationary object in cockpit and kicks. As boat swings upright, **A** is "scooped" into cockpit.

❹ **A** balances the boat and places it in the safety position (wind abeam, sails luffing) and then helps **B** aboard at stern.

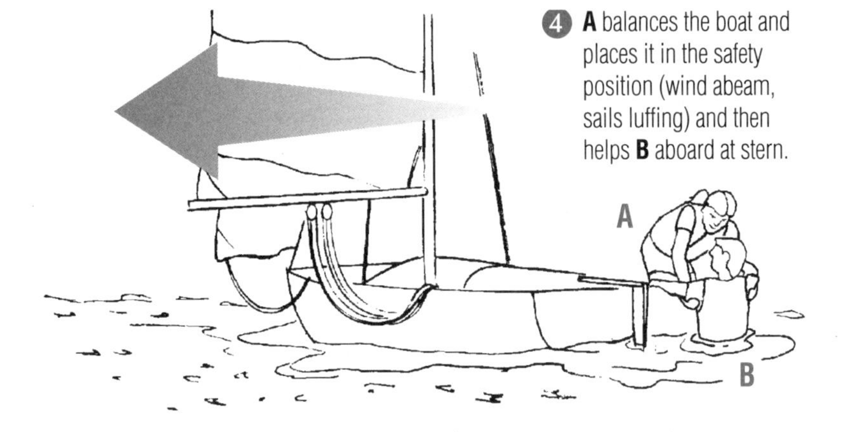


### *Multihull Tip...*

**Capsize Recovery**

Because multihulls are wider than monohulls and require greater leverage to right, there are a few differences in capsize procedure. Most involve the use of a righting line, which is usually attached to the dolphin striker.

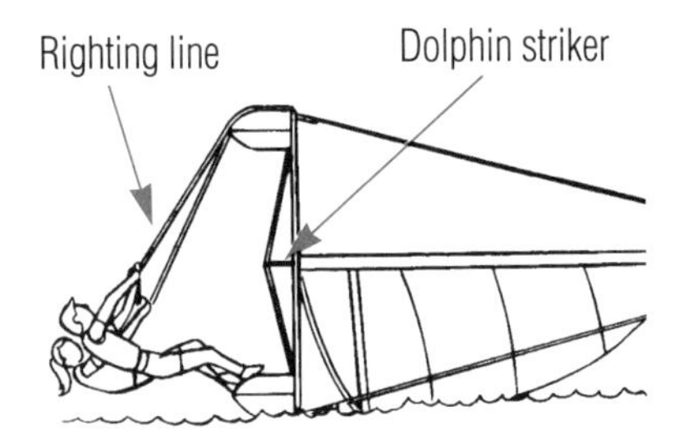


1. Uncleat the jib and main sheets.
2. Point the bows into the wind. By standing on and submerging the bow you can get the hull to swing around into the wind. Hanging on the righting line will help you balance and prevent the boat from turtling.
3. Stand on lower hull, holding righting line, and lean back to right the boat. Do this quickly to prevent the hull from rotating away from the wind.
4. Grab the dolphin striker or lower hull as boat is righted to prevent it from capsizing to the other side.

*NOTE: Be sure to position yourself so that the hull doesn't land on top of you when it is righted.*

## Traditional Recovery Method VIDEO 5

With the *traditional recovery method*, the boat is righted with no one in it. However, the boat can quickly capsize again, especially in stronger winds if no one is in the boat to balance and control it. To minimize this problem, position the boat with its bow pointed into the wind before it is righted. This may require the crew to rotate the boat in the water, which can be hard work. Once the boat is righted, the person at the bow holds the bow into the wind until the other person climbs in and takes control. Because of these problems, the scoop method is preferred, and gets you sailing again sooner.

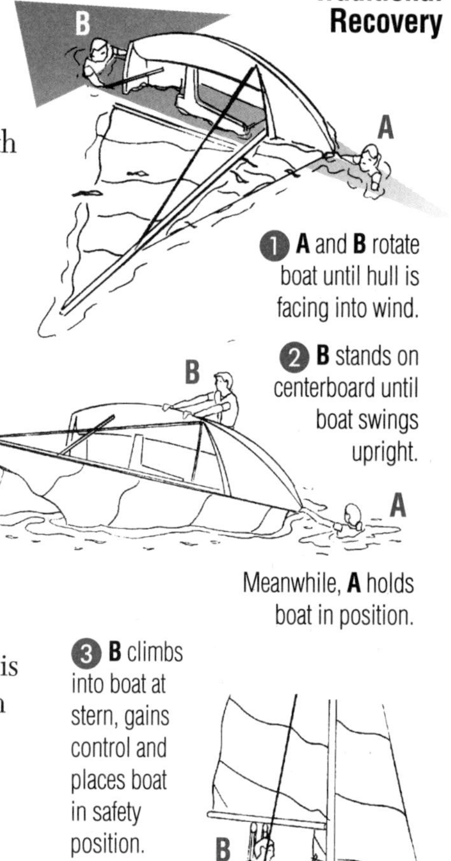


## Walkover Recovery Method VIDEO 5

Many sailboats can be righted as the capsize occurs by using the *walkover method* (this procedure requires practice and good timing). When a boat starts to capsize, it often drags its boom in the water — slowing the capsize. Acting quickly, a sailor can swing over the high side onto the centerboard before the boat goes all the way over. This part of the maneuver is the most difficult, and if the helmsman hesitates too long, the boat will tend to turn upside down.

Once over the top, the sailor should place both feet on the centerboard and grip the edge of the boat or gunwale. As you lean backward, the boat will start to come up and you can scramble back into the cockpit.

All of this should be done quickly, in one fluid motion. In good weather and warm water, practice capsizing the boat on purpose and righting it without getting wet by using this method.

### Walkover Method

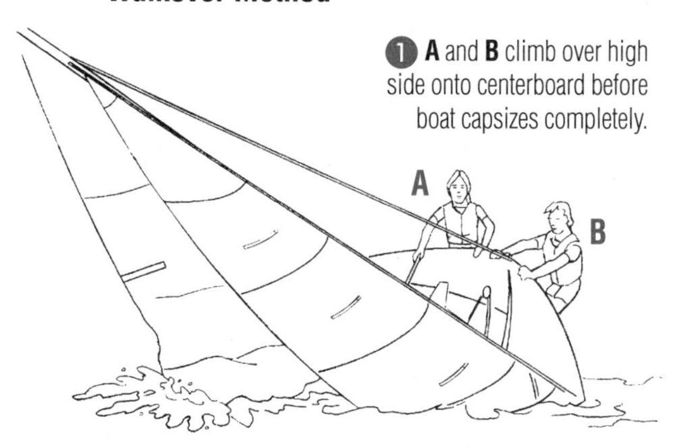


Boom drags in water, slowing capsize.

## Capsize Problems

When your boat capsizes, it's possible for it to continue turning over until it's upside down with the mast pointing straight toward the bottom. This type of capsize is called *turning turtle*, or *turtling*. (To help prevent this, some boats have flotation built into the mast or sewn into the top of the mainsail).

Righting a turtled boat can be difficult, since an upside-down hull is very stable and the submerged sails will resist efforts to spin the boat back upright. The centerboard or daggerboard can also slip back into its housing (no longer in the "down" position). Your first step is to rotate the turtled boat into a horizontal capsize position with the hull lying on its side and the sails pointed to leeward. Then you can follow the usual procedure for righting the boat.

**Turtled Recovery Method**
To rotate the boat to the normal capsize position, pull a sheet across the hull to the windward side, stand on the windward rail, and lean back.

When boat turtles, the centerboard will often slide back into trunk. Pull the centerboard back to its down position after boat has been turned onto its side.

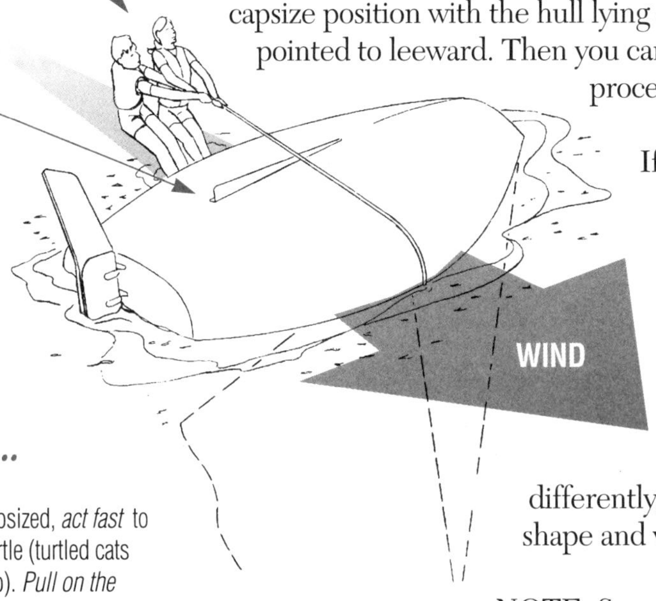

WIND

If you can't right the turtled boat by yourself, you will need help from your instructor or fellow sailors. However, you should learn how to right a turtled boat without assistance. Each boat will respond differently, depending on the size, shape and weight.

NOTE: Some older centerboard boats used to teach sailing do not have self-rescuing characteristics. For these, outside assistance will be needed to help get the water out of the boat or tow it to shore. The problem with this kind of boat is that once you have turned it back upright, it floats very low in the water. With the boat nearly awash, it tends to tip over unless you take extra care to balance it. A person outside the boat may have to steady the boat by holding the gunwale, while another person bails rapidly with a bucket. If you need outside assistance, remember to stay with the boat until help arrives.

### *Multihull Tip...*

**Turtled Recovery**

Once a catamaran has capsized, *act fast* to prevent it from turning turtle (turtled cats are difficult to get back up). *Pull on the righting line* (step 3 in Multihull Capsize Recovery Tip) *as soon as possible!* If your cat turtles anyway, here's what to do...

1. Move to leeward stern and pull on the righting line. The combination of your weight, wind and waves will hopefully lift your windward bow out of the water.
2. Once the windward bow is well out of the water, move to the center of the leeward hull while continuing to pull on the righting line. The boat will settle on its side. Continue pulling on the righting line until the mast is at the water's surface.
3. Follow the Multihull capsize procedure.
4. If you are unable to right your turtled catamaran, signal for help.

## Mast in the Mud

If a boat turtles in shallow water, the mast can stick into the mud or sand. You will need to act quickly to prevent the mast from becoming bent or breaking loose from the boat. The helmsman and crew should get off the boat quickly, so their weight won't make the mast dig deeper into the bottom. To free the mast, try swimming the bow into the wind. If the mast won't free up, you will need outside assistance.

## Entering and Exiting the Boat

During a capsize, there are preferred ways of leaving and reentering the boat. As the boat goes over, you should fall into the water feet first, *not* head first. Don't dive into the water. With a little practice, you will find it quite easy to drop into the water between the boom and the deck.

In a scoop recovery, one person is scooped into the boat and is then in a position to assist the second person. If both people are in the water when the boat rights, the stronger should enter the boat over the windward side of the transom, and put the boat in the safety position. Once in the safety position, the other person should be helped into the boat, also over the windward side of the transom. It may take a three-count to get the person into the boat. Lift using your legs, not your back.

### Quick Review

▶ Name three of the most common causes of a sailboat capsizing. *(answer on p.60-61)*

▶ Describe three ways to avoid capsizing. *(answer on p.61)*

▶ What is the most important safety rule after capsizing? *(answer on p.61)*

▶ Describe three capsize recovery methods. *(answer on p.62-63)*

### Think about it...

▶ What sail trim adjustments would be most helpful in preventing a capsize?

▶ After a capsize, what action would be most effective in preventing your boat from turning turtle (completely upside-down)?

**Helping a Person Back Aboard**

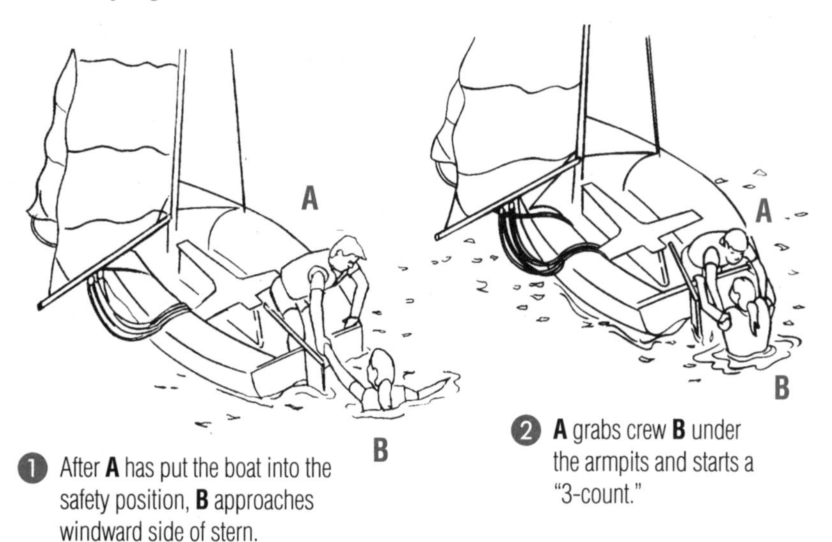


1. After **A** has put the boat into the safety position, **B** approaches windward side of stern.

2. **A** grabs crew **B** under the armpits and starts a "3-count."

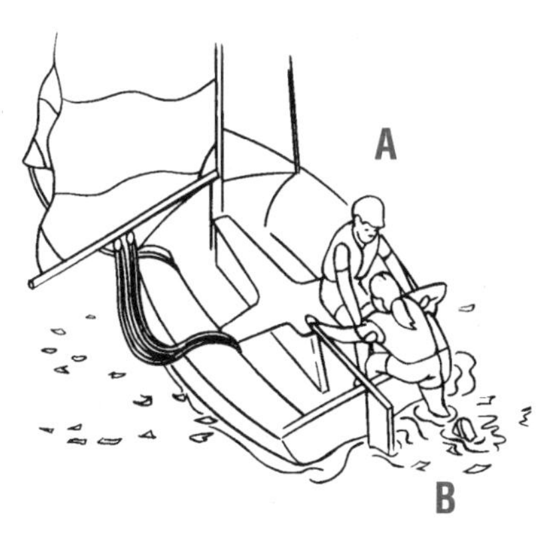


3. On the count of "3," **A** pulls **B** until his or her chest is over the transom. **B** swings a leg into the boat and climbs aboard.

CHAPTER 12

# Overboard Recovery

**KEY CONCEPTS**

- Overboard recovery methods
- Prevention
- Retrieval

Sometime during your sailing experience, you may have to rescue someone who has fallen off a boat. Falling overboard is serious. If you hear the words "CREW OVERBOARD!," you should assist in any way possible in making a recovery.

Learning overboard recovery procedure is easier than it first appears. The part that takes the most practice is putting the boat in position for the final approach to the person in the water. The key is to never let the boat luff directly into the wind, but instead to carefully approach the victim on a close reach, sheeting out the sails to stop the boat as you come alongside.

You should make contact with the victim from the windward side of the boat, then put the boat in the safety position while you help the person move to the transom and get in the boat (use method described on page 65). If the victim can't reach the boat, hold out a paddle or boat hook for the person to grab. During overboard recovery, it is important that you and/or your crew constantly keep watching and talking with the person in the water.

Practice with a five-gallon plastic jug filled with water as a "dummy." The weight of the water will give you an idea of the effort it takes to pull a wet sailor into a boat (it's a lot!).

*Multihull Tip...*

**Overboard Recovery**

1. Stop the boat immediately.
2. Perform the Dime Tack (see page 55).
3. Assume the Safety Position, and the boat will drift toward the sailor in the water. Changes in the direction of your drift can be made by sailing to windward or by sailing backward.
4. When close to the victim, approach slowly, placing the victim between the hulls. This will allow the victim to grab the dolphin striker and climb back aboard.

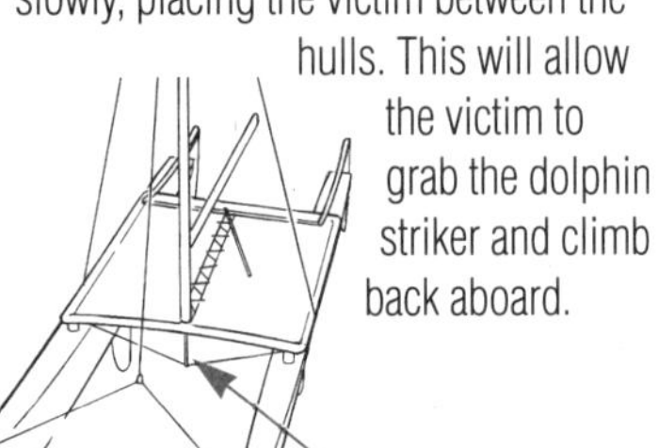


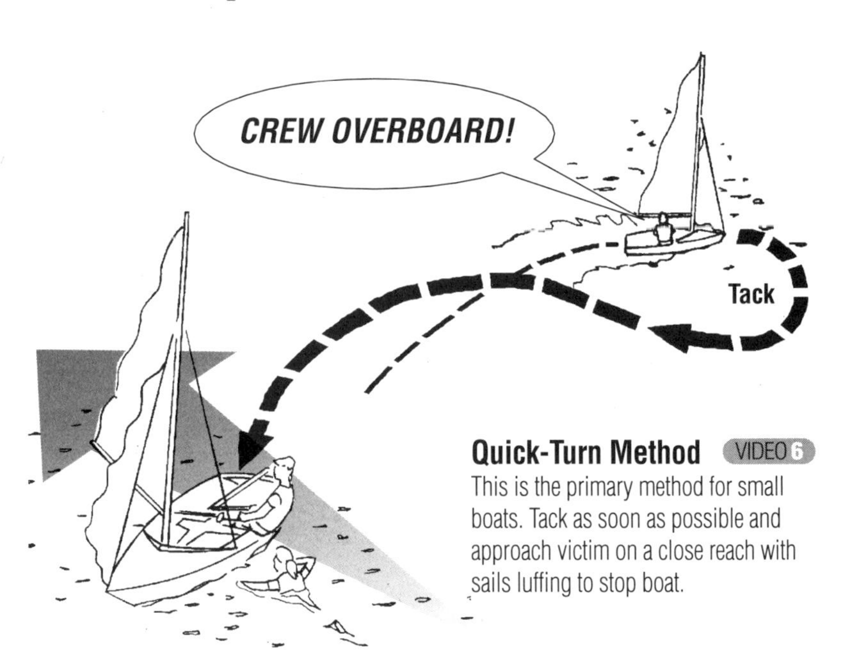


**Quick-Turn Method** VIDEO 6

This is the primary method for small boats. Tack as soon as possible and approach victim on a close reach with sails luffing to stop boat.

## Alternative Recovery Methods

An alternative method is *jibing* after the person has fallen in the water. A jibing recovery should only be used when the wind is light. In stronger winds, the jibe could result in a capsize if the boat is short-handed or the person in the boat is inexperienced.

Another alternative is the *heave-to* method, where the boat is tacked immediately, leaving the jib cleated. With the jib cleated, the boat turns and drifts toward the victim. As you drift downwind, the main is sheeted out fully and luffing. This method keeps the boat closer to the victim, which allows for better communication and visibility. It works best in light winds.

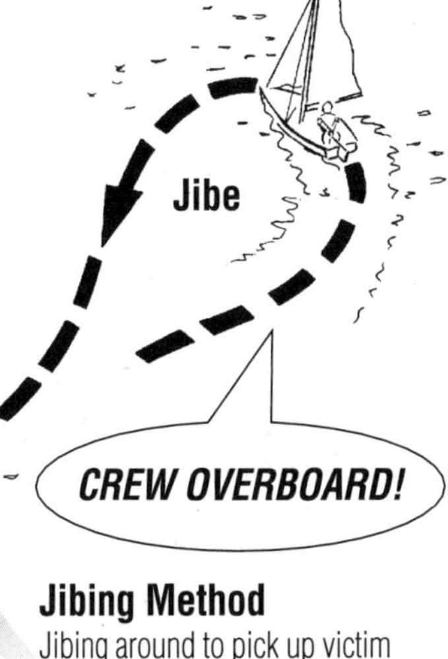


**Jibing Method**
Jibing around to pick up victim should only be done in light winds.

## Prevention

Most overboard accidents can be prevented through safety awareness. It is also important to make sure the boat and its equipment are in good condition.

- ▶ Check your boat thoroughly before sailing, especially hiking straps, tiller extension, and sheets.
- ▶ Wear nonskid shoes and hold onto the boat as you move about.
- ▶ Finally, listen to those marine forecasts and check the sky for threatening weather to avoid the heavy winds that can cause accidents.

**Heave-To Method**
Boat drifts down to victim with jib cleated to windward and mainsail luffing.

## Attachment and Retrieval

Getting an overboard victim back on board can be difficult, especially if the victim is weak. Therefore, the first thing to do when making a recovery is to attach the victim to the boat. This will vastly increase the probability of the victim's survival. If you are unable to get the victim back aboard, you can at least call for assistance. Attach the victim to the boat with a bowline knot through the D-rings of a life jacket or harness or around the victim. Never rely on the victim being able to hold onto a line for very long.

Other methods of getting a victim back on board high-sided boats include swimming ladders, foot loops or a double bowline harness. These methods are more common on small keelboats. Your instructor will review some of these methods with you.

### Quick Review

▶ Describe the three primary overboard recovery methods and the advantages and disadvantages or each. *(answer on p.66-67)*

▶ Describe three ways to prevent overboard occurrences. *(answer on p.67)*

### Think about it...

▶ What is the single most important part of a crew overboard recovery?

CHAPTER 13

# Leaving and Returning

**KEY CONCEPTS**
- Glide zone
- Mooring
- Docking

It's a bit ironic that almost any sailing experience begins and ends with perhaps its most challenging parts. Leaving and returning to a dock or mooring requires timing, judging speed and distance, and working with the wind to slow or maintain your speed as needed. By understanding a few simple principles, however, it will all fall into place.

## Leaving from a Dock or Mooring VIDEO 14

Leaving a mooring or a dock from the leeward side is easy, because the wind is pushing the boat away. Before leaving, lower the centerboard and raise the sails with the boat pointing into the wind (no-go zone). Then push or turn the bow of the boat away from the dock, ease the sails, and steer away on a reach.

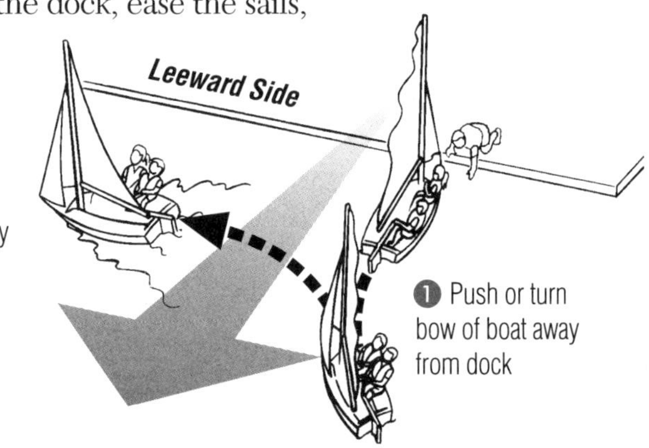


Leaving a dock from the windward side can be tricky, and requires careful timing. At the same time, you will need to be ready to sail upwind immediately as you leave. If you aren't prepared, the wind will tend to push you back onto the dock. If possible, move your boat to the leeward side and leave from there.

❸ Quickly trim in your sails for upwind sailing.

❶ As you raise your sails, make sure they are sheeted all-the-way out so they don't fill with wind.

❷ Push forward and away from the dock with enough speed to achieve steering and keep the boat from sideslipping back into the dock.

## Returning to a Dock or Mooring VIDEO 14

When returning to a dock or mooring, your goal should be to safely "glide" to a stop just as you reach your destination. The distance a boat takes to coast to a stop is called the *glide zone.* The length of a boat's glide zone is determined by how fast it is going, how much it weighs and the strength of the wind. More boat speed and/or more weight mean a longer glide zone. Stronger wind will slow down a boat more quickly. Having a feel for your boat's glide zone in different conditions is important when you dock, moor, and anchor.

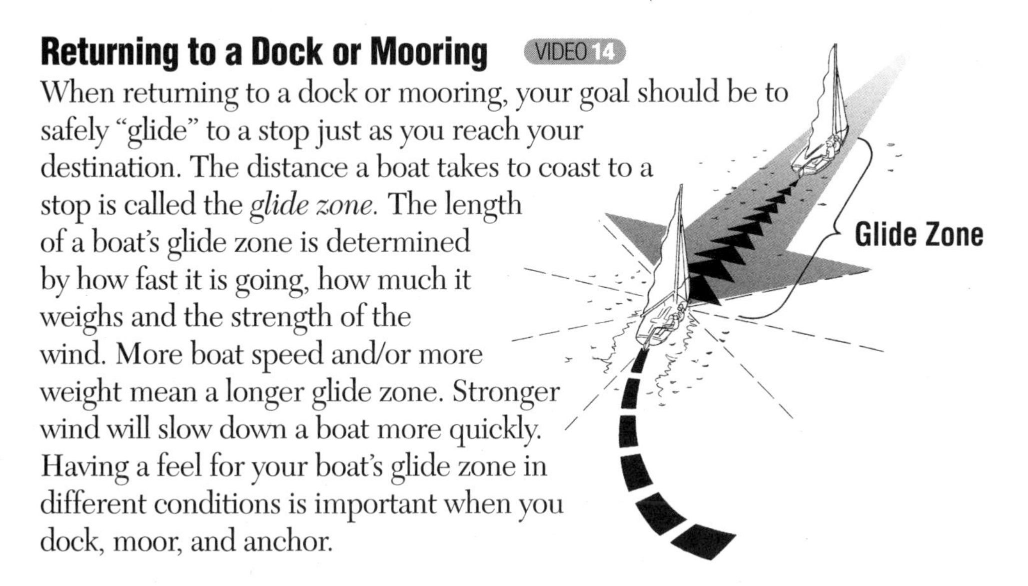


## Approaching a Mooring VIDEO 14

The best way to approach a mooring is to turn the boat into the no-go zone and glide to a stop just as you reach the mooring. Judging your glide zone in different conditions is challenging, so don't expect your approach to be perfect every time. Even experienced sailors sometimes make several approaches before they glide up to the mooring just as the boat is coming to a stop.

If you have trouble reaching a mooring this way, you can sail the boat upwind from the mooring, turn into the no-go zone, lower the sails, and drift or paddle downwind to the mooring.

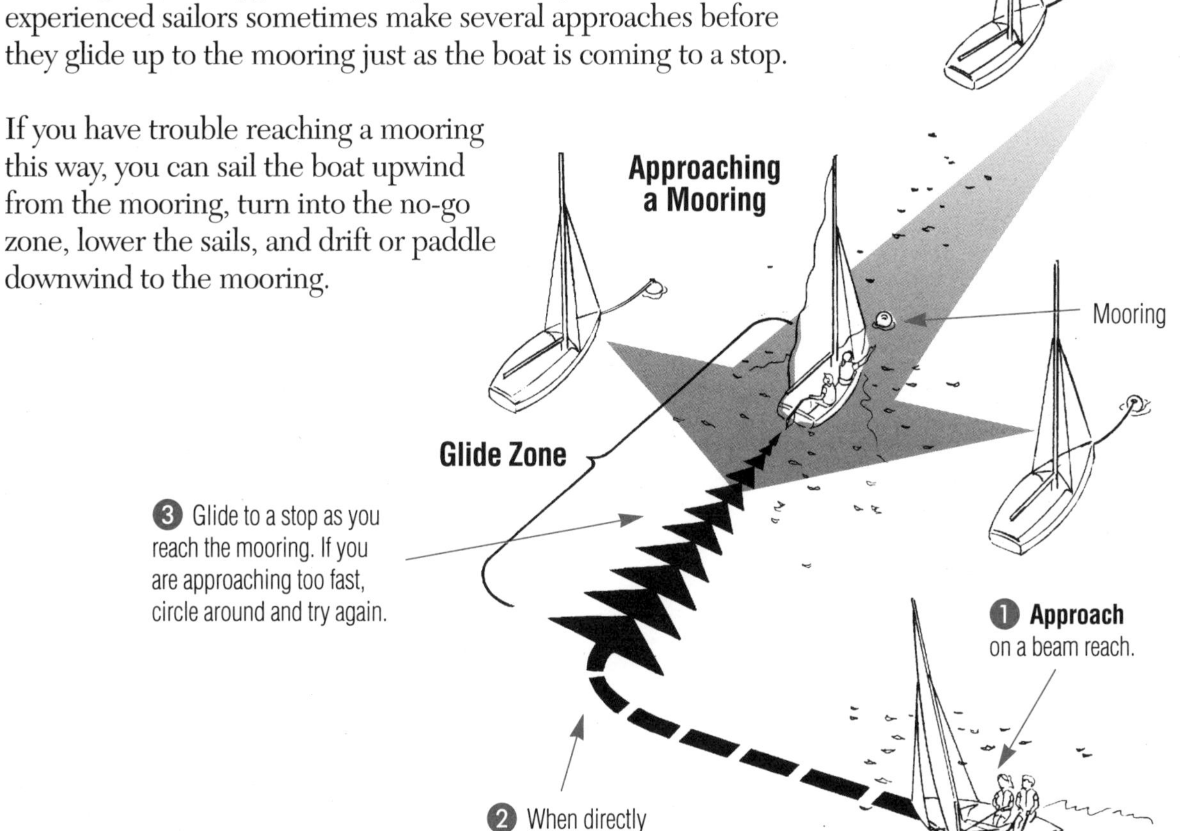

## Approaching a Dock - Leeward Side VIDEO 14

The easiest way for beginning sailors to return to a dock or mooring is to approach the dock slowly on a reach with the sails eased out until they are partially luffing. A better way is turning the boat into the no-go zone (similar to approaching a mooring).

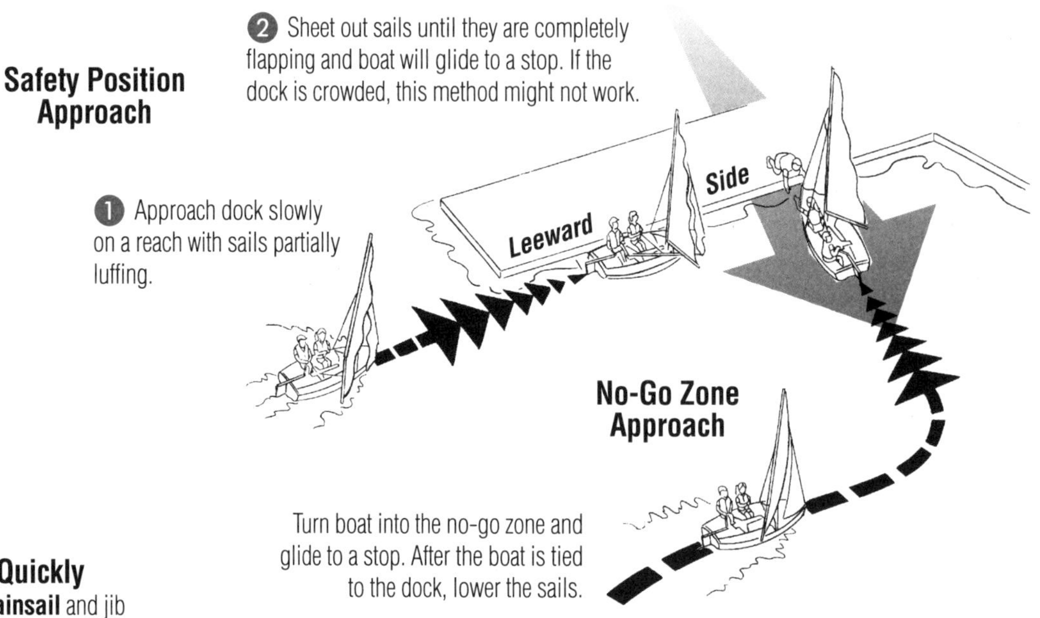


**Stopping Quickly**
**Back the mainsail** and jib by pushing them out all-the-way until the wind fills the back side of the sails.

Always plan an escape route in case you encounter a sudden wind shift, another boat or misjudge the glide zone.

If you approach a dock or mooring too fast, you can quickly slow the boat by *backing* (braking) with your mainsail. If you continue backing the mainsail, the boat will start to sail backward. Practice this maneuver in open water, clear of obstacles. It could help you out of an awkward situation.

## Approaching a Dock - Windward Side VIDEO 14

Similar to leaving a dock from the windward side, returning to the windward side can be challenging. Whenever possible, try to return on the leeward side of the dock. If returning to the windward side is necessary, use the Windward Side Approach (see next page).

NOTE: When coming back to a dock, it is not unusual to find the wind blowing from a different direction than when you left, so you may have to make your landing on a different side. For this reason, you should always think ahead and have a firm plan of how to leave and return to the dock safely from all directions.

Plan an *escape route*, in case you don't make it the first time, and visualize your glide zone. Remember, it's better to approach too slowly than too fast. Good judgment and planning are what it is all about.

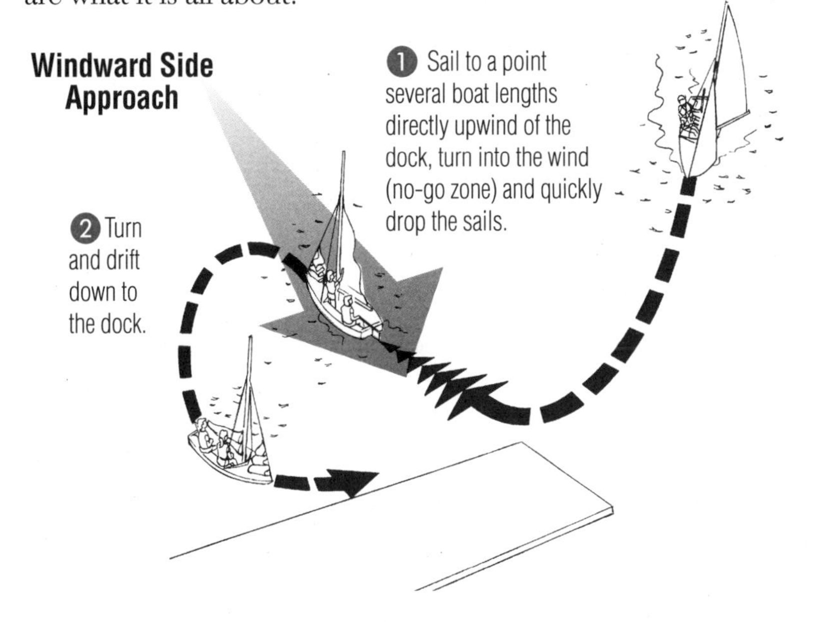


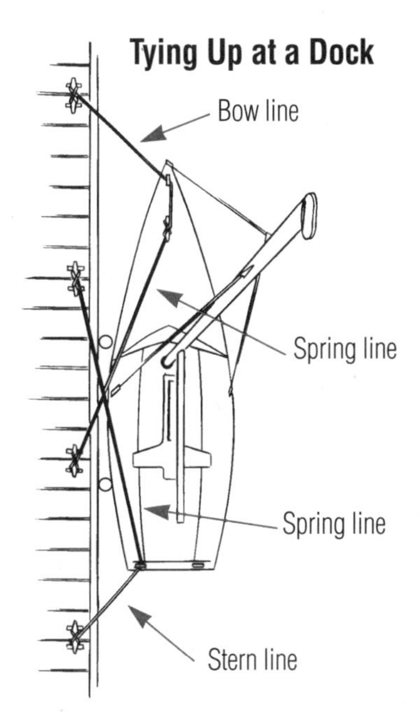


## Typical Docking Problems and Solutions

**Problem:** *Boat doesn't maneuver well - slides sideways when leaving.*

**Solution:** Make sure the centerboard and rudder are all-the-way down.

**Problem:** *The boat does not want to sail away from the dock on the windward side.*

**Solution:** Ask someone on the dock to give the boat a big push while you trim the sails quickly. You may also have to paddle a little to get going.

**Problem:** *I always under-shoot the dock.*

**Solution:** Time and practice will correct this. This problem is usually caused by turning the boat into the no-go zone too early. Practice by turning the boat into the no-go zone and see how far the boat will glide before it stops. Estimate the length of the glide zone in boat lengths. If you find it difficult to estimate boat lengths, try using a landmark close by. Just before you turn into the no-go zone, sight down the centerline of the boat to the landmark. If you under-shoot on your first approach, approach further upwind on your second approach, using the landmark as a reference.

**Problem:** *If I am sailing too fast and will over-shoot, how do I slow down quickly?*

**Solution:** First of all, make sure that you have turned your boat into the no-go zone and the sails are completely flapping. If you are still going too fast, you can quickly slow the boat by "backing" the sails.

### Quick Review

▶ Which side of a dock is it easier to leave from...*windward* or *leeward?* *(answer on p.68)*

▶ Define the "glide zone." *(answer on p.69)*

▶ Which side of a dock is it best to return to...*windward* or *leeward?* *(answer on p.70)*

▶ What is the best action to take if you are approaching a dock or mooring with too much speed? *(answer on p.71)*

### Think about it...

▶ Think of two drills that can help you develop a sense of your boat's glide zone.

▶ In how many ways is your glide zone affected by increasing wind, decreasing wind, current, sea conditions and boat speed?

▶ How would leaving and returning from a beach differ from leaving and returning to a dock or mooring?

CHAPTER 14

# Improving Your Skills

**KEY CONCEPTS**
- Sailing a course
- "In the groove"
- Depowering
- Weather helm
- Centerboard adjustment
- Sail trim
- Balance
- Water reading
- Safety habits

As you spend more time sailing, you will begin to refine your newly acquired skills. Sailing well involves developing a "feel" for when your boat is moving at its best. You'll become more adept at maintaining the proper angle of heel, moving crew weight fore-and-aft, making subtle adjustments in sail trim, and using centerboard position to keep your steering balanced. Sailing well also involves developing your awareness of currents, wind, weather, and safety.

## Sailing a Course VIDEO 13

One of the first things that a good sailor learns to master is sailing a course from point A to point B, no matter what the wind direction or conditions. While this may sound simple, there are many different ways of doing it.

WIND

When reaching or sailing downwind, sailing a course involves simply steering toward your destination and adjusting your sails to keep optimum trim.

If you must sail on a reach or run to get from **A** to **B**, the direct route is usually the best. Just aim your boat at the destination and sail. If the wind direction changes, you should change the trim of the sails to keep them working at their best.

If your destination is to windward — in the no-go zone — you will have to sail upwind on a zig-zag course to get there, tacking once or several times.

## Steering Upwind: "In the Groove"

As you steer upwind, you will react to changes in wind speed and direction by steering the boat either toward or away from the wind while keeping the telltales flowing back smoothly. You will soon discover that there is a *groove,* or lane, to steer in, where the boat is sailing upwind at its best. The sides of the groove can be "seen" by the telltales. If you start to cross the windward side of the groove (too high), the telltales on the windward side of the sails will flutter or stall while the telltales on the leeward side will continue flowing back smoothly. If you start to cross the leeward side of the groove (too low), the telltales on the leeward side of the sail will droop and stall, while the windward telltales will continue flowing smoothly.

When you are *in the groove*, both windward and leeward telltales will flow smoothly. The groove is not very wide. If you steer your bow back and forth just a few degrees, you will find the sides of the groove.

Because the wind is constantly changing, you should periodically check if you are in the groove. You can do this by gently steering the boat up until it nudges the windward side of the groove, and then steering back down into the groove. This technique keeps you sailing as close to the wind as possible while maintaining good boat speed. Experienced helmsmen may do this as often as every five or ten seconds. This may sound a little complicated at first, but after a little practice you will find yourself doing it automatically.

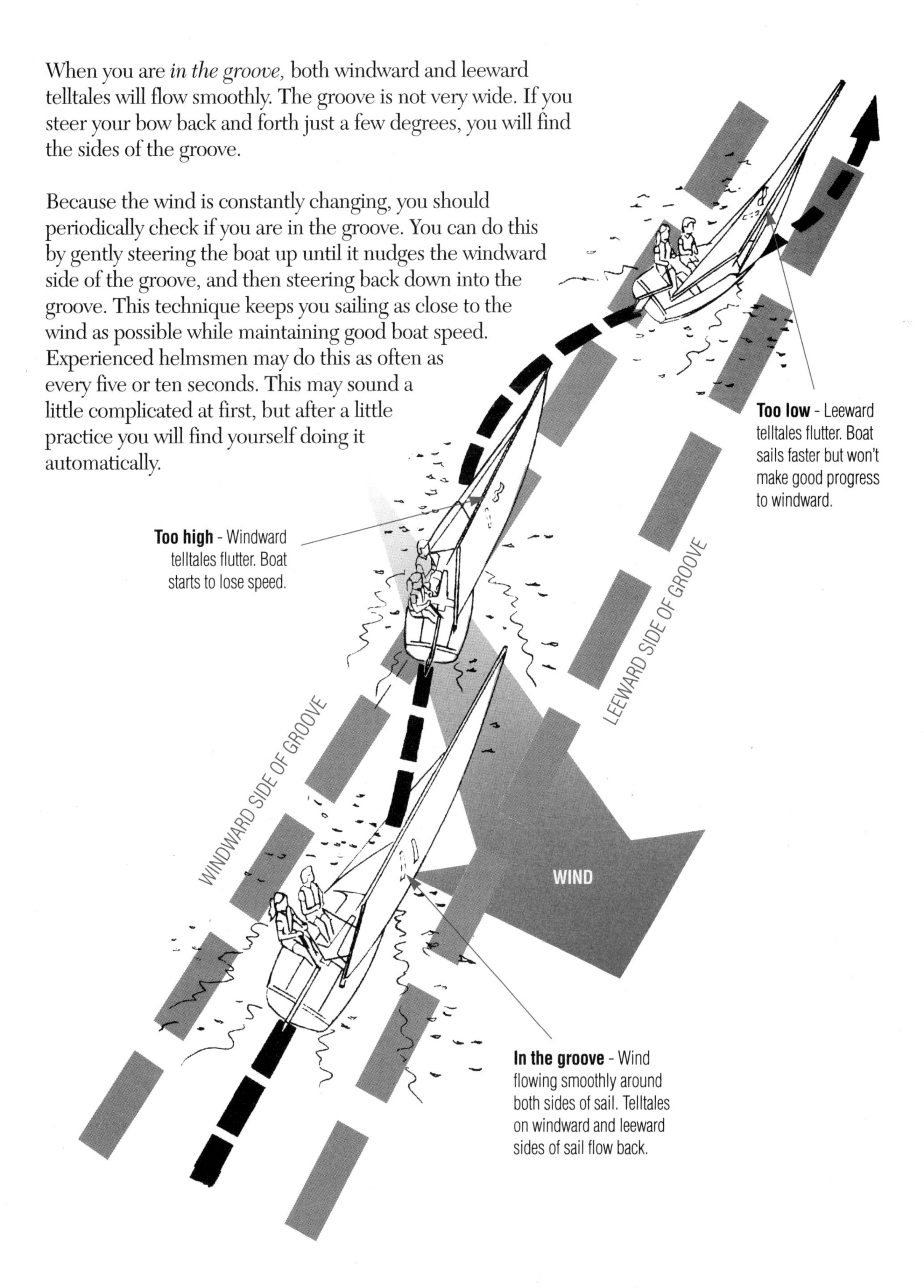

## Depowering by Feathering (Pinching)

As the wind increases or a puff hits, a boat can become overpowered. It will heel too much, lose speed and may even capsize. There are several ways to respond to this situation. You can move your weight to windward, adjust sail trim, or change the shape of the sails so that they produce less power.

Experienced helmsmen also use a steering technique called *feathering* or *pinching*, to help depower the boat and keep it stable. Feathering is simply steering the boat at the windward side of the groove for long periods of time. The sails, particularly the jib, will luff slightly, with the windward telltale stalling (at times the leeward telltale may also stall). It takes a bit of skill to feather the boat while keeping it moving forward. When feathering, the helmsman should steer with the tiller extension, and both helmsman and crew should be hiking, or leaning out over the windward side of the boat.

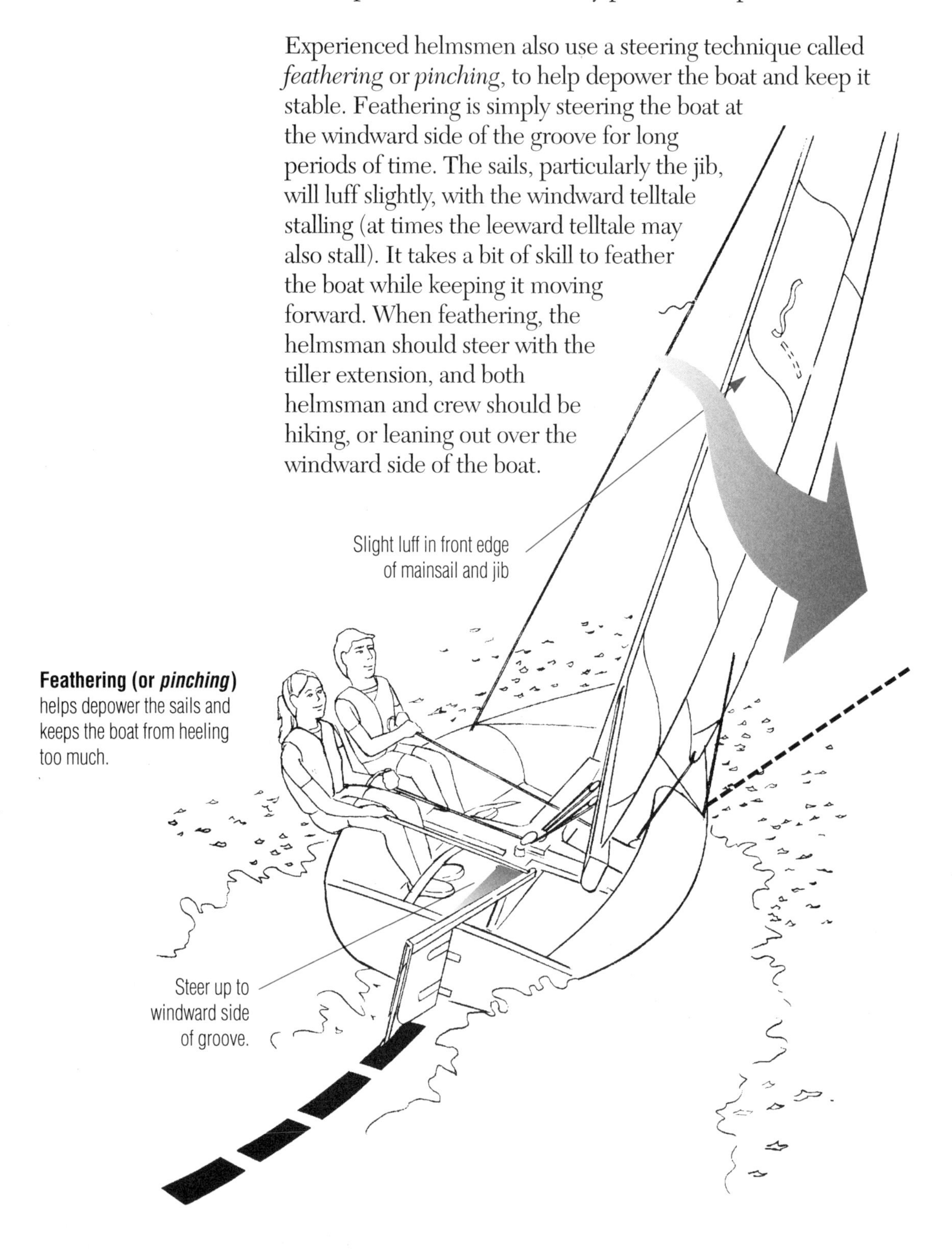


**Feathering (or *pinching*)** helps depower the sails and keeps the boat from heeling too much.

As the wind increases, the helmsman will usually have to pull harder on the tiller to counteract the boat's natural tendency to turn toward the wind. This is called *weather helm*. When sailing upwind, a small amount of weather helm actually helps to steer the boat close to the wind. But too much weather helm (on any point of sail) is a sign that the boat is heeling too much or is overpowered. The crew and helmsman can reduce weather helm by hiking out, sheeting out the mainsail a bit, or feathering the boat.

## Centerboard Position VIDEO 13

The centerboard or daggerboard has different positions for different points of sail. Upwind and on a close reach, the centerboard is kept all-the-way down. On a beam reach, the board is raised to about halfway up, and on a broad reach or downwind, it is raised about three-quarters of the way up.

When maneuvering upwind, you need all the centerboard to keep the boat from being pushed sideways. When sailing downwind, sideways force from the sails is less, so you do not need as much centerboard. Raising the centerboard for downwind sailing also reduces the amount of surface friction, which increases boat speed.

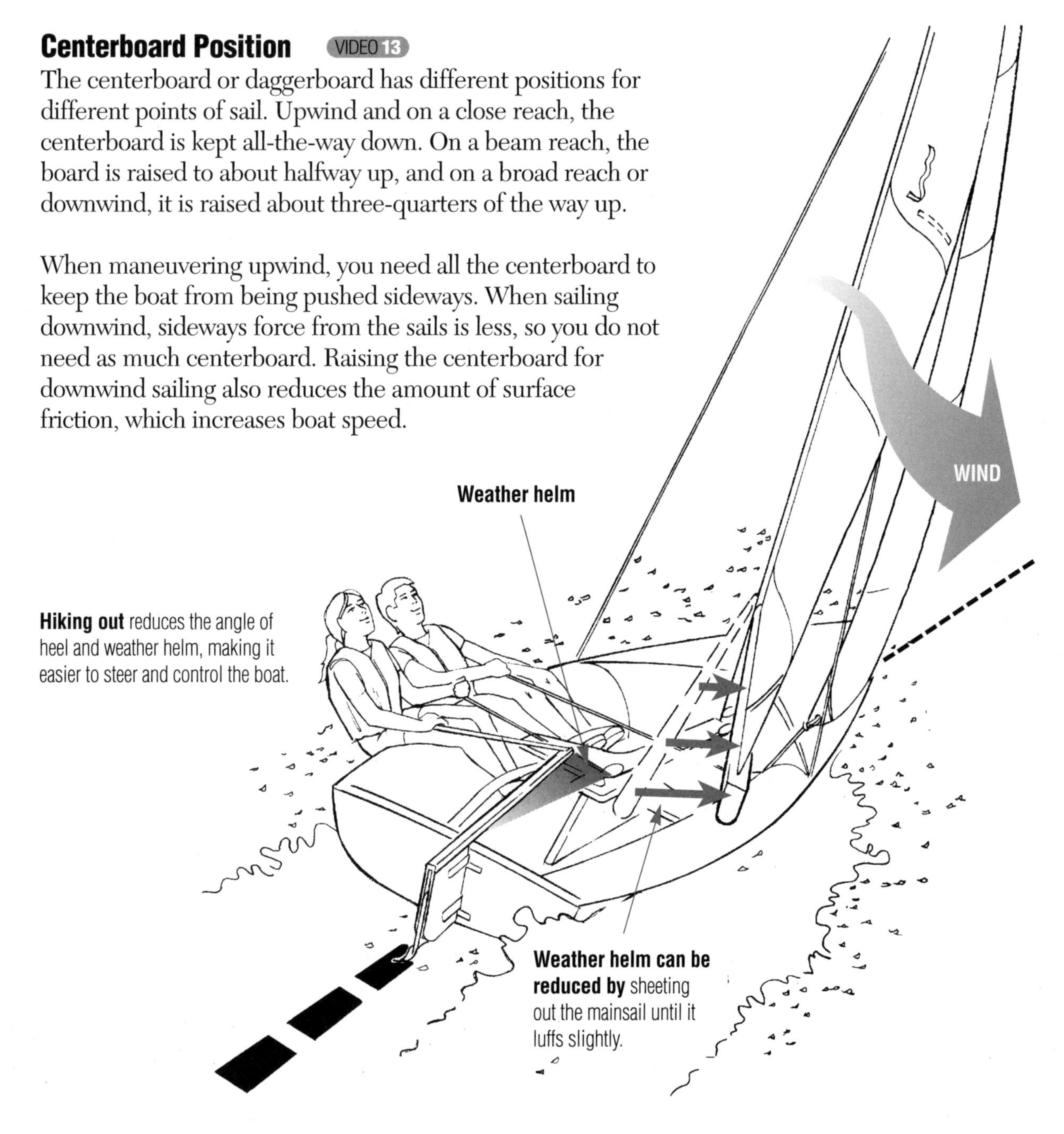

## Sail Trim VIDEO 13

As you become more sensitive to sail trim, you will find that sheeting in or out a few inches can make a noticeable difference in how the boat performs. You will also learn to coordinate the sheeting of the mainsail and jib. Helmsman and crew should sheet in (*trim*) and sheet out (*ease*) the sails in unison. You will generally sheet in the sails when turning toward the wind, and sheet out when turning away from the wind.

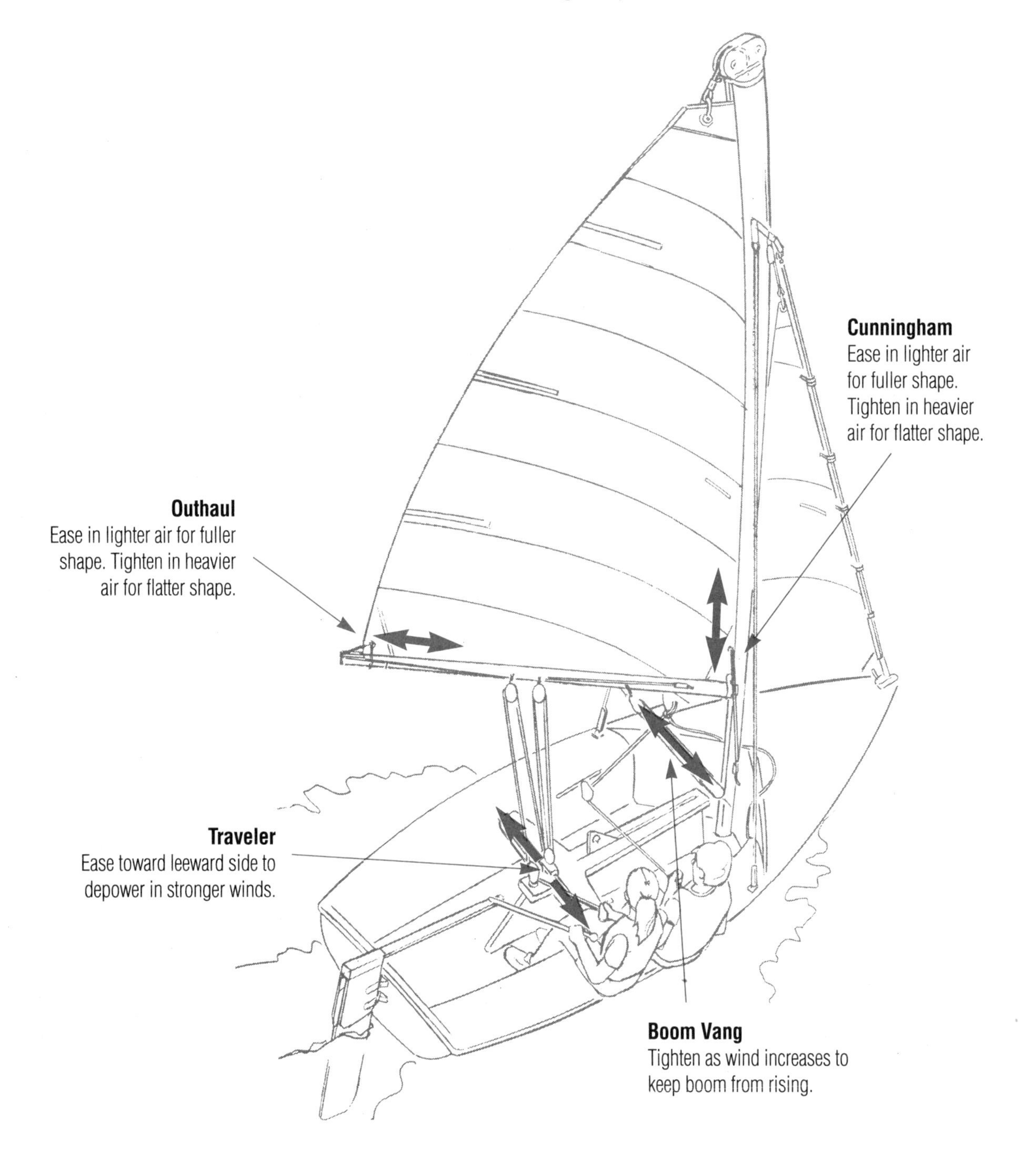

## Adjusting Sail Shape

You can also adjust the shape of your sails to suit different conditions using the *cunningham*, *boom vang*, and *outhaul*. Generally all three adjustments should be tightened as the wind increases. They work to flatten and "depower" the sail, making it easier to control the boat. In light air, they should be eased to make a fuller sail for greater power.

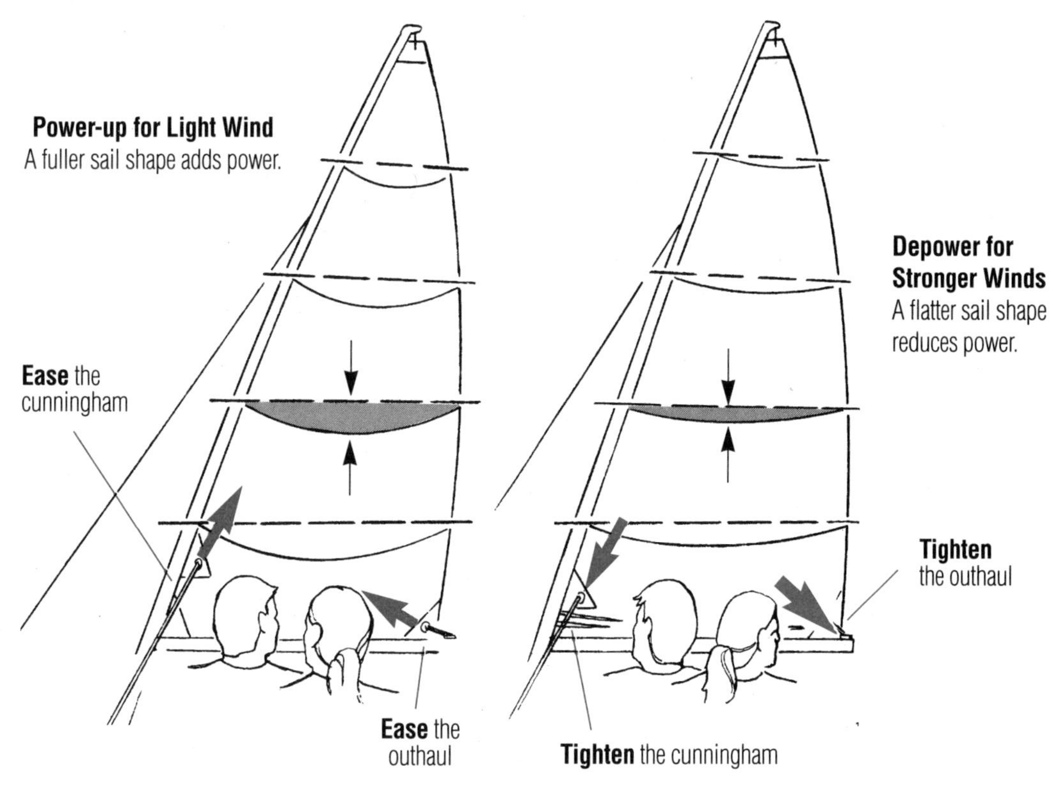


## Depowering with the Traveler

The *traveler* is another adjustment that allows you to change the angle of the mainsail without sheeting out the mainsheet and changing the sail's shape. Travelers are either *bridle types* or *track types*. Bridle travelers should be pulled tighter as wind increases. The sliding car on a track-type traveler should be moved toward the leeward side as wind increases. The traveler can be used effectively to reduce heeling in heavier air.

*"Can Bill trim, or what?"*

## Depowering by Shortening Sail

When the wind is too strong and your boat is heeling too much, shortening sail is another way to depower. The easiest way is to simply lower the jib, but a more significant depowering will result if you lower the mainsail.

## Boat Balance VIDEO 13

Your boat's angle of heel— or side-to-side angle—will differ for different points of sail. Upwind, heeling the boat slightly to leeward is good. Downwind, particularly in light and medium air, you may want the boat to be heeled slightly to windward to help neutralize weather helm and allow the sails to operate efficiently.

When the boat changes from one point of sail to another, try to move your weight smoothly to achieve the correct angle of heel. As the wind increases, you will have to move your weight further to the high (windward) side to maintain the proper angle of heel.

Earlier in Chapter 7, we discussed how to turn the boat by moving your weight from side to side. As you become more accomplished, you can use this concept when turning the boat. When you move the tiller to turn the boat toward the wind, move your weight a little to leeward at the same time, by leaning into the boat. This will help to turn the boat using less tiller movement. When you turn the boat away from the wind, move your weight a little to windward by leaning out.

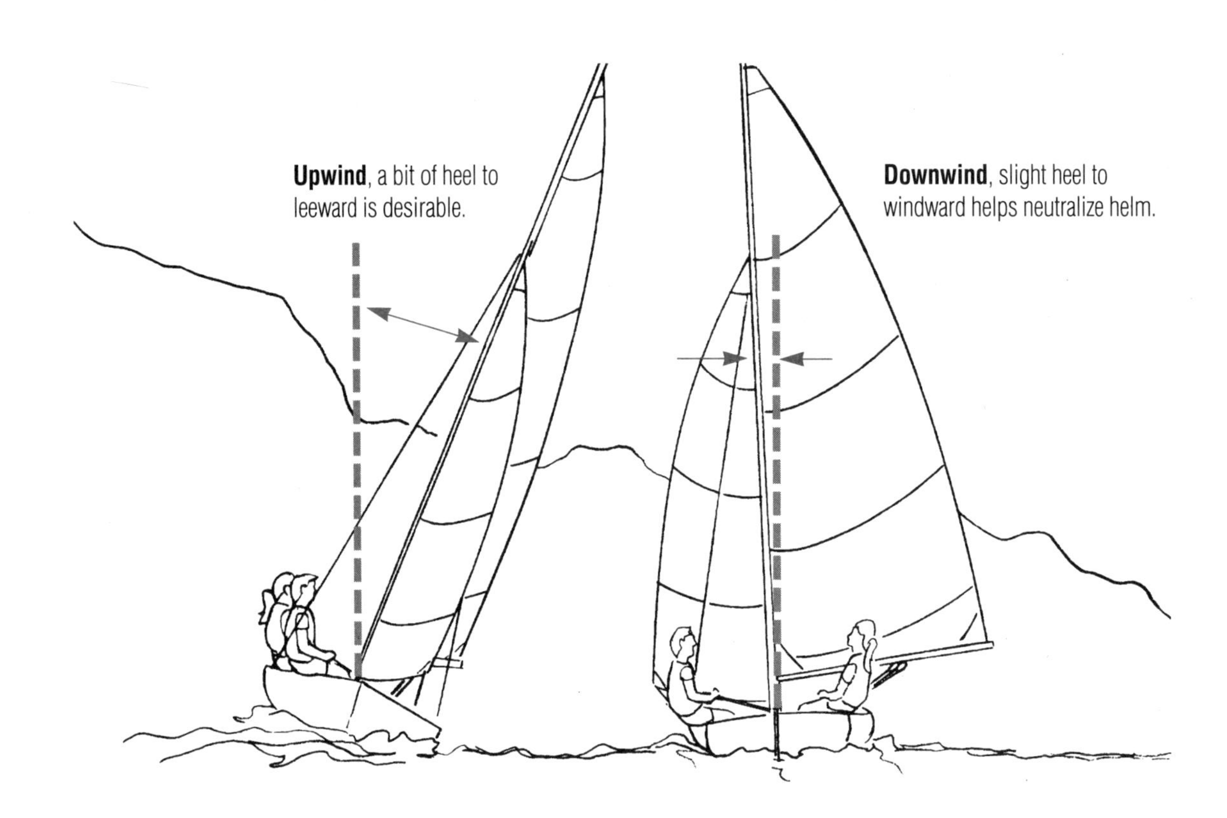

## Reading Wind on the Water

The water's surface can tell you a lot. By reading the ripples the wind makes on the water, you can detect puffs and lulls and determine the wind direction within a few degrees. Puffs on the water will look darker, while lulls will look lighter and smoother. When you see a puff approaching, you should begin easing the mainsail just before the puff hits. This will help keep the boat balanced and keep you in control.

## The "S" Word: SAFETY!

The most valued skill in sailing is seamanship, and the foundation of good seamanship is a constant and keen awareness of safety. As you develop your sailing skills, remember you also have an important responsibility for the well being of your boat and crew.

*Following is a checklist of items you should review every time you head out on the water:*

### Onshore Safety Checklist

- ☐ **Check the weather forecast.**
- ☐ **Bring the right clothing.** Remember that it is better to overdress than underdress.
- ☐ **Always wear your life jacket**, making sure it fits comfortably and is suitable for your body and weight.
- ☐ **Be sure you understand how to right a capsized boat.**
- ☐ **Make sure that you have required equipment** such as a paddle, bailer, spare line, and anchor.
- ☐ **Make sure that the boat is drained properly** and that the air tanks are empty and dry and the plugs are secured.
- ☐ **If the water is cold,** sail with a wet suit or dry suit, under a life jacket.
- ☐ **Establish an upper wind speed limit for your skill level.** If the wind blows harder, consider it unsafe to go sailing.
- ☐ **Always make sure that somebody onshore or at your sailing facility knows what time you expect to be back from your sail.**
- ☐ **Always bring sunblock, sunglasses and something to drink on hot sunny days.**

### Quick Review

- ▶ Describe sailing "in the groove." *(answer on p.72)*
- ▶ What are your best indicators to help you sail "in the groove?" *(answer on p.72-73)*
- ▶ Describe "feathering" and when this technique is useful. *(answer on p.74)*
- ▶ Describe two ways to reduce excessive weather helm. *(answer on p.75)*
- ▶ Describe how sail shape affects power. *(answer on p.77)*
- ▶ What sail shapes are best for light winds and stronger winds? *(answer on p.77)*

### Think about it...

- ▶ What do sailing "in the groove" and "feathering / pinching" have in common?
- ▶ Name two indicators — other than telltales — which help you know if you are sailing "in the groove."
- ▶ Describe how you would adjust sail shape sailing upwind in light winds, medium winds and strong winds.
- ▶ Carefully review the onshore safety checklist, then review it each time you go sailing until it becomes automatic. At most, it can save your life. At least, it will ensure a good time on the water.

CHAPTER 15

# Right-of-Way

**KEY CONCEPTS**

- Avoiding collisions
- Right-of-way
- Basic Navigation Rules

So far we've concentrated on your skills, your crew and your boat. But you are not out there alone. As a matter of fact, sometimes it can get downright crowded out on the water. Just as there are rules for automotive traffic, the sailing community has "rules of the road," called *Navigation Rules*, for sailboats and powerboats to avoid collisions. As you learn to sail you can safely operate your boat by understanding just a few basic Navigation Rules.

## Avoiding Collisions

VIDEO 13

The basic purpose of the Navigation Rules is to avoid collisions. The boat that has right-of-way is the *stand-on vessel* and should maintain course and speed. The *give-way vessel* must keep out of the way and should make its change of course obvious and early. It is always a vessel's obligation to avoid collisions even if it has the right-of-way. Unless the danger is straight ahead, one of the best ways to avoid a collision is simply to push or pull the *tiller toward trouble*, which will turn the boat away from it. You can also avoid a collision by slowing or stopping the boat. Don't be intimidated. In a short while, you will feel as natural encountering on-the-water traffic as you do on land.

Also remember to look around before you tack or jibe and check for other boats to leeward. Check those blind spots behind the sails frequently.

**Turning the tiller toward trouble** turns the boat away from danger. (Remember the 3 T's: **T**iller **T**oward **T**rouble.)

## Right-of-Way VIDEO 13

Whenever two boats meet, one boat will have *right-of-way*. When two or more sailboats are involved, you need to know what tack and what point of sail they are sailing on to determine which boat has right-of-way.

## Basic Rule 1: Starboard Tack over Port Tack VIDEO 13

When sailboats approach on opposite tacks, the boat on starboard tack has the right-of-way and is the stand-on vessel. The port tack boat, or give-way vessel, should change course to pass behind the other boat.

You should politely hail the sailor on port tack, *"Starboard!"* or *"I have right-of- way!"* This will remind them that you are the right-of-way boat and they must stay clear of you.

When a sailboat is on starboard tack, wind is coming over the starboard (right or green) side of the boat, which will be the "high" side when sailing upwind. When a sailboat is on port tack, the wind is coming over the port (left or red) side, or the "high" side when sailing upwind.

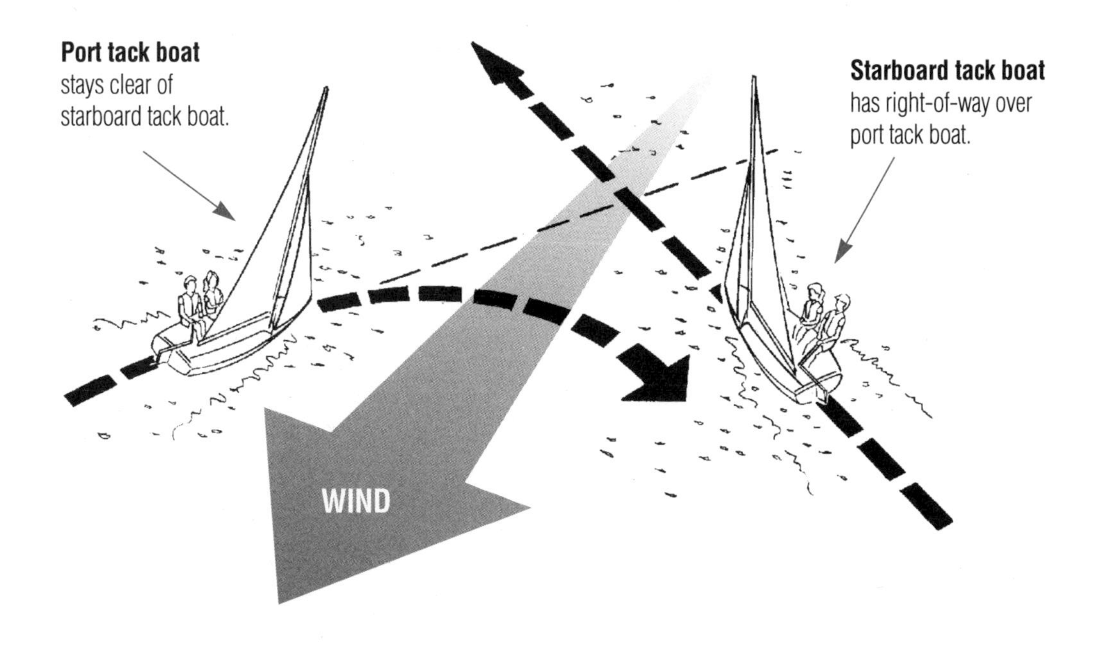

## Basic Rule 2: Leeward over Windward VIDEO 13

When two sailboats meet on the same tack, the upwind (*windward*) boat is the give-way vessel and should steer behind the leeward boat, which is the stand-on vessel. To remind the windward boat, the leeward boat should say, *"I'm leeward boat - please stay clear!"*

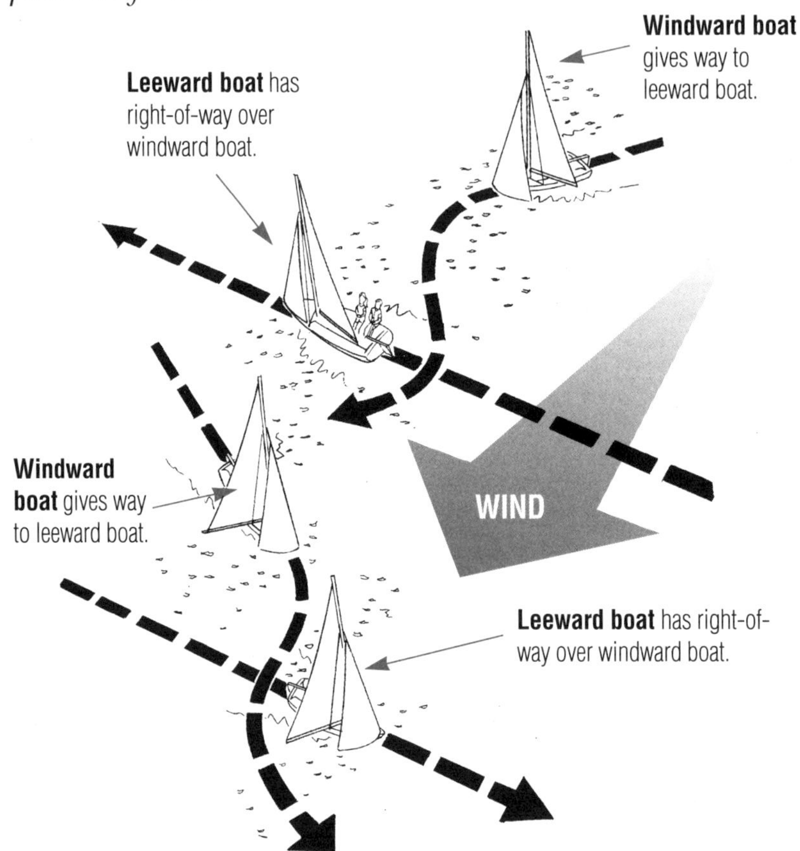


## Basic Rule 3: Overtaken over Overtaking VIDEO 13

The boat that is doing the passing is the give-way vessel and may pass to either side of the stand-on vessel. The stand-on vessel should hold its course.

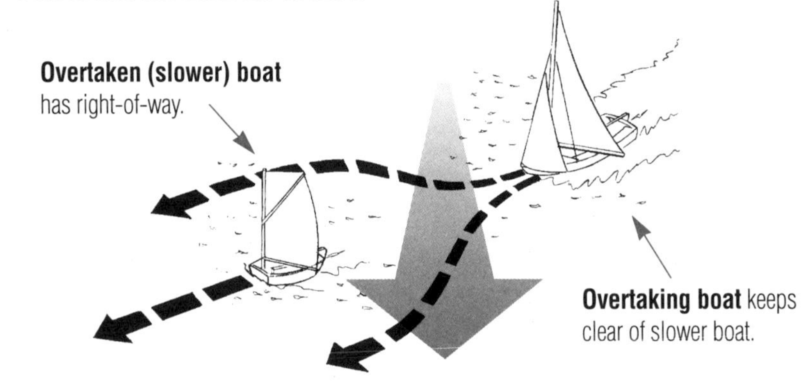

## Basic Rule 4: Sailboats over Powerboats

VIDEO 13

When sailboats and powerboats meet, the sailboat is the stand-on vessel. The powerboat is the give-way vessel because it is more maneuverable.

Remember, when on the water, keep up your environmental awareness and make sure that you are staying clear of other boats and obstacles. If you're in a sailboat and you encounter a muscle-powered boat (rowboat, canoe, kayak, etc.), you should treat it as a stand-on vessel and change your course. Always be on the lookout for other boats — especially to leeward of you, which are difficult to see behind the sails. Finally, *if in doubt, stay clear!*

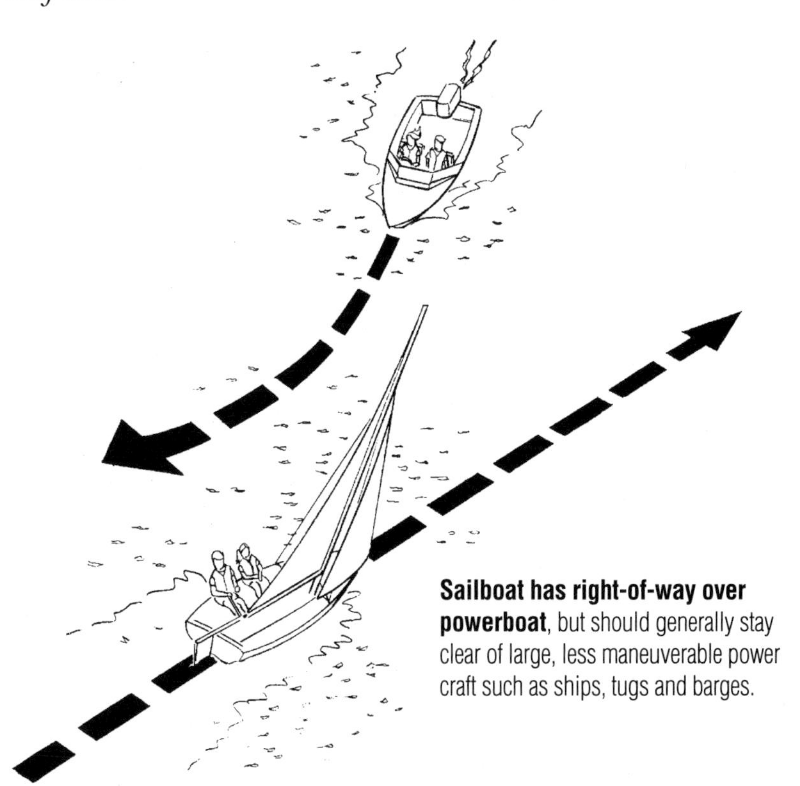

**Sailboat has right-of-way over powerboat**, but should generally stay clear of large, less maneuverable power craft such as ships, tugs and barges.

### Quick Review

TRUE or FALSE

- When danger approaches, you should turn the tiller toward the danger. *(answer on p.80)*
- A boat on port tack has right-of-way over a boat on starboard tack. *(answer on p.81)*
- A leeward boat has right-of-way over windward boats on the same tack. *(answer on p.82)*

### Think about it...

- What is the crew's role in avoiding collisions?
- Usually, a powerboat gives way to a sailboat. Think of two situations where a sailboat should give way to a powerboat.

## Basic Rule 5: Commercial Vessels over Pleasure Craft

Ships in channels, tugboats with tows and working commercial fishing vessels are stand-on vessels and have the right-of-way over sailboats.

# CHAPTER 16 Backup Skills

**KEY CONCEPTS**
- Paddling and sculling
- Anchoring
- Towing
- Coming alongside

There are several important skills that serve as a backup to sailing's endless variables. Rowing, paddling, sculling, anchoring, towing and coming alongside an anchored boat are maneuvers that every sailor will probably need to perform...sooner or later.

## Rowing, Paddling and Sculling

When maneuvering near a dock or in other restricted areas, muscle power may be your safest and best method of propulsion. There are three ways a sailboat can be powered without using the sails: paddling, rowing or sculling. Paddling and rowing can be done for extended periods, while sculling is more often used for short distances.

Paddling works best with at least two people in the boat. One person steers with the rudder while the other paddles from the side of the boat. If the centerboard is all-the-way-down, the boat will track nicely through the water, and the paddler need only paddle from one side.

For short distances, it is often easiest to scull the boat. In sculling, you move the tiller and rudder repeatedly back and forth, using it like a fish tail at the stern. If you have lowered the sails, they should be furled or stowed, so they won't blow in the water or get in your way.

**When paddling**, keep the boat level. The person paddling should use long, even strokes.

**Sculling** is best for short distances.

## Anchoring

If the wind dies and the current is carrying you in the wrong direction, you will want to anchor until the current changes or the wind increases. You may want to stop sailing to have lunch, or a squall might be approaching.

Before anchoring, take down and stow the jib. Make sure the anchor line is neatly coiled so it will run freely, and that one end is tied securely to the boat and the other end to the anchor. The ratio of anchor line length to the water depth is called *scope*. A scope of 7:1 is considered adequate for most conditions. This means that if the depth of water where you are anchoring is 10 feet, you should let out 70 feet of anchor line. It is important to know the water depth where you sail so you can have enough anchor line on board.

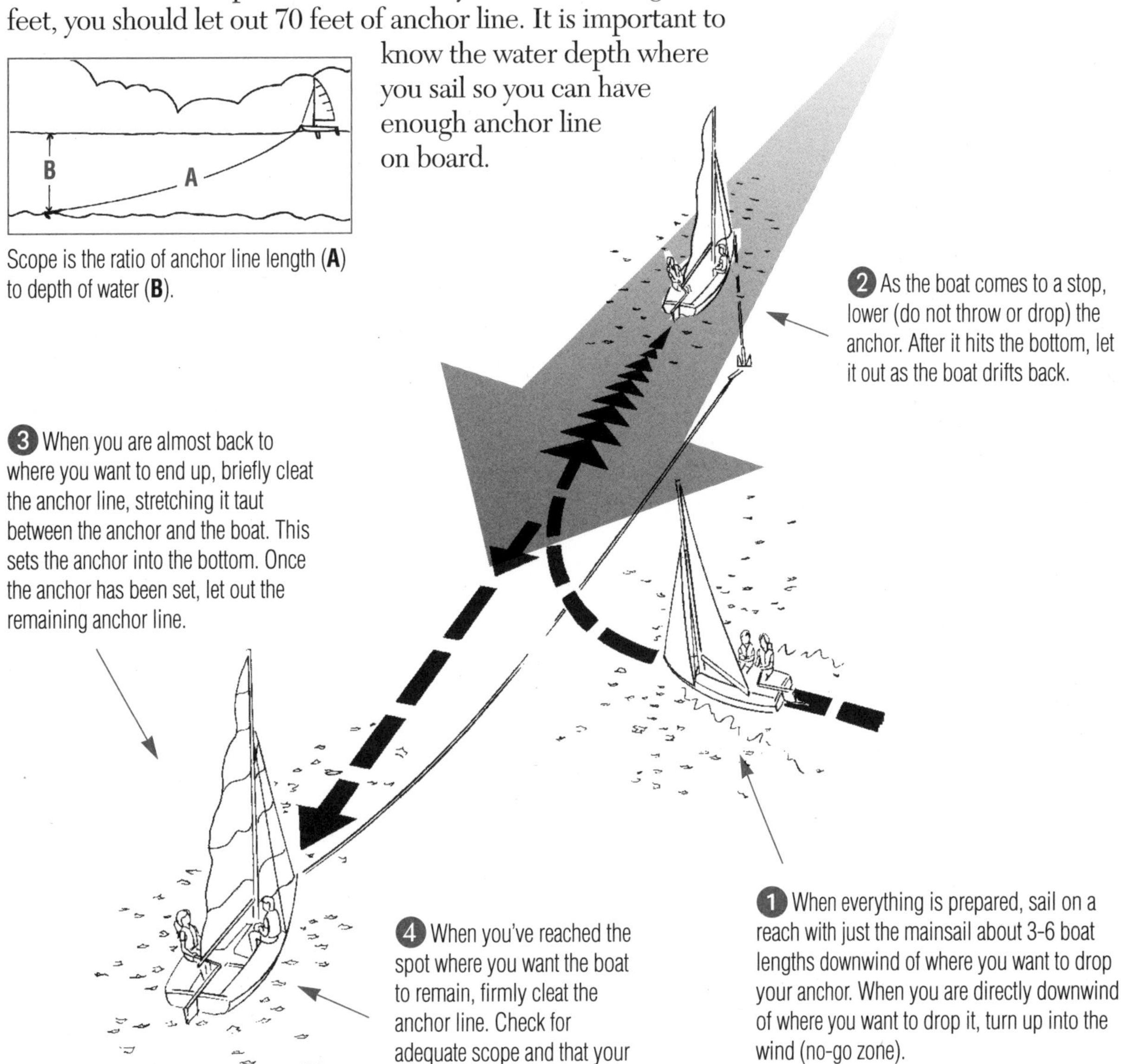


Scope is the ratio of anchor line length (**A**) to depth of water (**B**).

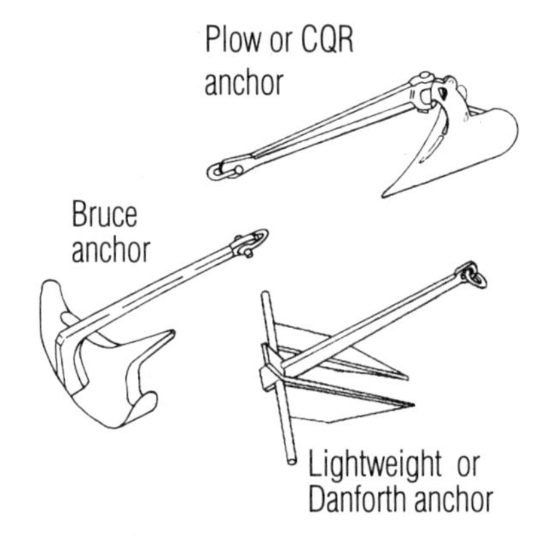

A plow or lightweight anchor digs into the sea bottom when pulled at a narrow angle to the bottom, and releases when pulled up vertically.

## Raising the Anchor

When pulling up the anchor, pull in the anchor line until the boat is over the anchor. Then pull it directly upward, breaking the anchor free from the bottom. Coil the line as you bring the anchor up. If it is dirty, swish it back and forth in the water to clean it. When the anchor is back in the boat, stow it so it won't get in your way or get lost if you capsize. Always coil the anchor line neatly in case you have to use the anchor in an emergency.

## Towing

If you are becalmed or your boat has a breakdown, you may need a tow back to shore. It's important to understand the best way to pick up or throw a towline. Towlines will be either thrown to you or slowly dragged through the water close by your boat. Fasten it to a strong point on the boat, which is often the mast.

Many sailing dinghies have a line, called a *painter*, permanently attached to the bow of the boat. If you use the painter for towing, the tow boat will usually pass alongside and take it. If the tow boat plans to tow a group of sailboats, it may drag a long line behind for you to tie your painter to. A polypropylene line is often used as a towline because it floats on the water and is easy to see. To pick it up, position your boat parallel to the towline and grab it as the line comes by. Tie the end of your painter to the towline using a *rolling hitch* (see page 95).

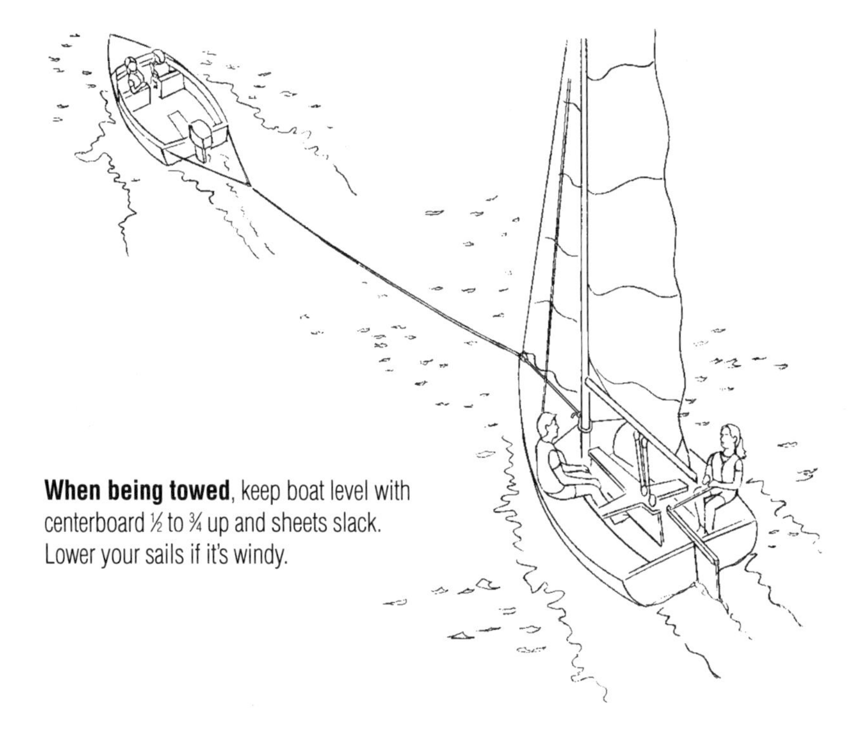

**When being towed**, keep boat level with centerboard ½ to ¾ up and sheets slack. Lower your sails if it's windy.

## Coming Alongside Another Boat

Sometimes it may be necessary to come alongside another boat to change crew or pick up equipment. This can be done without lowering your sails. If a boat is anchored in little or no current, its bow will be pointing into the wind. There are two ways to come alongside such a boat using the glide zone. Approach the anchored boat on a reach, turn the boat into the wind (the no-go zone), and slowly coast or glide to a stop alongside the boat. Be careful that your fingers don't get between the boats.

The second method is to approach the anchored boat slowly on a beam reach with the sails luffing. Stop at the back end (*transom*) of the boat by sheeting out the sails until they flap (*safety position*).

It is important when you come alongside that you do it slowly. It is better to undershoot your destination and try again than come in too quickly and collide. Never come alongside a boat sailing on a broad reach or run. You cannot stop the boat on these points of sail. Remember, the best way to stop a boat is either to luff the sails or to turn the boat into the wind. You can practice coming alongside by sailing up to a mooring or buoy instead of an anchored boat.

### Quick Review

- Name three ways a sailboat can be powered without using its sails. *(answer on p.84)*
- Is sculling best for long or short distances? *(answer on p.84)*
- Define scope. *(answer on p.85)*
- What is recommended scope for anchoring a sailboat? *(answer on p.85)*
- When being towed, should your centerboard be up or down? *(answer on p.86)*
- Describe two ways of coming alongside another boat. *(answer on p.87)*

### Think about it...

- Name four reasons why anchoring skills can be important.
- Why is adequate scope important when anchoring?

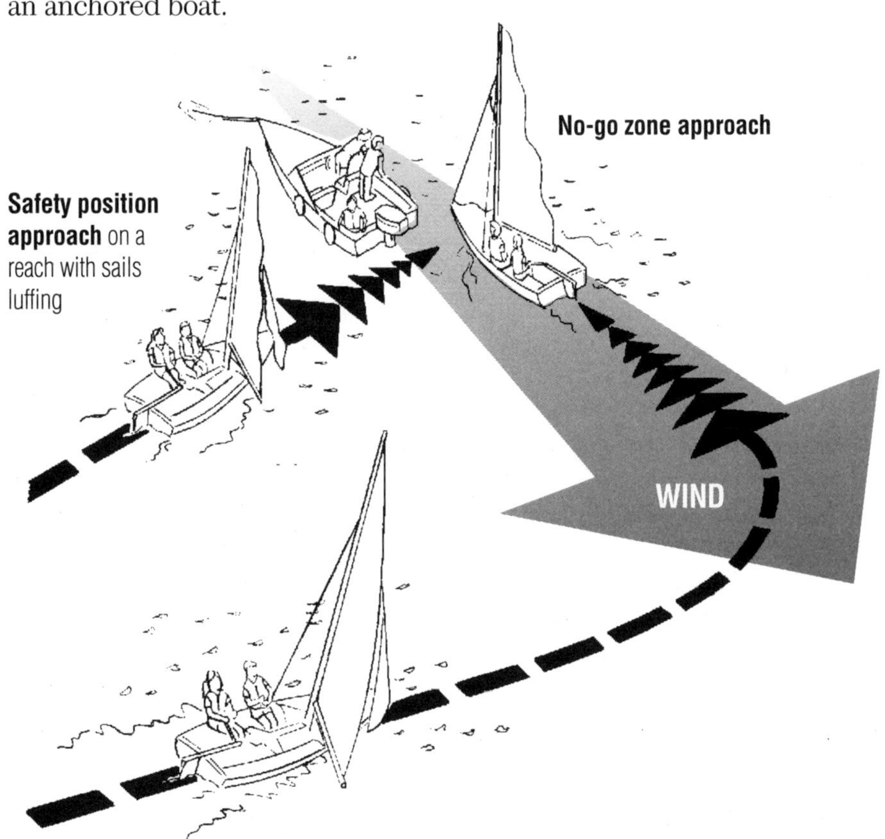

# Weather, Tides & Currents

**KEY CONCEPTS**

- Barometer
- Anemometer
- High pressure
- Low pressure
- Wind movement
- Offshore wind
- Onshore wind
- Bad weather signals
- Tides and currents

One of the first things sailors learn is that the weather is constantly changing. No two days are ever exactly the same. Even if today's wind is blowing from the same direction as yesterday, the waves and wind speed will almost certainly be different. An important part of good seamanship is learning to identify the signs of good sailing weather and the warning signs of poor weather.

## Weather Information VIDEO 12

You can obtain weather information from numerous sources. The U.S. Coast Guard and the National Weather Service issue reports regularly, but weather information is also available from everyday sources such as newspapers (which publish detailed weather maps), and local radio and TV/cable stations. The best sources for wind speed and up-to-the-minute weather projections are marine forecasts and aviation reports—often available by telephone. The U.S.

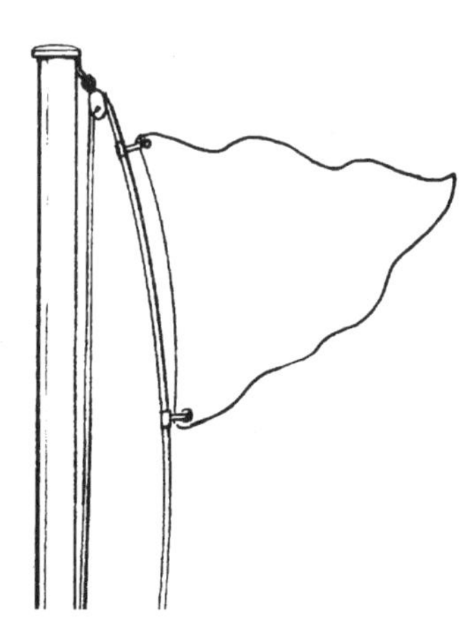

**Small craft advisory signal** (a single red triangular flag) is flown onshore to indicate winds up to 33 knots and conditions unsafe for small boats.

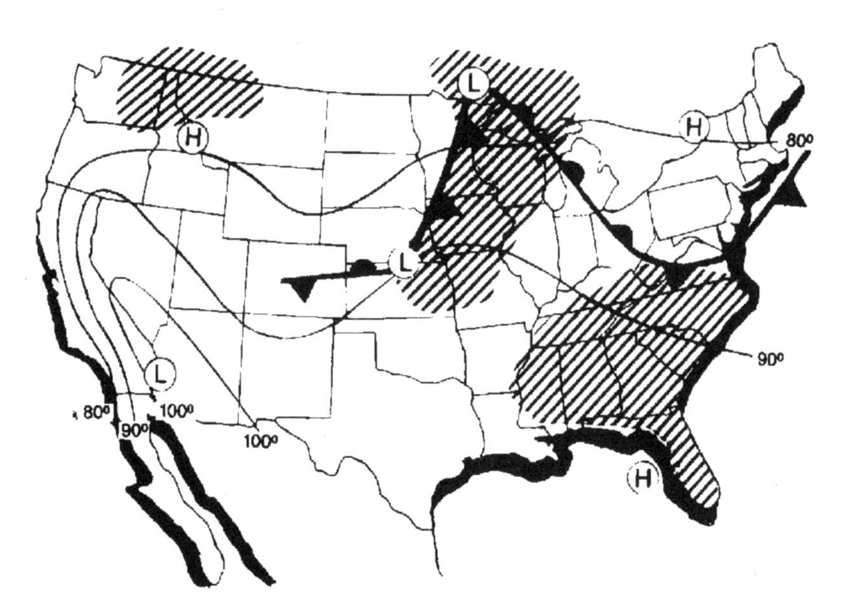


**Weather maps** show high pressure (H) and low pressure (L) systems moving across the country from west to east. Weather maps are found in many newspapers.

Coast Guard also uses an advisory system that displays different flags to indicate wind speed and warnings.

## Measuring Weather

One of the best aids for predicting weather is the *barometer*, which indicates atmospheric pressure changes. Generally, when the barometer is rising, it indicates fair weather and good sailing conditions. When the barometer starts to fall, poor weather may be on its way. Television weather reports usually give the barometric pressure and indicate whether it is rising or falling.

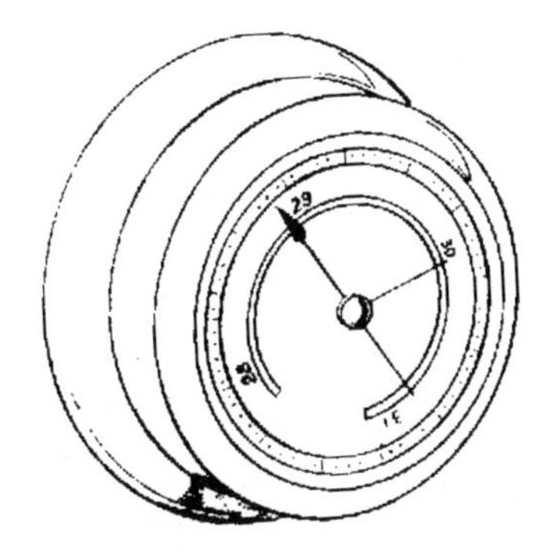

**A barometer** measures atmospheric pressure. Rising pressure indicates fair weather. Falling pressure usually indicates poor weather approaching.

An *anemometer* is used to detect wind speed. Many sailing sites have an anemometer that shows how strong the wind is blowing at the waterfront. It is a good idea to check the anemometer before you go out on the water, especially when the wind is blowing away from the shore and the surface of the water is difficult to judge.

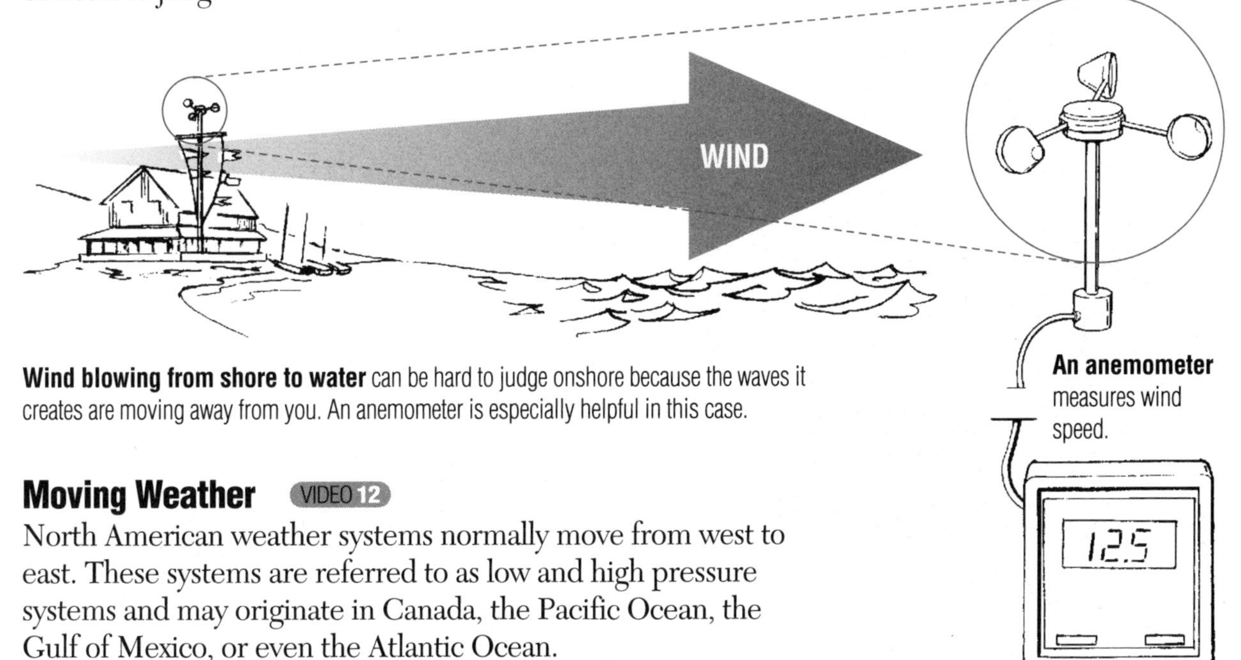


**Wind blowing from shore to water** can be hard to judge onshore because the waves it creates are moving away from you. An anemometer is especially helpful in this case.

**An anemometer** measures wind speed.

## Moving Weather VIDEO 12

North American weather systems normally move from west to east. These systems are referred to as low and high pressure systems and may originate in Canada, the Pacific Ocean, the Gulf of Mexico, or even the Atlantic Ocean.

A *high pressure system*, identified by a large "H" on a weather map, usually denotes drier, cooler air, and you can generally expect good sailing conditions. Cool air tends to sink to the earth's surface and cause an increase in pressure.

A *low pressure system* is identified by an "L" on a weather map and usually denotes relatively warm air that has a tendency to rise, creating lower pressure and a fall in the barometer. Low pressure systems can have strong winds, rain, and storms.

Higher up above the clouds is the *Jet Stream*, a snake-like river of air that circles the earth at an altitude of about 35,000 feet. It influences the movement of high and low pressure systems.

*"Local showers."*

## Wind Movement VIDEO 12

Wind is created by pressure differences in the atmosphere, with air usually flowing from high pressure areas to low pressure areas. Its direction and speed can be greatly affected by local

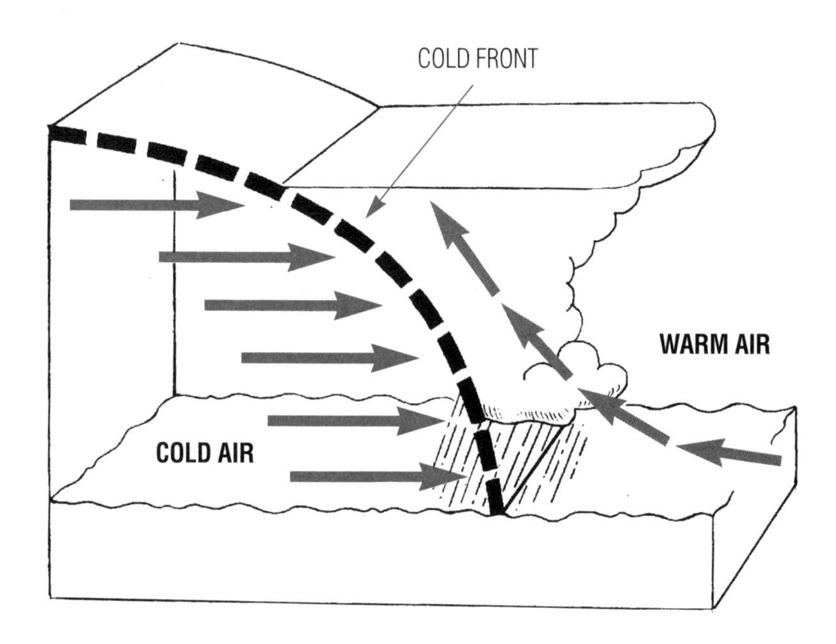


**Cool, dry air** sinks to the earth's surface. When a cool air mass moves into a warmer air mass, clouds, rain and strong winds can occur, sometimes accompanied by thunder and lightning. The border where a cold air mass pushes into a warm air mass is called a *cold front*.

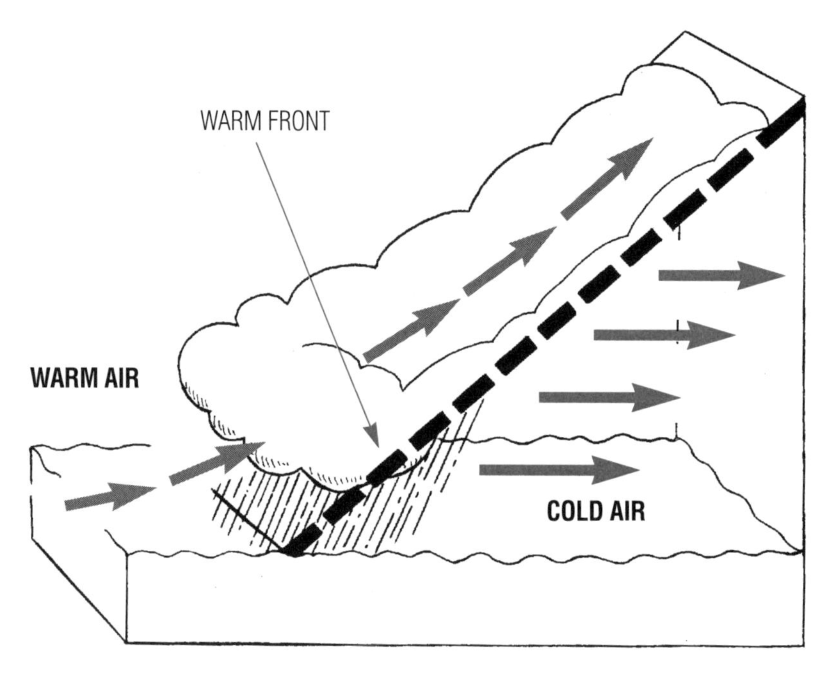


**Warm air masses** have a tendency to rise, so the rain and wind created when they meet cold air masses is less violent. The border where a warm air mass pushes into a cold air mass is called a *warm front*.

topography. As you sail on a body of water surrounded by large buildings or hills, you will notice the wind speed and direction changing often. This is a unique aspect of sailing which is fun to discover and learn. Your environmental awareness will help you react to these changes.

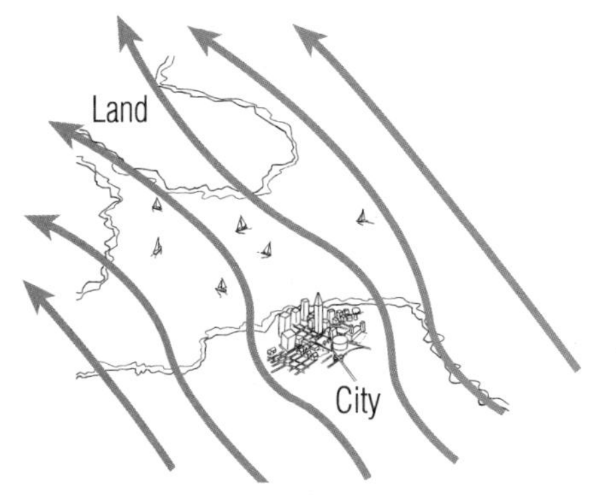


**Wind direction and strength** can be affected by local topography.

## Offshore and Onshore Winds VIDEO 12

Some winds are referred to as either offshore or onshore. *Offshore winds* blow from the land out onto a body of water and are affected by local topography. Standing on land and looking out over the water, an offshore wind can seem calmer than it really is because you are seeing the backs of the waves. As you move out onto the water you may find the wind to be stronger than you expected.

*Onshore winds* or *sea breezes* occur when the air blows from the water onto the shore. They are a result of cooler air over water being pulled in by the hotter air rising over the land. Onshore winds typically build in strength in the afternoon as the land heats up. A light to medium sea breeze provides ideal wind for a novice sailor.

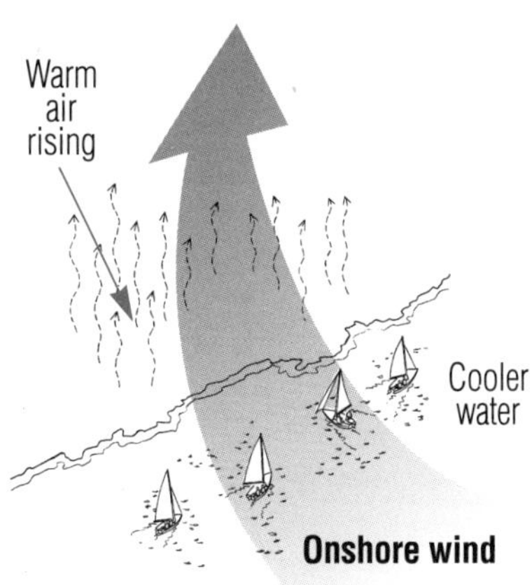


**Local winds** can be caused by differences in temperature between land and water.

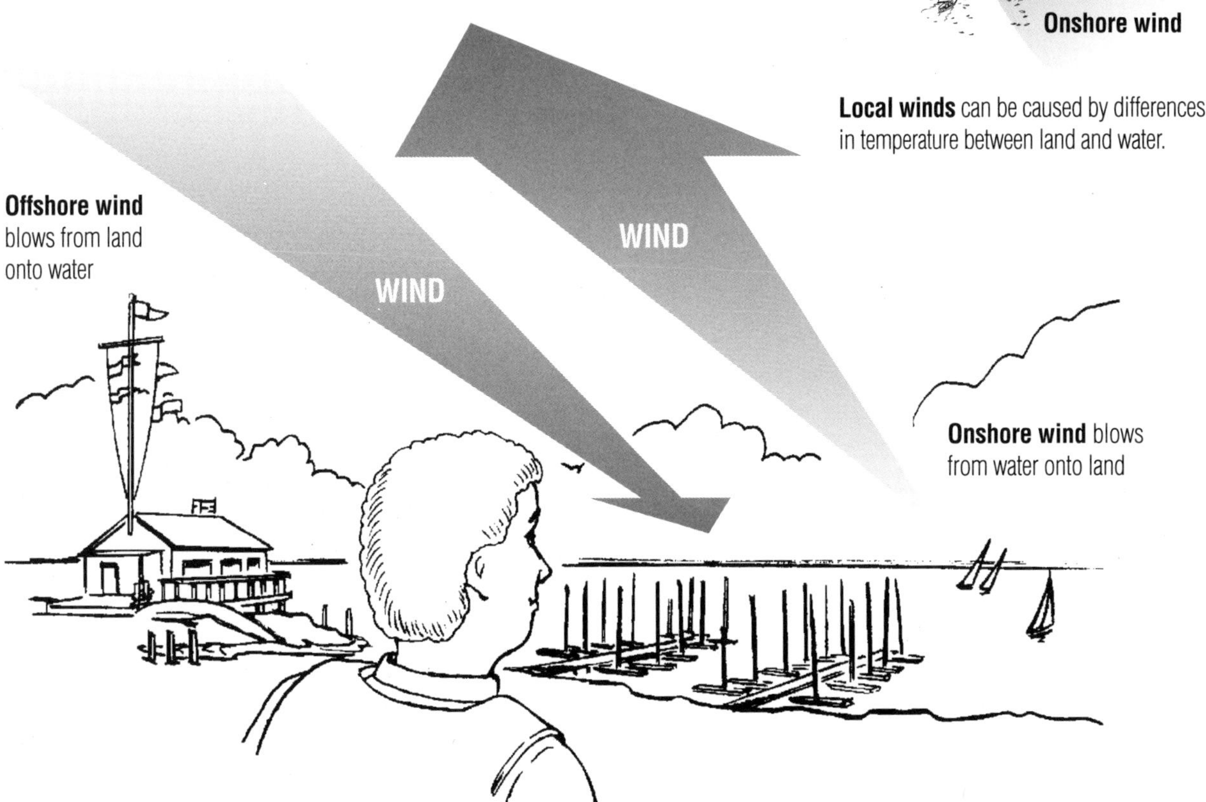


**Offshore wind** blows from land onto water

**Onshore wind** blows from water onto land

At the first sign of threatening weather, it is smart to head for shore.

## Bad Weather Signals

A good sailor is always on the lookout for changes in weather. Television or radio forecasts are the first step in determining whether it's safe to sail. You should also know some of the early signals of approaching bad weather.

- Increase in cloud cover and darkening skies.
- Sudden decrease or increase in wind velocity.
- Change in wind direction.
- Lightning nearby or in the distance.
- Thunder in the distance.
- Gusty wind conditions.

On the water, weather can change quickly. If there is any sign of bad weather approaching, don't hesitate to head for shore.

## Tides and Currents VIDEO 12

Tides and currents will have an important influence on just about every aspect of your sailing, especially docking, mooring and sailing a course. *Tides* are the *vertical* movement of water caused by the gravitational pull of the earth and moon. *Current* is the *horizontal* flow of water caused by tide or the natural flow of water from higher elevations to lower (such as rivers). Tides occur daily at regular intervals, but the difference in height between low and high tide varies in different locations. Most fresh water lakes do not have tides.

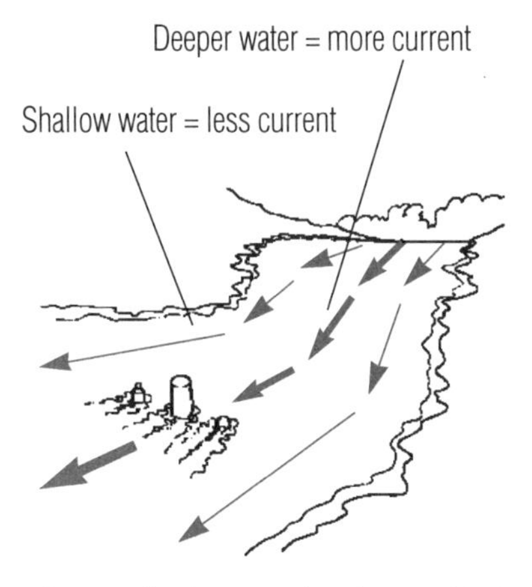


**Current** flowing around stationary objects will create a swirl or "wake" that can help you determine its direction.

Currents and tides are both affected by water depth. Deep water will increase the speed of the current or tide, and shallow water will reduce it. You can determine the direction and speed of current by using certain indicators. A floating object, such as a stick being carried along by the moving water, or water swirling past a fixed buoy or dock are good current indicators. The vertical movement of tides can be seen as the water rises or falls on a piling or beach. A falling tide will leave a wet beach or piling next to the water's edge. A dry beach or piling next to the water signifies a rising, or high tide.

## Currents and Tides: Questions and Answers

**Q: How do you detect the direction current is flowing?**

A: By looking at a stationary object such as a buoy, mooring, or lobster pot. Current flowing past these objects can create a swirl or '"wake" that moves in the direction of the current.

---

**Q: If I can't sail against the current, what should I do?**

A: The best solution is to anchor the boat and wait for the wind to increase, wait for the current to change direction or wait for a tow.

---

**Q: How do I find out if the tide is rising or falling?**

A: Marine forecasts usually have tide reports. Tide tables can also be bought at local marine stores. A wet beach or piling indicates a falling tide, and a dry beach or piling signifies a rising tide.

---

**Q: The boat keeps going sideways or downstream from the point that I'm aiming for. What can I do?**

A: Steering upstream and overcorrecting will help (see below).

---

**Q: Do I have to compensate for current when returning to a dock or mooring?**

A: Yes. The first step is to determine the direction and speed of the current. Then you correct for current during your approach. This may take some practice.

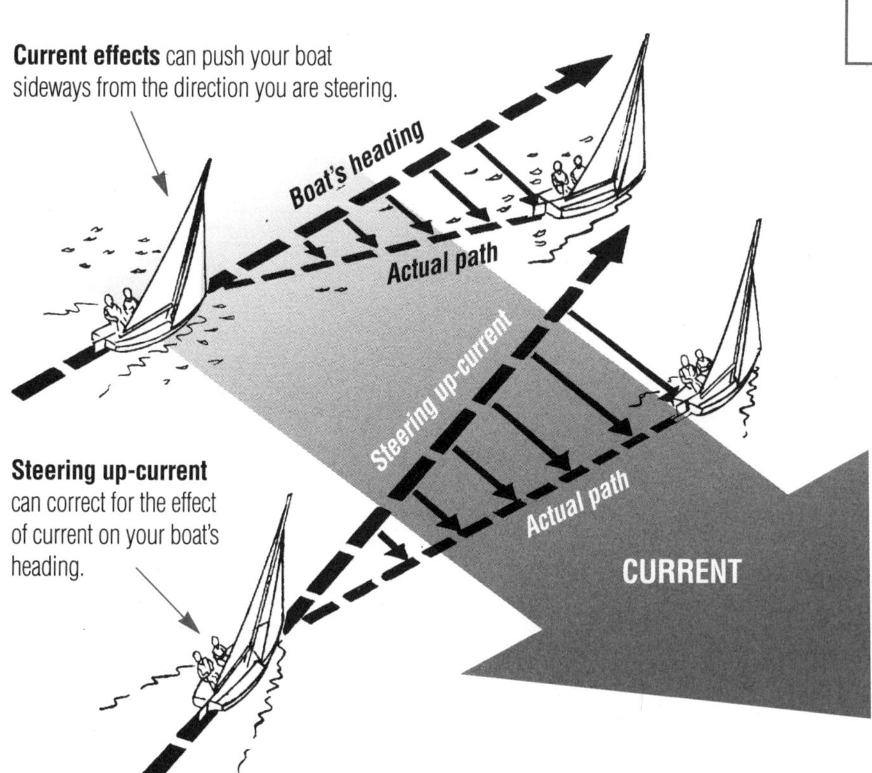


**Current effects** can push your boat sideways from the direction you are steering.

**Steering up-current** can correct for the effect of current on your boat's heading.

### Quick Review

- Do high pressure weather systems usually bring good weather or bad? *(answer on p.89)*
- In which direction does an onshore breeze blow? *(answer on p.91)*
- Name four signs in the sky of approaching bad weather. *(answer on p.92)*
- How can you tell what direction current is running while you are out on the water? *(answer on p.92)*
- Does current run faster in shallow water than it does in deeper water? *(answer on p.92)*
- If you were crossing a body of water with current running from left to right, how would you compensate your course for the current? *(answer on p.93)*

### Think about it...

- What are the prevailing weather patterns in your sailing area?
- Name two places where tides are of no concern to sailors.

CHAPTER 18

# Knots and Lines

**KEY CONCEPTS**

- Types of line
- Bowline
- Figure-8
- Cleat hitch
- Clove hitch
- Two half hitches
- Rolling hitch
- Throwing and coiling a line

You'll probably be surprised to see how often knots are used in sailing. Learning how to tie knots correctly is an important skill, and could save your life. A few basic knots are all you need to get started sailing, and they're easy to practice at home.

All ropes used on a sailboat are called *lines*. Different lines are made of different materials for different uses. Nylon, for example, is stretchy and is used for anchoring and docklines. Dacron™ (the Dupont trademark for polyester fiber) has very low stretch and is used for halyards and sheets. Polypropylene line floats and is often used for mooring pick-up lines. The lines that you will probably use most — the jib sheets and the main sheet — will usually be Dacron.

The six knots illustrated here are the only ones you need to know to get started. VIDEO 3

The **bowline** (pronounced "BOE-lin") is for tying a non-slip loop for a variety of purposes. The bowline is widely used in sailing.

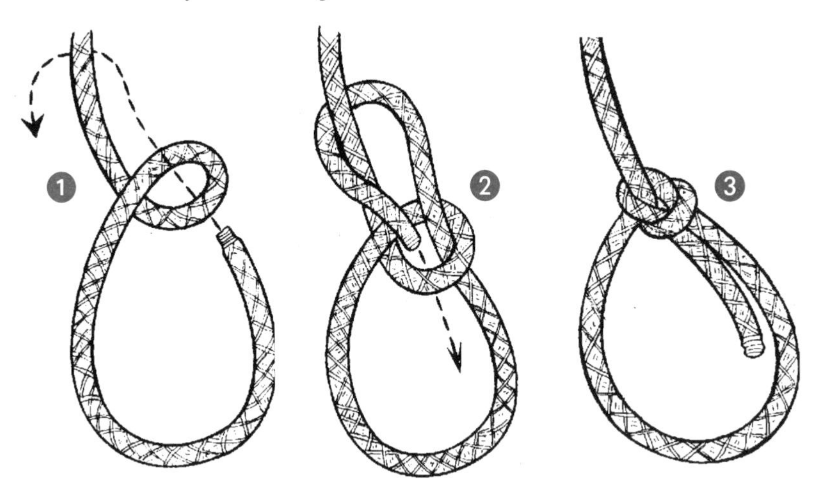


The **clove hitch** is used for tying to a post, ring or eye. It is not a very secure knot, and is often used as a temporary hitch.

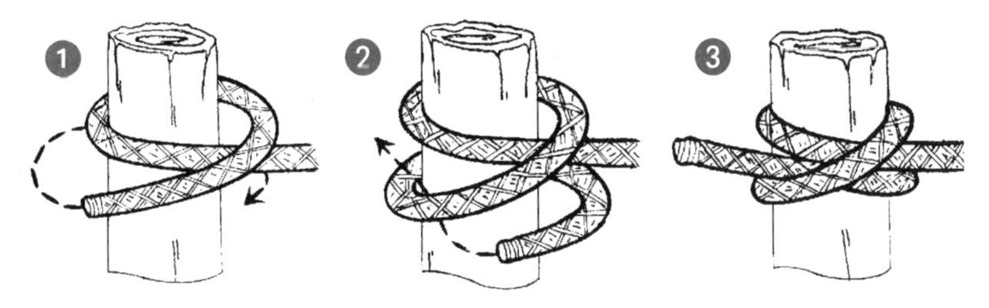

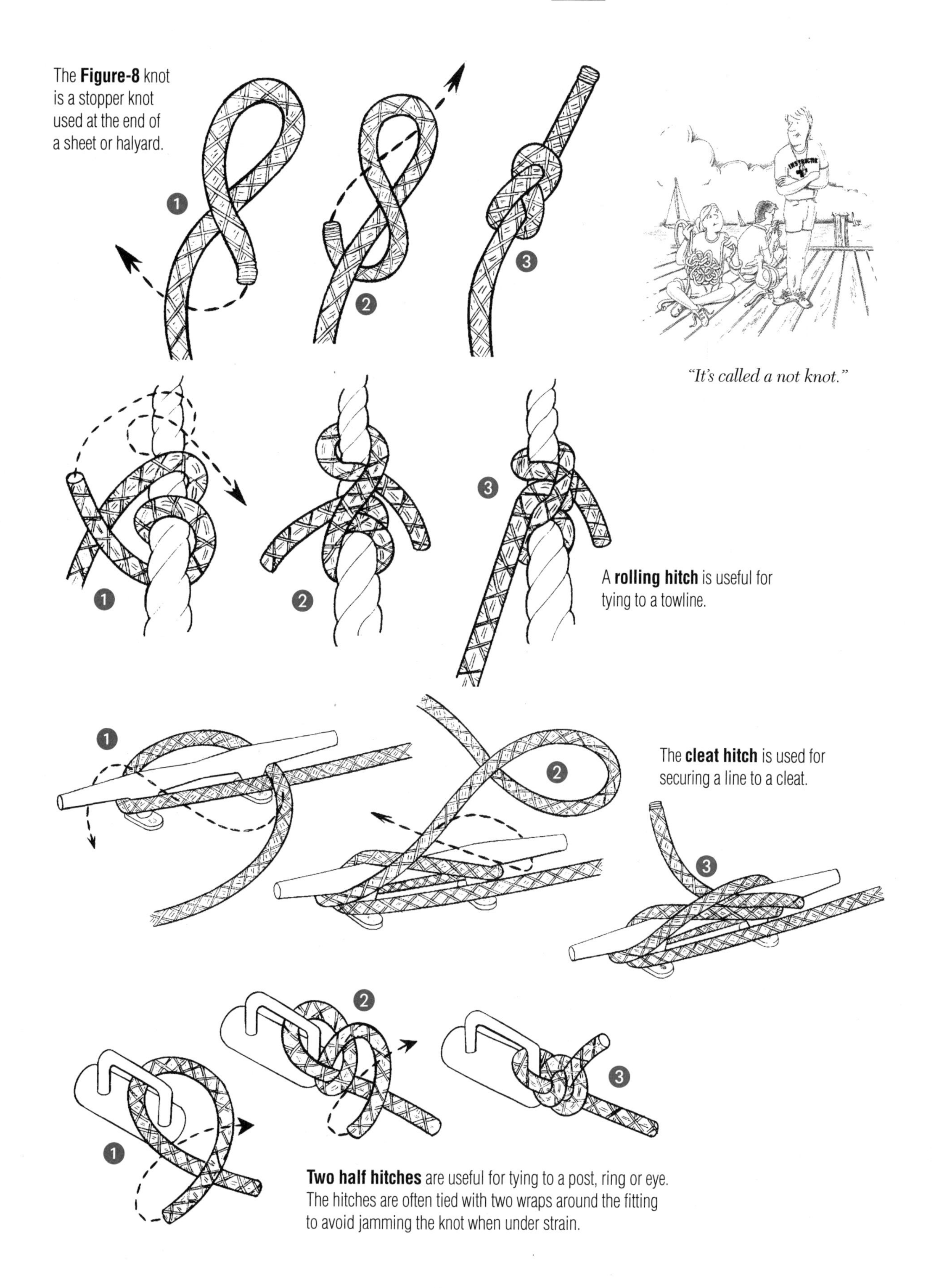

The **Figure-8** knot is a stopper knot used at the end of a sheet or halyard.

*"It's called a not knot."*

A **rolling hitch** is useful for tying to a towline.

The **cleat hitch** is used for securing a line to a cleat.

**Two half hitches** are useful for tying to a post, ring or eye. The hitches are often tied with two wraps around the fitting to avoid jamming the knot when under strain.

Throwing a line is sometimes necessary when docking or towing a boat. A line should always be coiled first, before throwing. Though it looks easy, you should practice throwing a line to make sure you can do it quickly and accurately. Stowing a line is best done by coiling the line and then tying it so that it is ready to use. Knowing how to use the knots and how to coil and throw a line will make life around the sailboat much easier.

▶ Describe the different uses of nylon, dacron and polypropylene line. *(answer on p.94)*

▶ Why are sheets usually made from dacron? *(answer on p.94)*

▶ What is the most widely used sailing knot? *(answer on p.94)*

**Think about it...**

▶ Name two important reasons why it is important to coil spare lines and halyards.

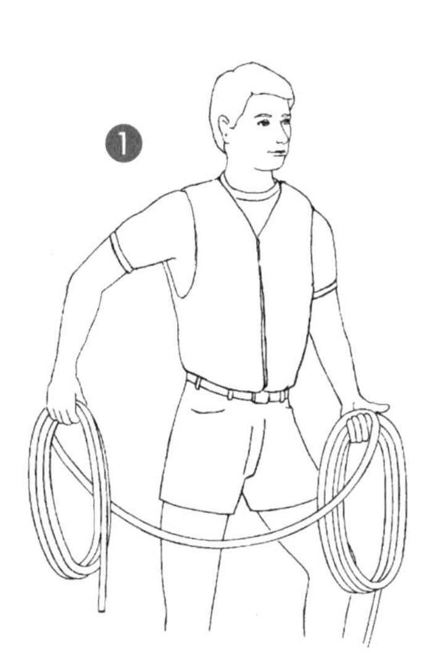


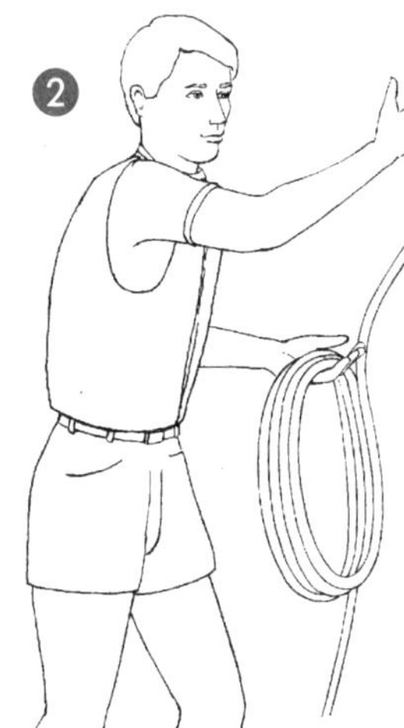


**Throw a line** by separating the coil into two sections ❶, then throwing the smaller coil and letting the rest of the line uncoil from the other hand.

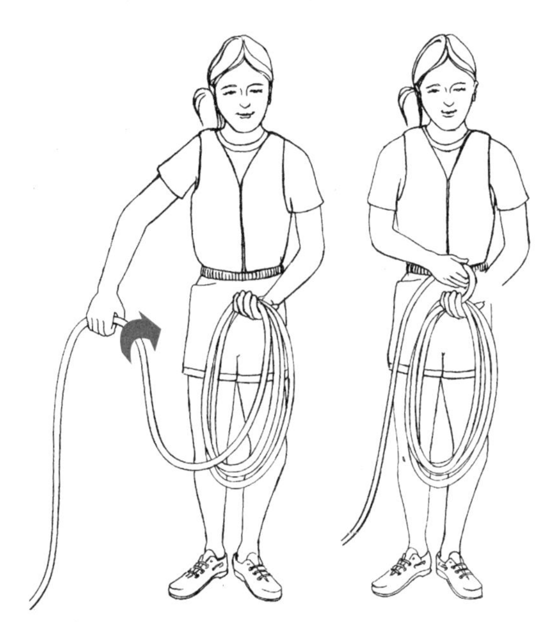

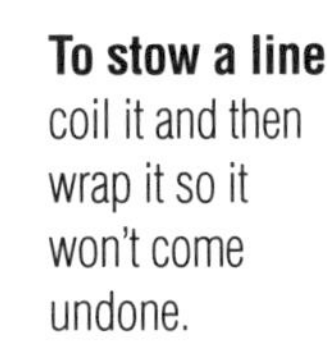

**To stow a line** coil it and then wrap it so it won't come undone.

**Coiling a line** is easy with practice. With some lines it helps to twist the line as you coil to compensate for natural twist in the line.

# Appendix

## Types of Sailboat Rigs

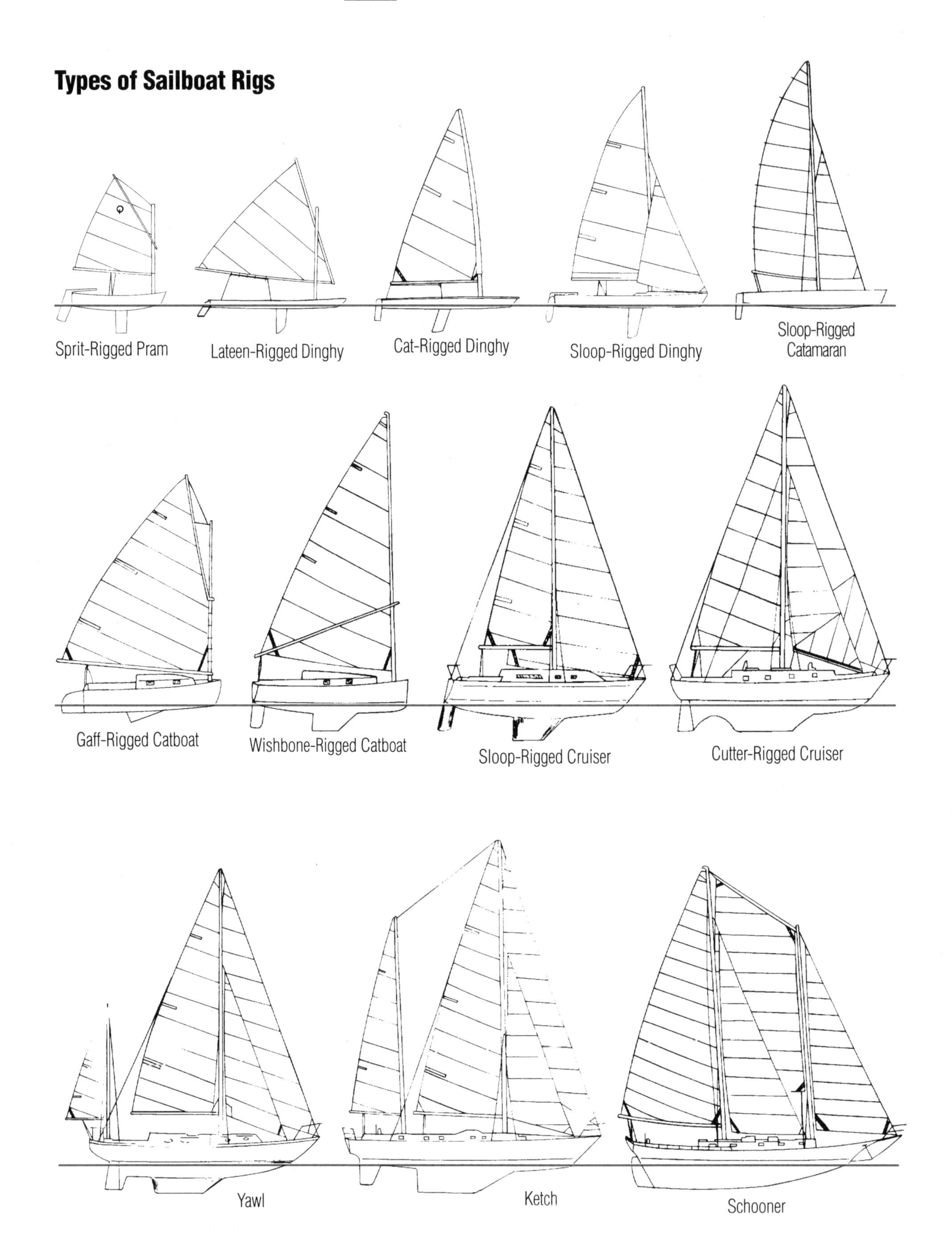

## Car-topping and Trailering

When car-topping a boat, it can be loaded on top of the car from the rear or from the side. Be sure to have enough people to lift the boat comfortably to avoid possible injury or damage.

Tie down the boat securely on car top with straps or lines across the boat and lines from bow and stern to forward and rear bumpers — preferably to each corner (see below).

Trailering is necessary for larger boats. While trailer designs and features vary, proper trailer maintenance can help prevent breakdowns on the road.

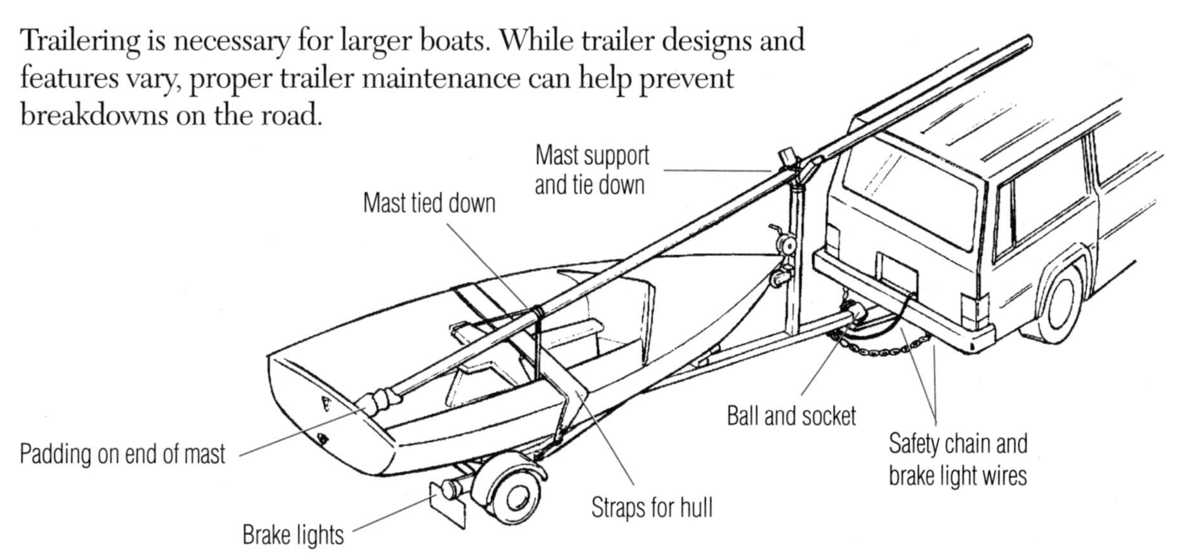

## Glossary of Important Sailing Terms and Expressions

Following is a comprehensive list of sailing vocabulary and terms used in this book and in the world of sailing. Words having the similar meaning (synonyms) are also included to assist in word association and account for regional differences in the sailing language.

### ▸A

**Abeam.** A direction off the side of a boat, at right angles to a line from bow to stern. Syn. *On the Beam.*

**Aerobic.** Exercise activity such as bicycling, jogging, or swimming which stimulates the cardiovascular system.

**Aft.** 1. Toward, near, or at the back end of a boat. Syn. *Astern.* 2. A direction behind the stern of a boat. Syn. *Astern.*

**Amidships.** The middle of a boat.

**Anaerobic Exercise.** Activity such as lifting weights which helps promote strength, flexibility, and muscle development.

**Anchoring.** Stationary positioning of a boat in the water by a weighted object connected to the boat by a rope and/or chain.

**Anemometer.** A device used to indicate wind speed.

**Apparent Wind.** The wind that flows over a moving boat, which is the result of the "true wind" affected by the movement of the boat.

**Appendage.** An underwater fin, such as a centerboard, daggerboard, leeboard, keel, or rudder.

**Astern.** See **Aft.**

**Athwartships.** A sideways direction on a boat that is at a right angle to the line from bow to stern.

### ▸B

**Back.** To push a sail out against the wind to help turn the boat, slow it, or move it backward.

**Backstay.** The standing rigging running from the stern to the top of the mast, keeping the mast from falling forward.

**Backwind.** The wind flowing off the trailing edge of a jib or mainsail.

**Bailers.** Openings in the bottom or transom of a boat to remove water when sailing. Syn. *Self-Bailers.*

**Ballast.** Weight used to give a boat stability. On large boats, ballast in the keel (usually lead) provides stability. On smaller boats, stability is usually provided by the weight of the sailors.

**Barometer.** A device used to indicate atmospheric pressure.

**Batten.** A thin wooden or plastic stiffener inserted into a pocket on the back part (leech) of a sail.

**Beam.** The width of a boat.

**Beam Reach.** Sailing at approximately 90 degrees to the wind source with the wind coming from abeam and the sails let out about halfway. (One of the points of sail.)

**Bear Away.** See **Head Down.**

**Bear Off.** See **Head Down.**

**Bear Up.** See **Head Up.**

**Beating.** Sailing toward the wind source, or against the wind, with the sails pulled in all-the-way, tacking as you go, to reach a destination upwind.

**Bilge.** The lowest part of a boat inside the hull.

**Block.** The nautical term for a pulley. It can have one or more sheaves, or wheels.

**Bolt Rope.** The rope sewn into the forward (luff) and bottom (foot) edges of the mainsail.

**Boom.** A spar used to hold out or anchor the bottom of a sail.

**Boom Vang.** A control line, usually a multi-purchase tackle, secured to the boom to prevent it from lifting when wind hits the sail. Syn. *Vang*

**Bow.** The forward end of a boat.

**Breeze.** Wind.

**Broad Reach.** Sailing with the wind coming over the rear corner of the boat, or with the bow approximately 135 degrees to the wind source. (One of the points of sail.)

**By the Lee.** Sailing downwind with the wind blowing over the leeward side of the boat, increasing the possibility of an unexpected jibe.

### ▸C

**Capsize.** A boat turned over on its side or upside down.

**Cast Off.** To untie a line and let it go, or to remove a line from a cleat and let it go.

**Cat.** See **Catamaran.**

**Catamaran.** A boat with two parallel hulls. Syn. *Cat.*

**Catboat.** A boat that has only a mainsail, with the mast located at the bow.

**Centerboard.** A pivoting plate of wood, fiberglass, or metal, projecting below the bottom of a sailboat to help prevent the boat from sliding sideways.

**Centerline.** An imaginary line that runs down the center of the boat from the bow to the stern.

**Chart.** A nautical map showing water depths, obstructions, restricted areas, markers and buoys.

**C-Jibe.** A course steered through a downwind turn (jibe) which results in the mainsail suddenly crossing from one side to the other side uncontrolled. The path of the boat makes a "C." *Syn. Slam Jibe, Flying Jibe.*

**Class.** A category into which boats of similar design are grouped.

**Cleat.** A wooden, plastic, or metal device which is used to hold or secure lines.

**Clew.** The lower back corner of a mainsail or jib.

**Close-Hauled.** Describes a boat sailing as close to the wind as possible with its sails pulled in all the way. Syn. *On the Wind, Sailing to Weather, Sailing to Windward, Sailing Upwind.* (One of the points of sail.)

**Close Reach.** Sailing with the wind just forward of abeam, or with the bow approximately 70 degrees to the wind source. (One of the points of sail.)

**Cockpit.** The open well in a boat where the helmsman and/or crew sit or put their feet.

**Come About.** To turn the bow of a sailboat through the wind, or no-go zone, so that the sails fill on the opposite side. Syn. *Tack.*

**Come Down.** See **Head Down.**

**Come Up.** See **Head Up.**

**Coming About.** See **Tacking** and **"Hard a-Lee."**

**Compass.** An instrument used to determine the direction that a boat is headed, or to take a bearing (sight) on an object.

**Constant Angle to the Wind.** The correct angle of the wind to a sail, which remains the same for all points of sail when the sail is correctly trimmed (positioned), except when the wind is blowing from behind the stern.

**Control Line.** A rope used to adjust and trim a sail, such as a sheet, outhaul, downhaul, cunningham or boom vang. Syn. *Running Rigging, Sail Controls.*

**Control Signals.** Hand signs used between instructors and sailors to communicate while on the water.

**Course.** The direction that a boat is steered to reach a destination.

**Crabbing (to Weather).** See **Feathering.**

**Crew.** The people who help the helmsman sail a boat.

**Cunningham.** A control line that tensions the forward edge (luff) of a sail.

**Cunningham Hole.** A hole in the tack of a sail through which the cunningham line runs to tension the forward edge (luff) of the sail.

**Current.** The horizontal movement of water caused by tides, wind, or change in elevation.

## ▶ D

**Daggerboard.** A movable plate of wood, fiberglass, or metal let down below the bottom of a boat to help prevent the boat from sliding sideways. Similar to the centerboard, except it is raised and lowered vertically rather than pivoted.

**Dead Downwind.** See **Run.**

**Deck.** The top (horizontal) surface of the hull.

**De-Rigging.** Removing a boat's mast, boom and equipment.

**Displacement.** The weight of water displaced by a floating boat. The weight of water is equal to the weight of the boat; therefore, a boat's weight is often called its displacement.

**Dolphin Striker.** A metal compression rod positioned on the underside of a multihull's forward crossbeam, directly underneath the mast.

**Downhaul.** A control line that adjusts and tensions the luff of a sail by moving the end of the boom at the mast. The movable fitting joining the mast and boom is called the "gooseneck."

**Downwind.** In the opposite direction from the wind source, or where the wind is blowing to. Syn. *Leeward.*

**Downwind Sailing.** Sailing away from the wind source with the sails let out. Syn. *Broad Reach, Run, With the Wind.*

**Downwind Side.** See **Leeward Side.**

### ▶E

**Ease.** To let out a line or sail. The opposite of pull. Syn. *Let Off, Sheet Out.*

**Electrical Hazards.** Overhead power lines, electrical cables, electrical power tools and equipment used near the water, or near launching and boat storage areas.

**Environmental Awareness.** The continuous monitoring of wind, weather, sea conditions, current, and distance from the shore.

### ▶F

**Fairlead.** A fitting, such as a ring, eye, block or loop which guides a rope in the direction required.

**Fall Off.** See **Head Down.**

**Feathering.** Sailing upwind so close to the wind that the forward edge of the sail is stalling or luffing, reducing the power generated by the sail and the angle of heel. Syn. *Crabbing (to Weather), High, Light, Pinching, Sailing Thin.*

**Fly.** See **Telltales.**

**Flying Jibe.** See **C-Jibe.**

**Foot.** The bottom edge of a sail.

**Fore.** Toward, near, or at the bow.

**Fore and Aft.** Toward, near, or at both ends of a boat.

**Fore-and-Aft Line.** An imaginary line that runs lengthwise on a boat.

**Forestay.** A support wire connecting the mast to the bow. Part of the standing rigging.

### ▶G

**Give-way Vessel.** The vessel required to give way to another boat when they may be on a collision course.

**Glide Zone.** The distance a sailboat takes to coast to a stop after turning into the no-go zone or letting out the sails.

**Go Up.** See **Head Up.**

**Gooseneck.** The joint fitting that connects the boom to the mast.

**Gunwale** (GUN-nle)**.** The edge of a sailboat where the deck and hull meet.

**Gust.** See **Puff.**

**Gybe.** See **Jibe.**

**Gybing.** See **Jibing.**

### ▶H

**Halyard.** A line used to raise or lower a sail.

**"Hard a-Lee."** A command made by the helmsman when the tiller is moved to leeward to tack a sailboat. Syn. *"Coming About," "Helm's a-Lee," "Tacking."*

**Harden Up.** See **Head Up.**

**Head.** The top corner of a sail where the halyard is attached.

**Head Down.** To turn the boat away from the wind. Syn. *Bear Away, Bear Off, Come Down, Fall Off, Head Off*

**Head Off.** See **Head Down.**

**Head Up.** To turn the boat toward the wind. Syn. *Bear Up, Come Up, Go Up, Harden Up, Luff Up.*

**Heading.** The direction in which a boat is pointing.

**Head-to-Wind.** When the bow of a boat is pointing directly into the wind, or in the middle of the no-go zone.

**Heat Emergencies.** See **Hyperpyrexia.**

**Heave-to.** A position with the sails and rudder countering each other as the boat slowly drifts downwind and forward.

**Heel.** 1. When a boat leans over or tips to one side. 2. The lower end of the mast.

**Helm.** 1. The tiller or wheel of a boat. 2. The tendency of a sailboat to turn toward or away from the wind on its own. If the boat wants to turn toward the wind (to weather), it has a weather helm. If it wants to turn away from the wind (to leeward), it has a lee helm.

**"Helm's a-Lee."** See **"Hard a-Lee."**

**Helmsman.** The person who steers or drives a boat. Syn. *Skipper.*

**High Pressure.** Higher atmospheric pressure generally associated with fair skies and good weather.

**High Side.** The side of a sailboat nearest to the wind source. Syn. *Weather Side, Windward Side, Upwind Side.*

**Hiking.** When a person leans over the side of a boat to counteract heel.

**Hiking Stick.** See **Tiller Extension.**

**Hole (in the Wind).** See **Lull.**

**Hull.** The body of a boat, excluding rig and sails.

**Hull Speed.** The maximum speed that a boat can achieve without planing.

**Hyperpyrexia.** Increase in body temperature caused by prolonged exposure to the sun, heat, and humidity. Syn. *Heat Emergencies.*

**Hypothermia.** Reduction in body temperature caused by prolonged exposure to cold temperatures or cold water.

## ▶ I

**In Irons.** When a boat is pointed into the wind and has stopped or is moving backward through the water, and is temporarily unable to turn onto either tack. Syn. *In Stays.*

**In Stays.** See **In Irons.**

**In the Groove.** When a sailboat is moving well with proper balance and sail trim, and is steered so the sails are working at their best with the telltales flowing properly.

## ▶ J

**Jet Stream.** A snake-like river of air at about 35,000 feet in the atmosphere which affects the position and movement of high and low pressure systems.

**Jib.** The smaller triangular sail in front of the mast.

**Jibe.** Changing from one tack to the other when sailing downwind. The mainsail swings across the boat, which can be a controlled maneuver or can happen unexpectedly as the wind crosses the stern. Syn. *Gybe, Jibing, Gybing*

**"Jibe Ho."** A command made by the helmsman as he or she starts to jibe. Syn. *"Jibing"*

**Jibing.** 1. The maneuver of changing from one tack to the other when sailing downwind. Syn. *Gybing, Jibe, Gybe.* 2. A command made by the helmsman as he or she starts to jibe. Syn. *"Jibe Ho."*

**Jury Rig.** A temporary fix to damaged equipment enabling a boat to be sailed.

## ▶ K

**Keel.** The fixed underwater fin on a sailboat hull which helps provide stability and prevents the boat from slipping sideways.

**Knot.** One nautical mile per hour. 1 knot equals 1.15 miles per hour.

## ▶ L

**Land Breeze.** See **Offshore Wind.**

**Leech.** The back edge of a sail (between the head and clew) where the battens are located.

**Leeward.** In the opposite direction from the wind source, or where the wind is blowing to. Syn. *Downwind.*

**Leeward Side.** The side of a sailboat or sail away from the wind source. Syn. *Downwind Side, Low Side.*

**Leeway.** The distance a boat is pushed to leeward of its course by the action of the wind or current.

**Lift.** 1. The aerodynamic or hydrodynamic force that results from air passing by a sail, or water flowing past a centerboard or rudder. 2. A change in wind direction which lets the boat head up.

**Light.** When only the forward edge of a sail is stalling or luffing. Syn. *Feathering, High, Luffing, Pinching, Soft.* 2. Description for low wind speed. Syn. *Soft.*

**Line.** A rope used for a function on a boat, such as a sheet, halyard, cunningham or painter.

**Low Pressure.** Lower atmospheric pressure generally associated with clouds, rain, and inclement weather.

**Low Side.** The side of a sailboat away from the wind source. Syn. *Downwind Side, Leeward Side.*

**Luff.** 1. The forward edge of a sail. 2. To stall or flap the sail at its forward edge, or over the entire sail.

**Luff Rope.** The rope sewn into the forward edge (luff) of the mainsail, which is usually attached to the groove or track on the mast. Syn. *Bolt Rope.*

**Luff Up.** See **Head Up.**

**Luffing.** When the sail is stalling or flapping at its forward edge, or the entire sail is flapping. Syn. *Feathering, High, Light, Pinching, Soft.*

**Lull.** A decrease in wind speed for a short duration. Syn. *Hole.*

## ▶ M

**Main.** See **Mainsail.**

**Mainsail.** The sail which is attached to the mast and boom. Syn. *Main.*

**Mast.** A spar placed vertically in a boat to hold up the sails.

**Masthead.** The top of a mast.
**Masthead Fly.** A wind direction indicator at the top of the mast.
**Monohull.** A boat with only one hull.
**Moor.** To fasten a boat to a mooring.
**Mooring.** A permanent anchor connected to a buoy by a rope and/or chain, to which a boat may be fastened.
**Multihull.** A boat with more than one hull, such as a catamaran or trimaran.

## ▶ N

**Navigation Rules.** Laws establishing right-of-way in different situations that are intended to prevent collisions on the water. Syn. *"ColRegs," Collision Rules.*
**No-Go Zone.** The area into the wind where a sailboat cannot sail, even with the sails pulled in all-the-way. The zone covers the direction pointing directly into the wind source and extending to about 45 degrees on either side of it. Syn. *No-Sail Zone.*
**No-Sail Zone.** See **No-Go Zone.**

## ▶ O

**Off the Wind.** Any of the points of sail, except sailing upwind.
**Offshore.** Away from the shore.
**Offshore Wind.** Wind blowing away from the shore to the water. Syn. *Land Breeze.*
**On the Beam.** See **Abeam.**
**On the Wind.** See **Close-hauled.**
**One-Design.** Any boat built to conform to rules so that it is identical to all others in the same class.
**Onshore.** Toward the shore.
**Onshore Wind.** Wind blowing from the water to the shore. Syn. *Sea Breeze.*
**Outhaul.** A control line that is attached to the clew of the mainsail that adjusts tension along the bottom (foot) of the sail.

## ▶ P

**Painter.** A rope attached to the bow of a small boat, which is used to fasten the boat to a dock or mooring.
**PFD.** A personal flotation device. Syn. *Life Jacket, Life Vest.*
**Pinching.** See **Feathering.**
**Planing.** When a boat accelerates enough to break loose from its bow wave and ride on top of the water.
**Points of Sail.** The headings of a sailboat in relation to the wind, i.e., close-hauled, close reach, reach, broad reach, run.
**Port.** The left side of a boat (when looking forward).
**"Prepare to Tack."** See **"Ready About."**
**Pterygium.** An eye disease caused by the prolonged exposure to sun and salt water.
**Puff.** A sudden increase in wind speed.
**Push-Pull Principle.** The way a sail generates power to propel a boat through the water. The wind acts to either push or pull the boat.

## ▶ R

**Reach.** Sailing with the wind coming over the side, or abeam. (One of the points of sail.)
**"Ready About."** A command made before tacking to ensure everyone is ready to tack. Syn. *"Prepare to Tack," "Ready to Tack."*
**"Ready To Tack."** See **"Ready About."**
**Reef.** To reduce the area of a sail.
**Rig.** 1. The spars, standing rigging, sails, or their configuration, which determines the type of sailboat, such as a catboat, sloop, yawl or schooner. 2. To prepare the boat for sailing.
**Right-of-Way.** A right of the stand-on vessel to maintain its course.
**Roller Furling.** A way of stowing a sail by rolling it up around its front edge (luff), like a window shade.
**Rudder.** An appendage in the water, which is used to steer or scull the boat.
**Run.** Sailing away from the wind source with the sails let out all-the-way. Syn. *Downwind, With the Wind.* (One of the points of sail.)
**Running Rigging.** The lines and associated fittings used to adjust and trim the sails, such as halyards, sheets, outhaul, downhaul, cunningham or boom vang. Syn. *Control Line, Sail Controls.*

## ▶ S

**Safety Position.** When a boat is stopped with the sails eased and flapping with the wind coming from the side.

**Sail Controls.** Ropes used to adjust and trim the sails, such as sheets, outhaul, downhaul, cunningham, boom vang. Syn. *Control Lines, Running Rigging.*

**Sail Trim.** The positioning and shape of the sails to the wind. Syn. *Set.*

**Sailor's Code.** Standards of behavior and courtesy demonstrated by sailors to other boaters.

**Scoop Recovery Method.** The method of righting a capsized boat while "scooping" a person into the cockpit as the boat rights.

**Scope.** The ratio of the length of anchor rope let out to the depth of the water.

**Scull.** 1. To propel a sailboat forward by moving the rudder and tiller side to side repeatedly. 2. To propel a boat forward by using an oar or paddle in a figure eight motion at the stern of the boat.

**Sea Breeze.** Wind resulting from cooler air over the water moving in to replace the warm air that rises over the land. Syn. *Onshore Wind.*

**Sea Conditions.** The size, shape, and frequency of the waves.

**Secure.** Fasten, put away or stow.

**Self-Bailers.** See **Bailers.**

**Self-Bailing.** The automatic draining of water from a boat through openings in the bottom or transom when sailing.

**Self-Reliance.** The ability to sail and react to changing conditions by oneself without needing outside assistance.

**Self-Rescue.** 1. The maneuver of righting a capsized boat and removing any water quickly without outside assistance. 2. An important design characteristic of a sailboat which allows it to be righted and bailed out quickly after a capsize without outside assistance.

**Set.** 1. To raise and trim a sail. 2. The direction in which a current flows.

**Shackle.** A U-shaped fitting closed with a pin and used to secure sails to lines or fittings, and lines to fittings.

**Sheet.** 1. The rope which pulls in or lets out a sail. Syn. *Line.* 2. To adjust a sail by using the sheet. Syn. *Set, Trim, Sheet In, Pull In, Take In.*

**Sheet Out.** To let out a sail. Syn. *Ease, Let Off*

**Sheeting.** Pulling in or letting out the sail. Syn. *Setting, Trimming.*

**Shrouds.** Wires which support the mast on either side. Syn. *Standing Rigging.*

**Side-to-Side Balance.** Using body weight to achieve proper angle of heel for the boat.

**S-Jibe.** A method of jibing a sailboat which results in the mainsail crossing the boat under control. The path of the boat makes an "S."

**Skipper.** See **Helmsman.**

**Slam Jibe.** See **C-Jibe.**

**Soft.** See **Light.**

**Spar.** A wooden or metal pole used to support a sail, such as a mast or boom.

**Spinnaker.** A lightweight, three-cornered balloon type sail used when sailing downwind.

**Spreader.** A support strut extending athwartships from the mast, used to support the mast and guide the shrouds from the top of the mast to the chainplates.

**Squall.** A strong wind of short duration, usually appearing suddenly and accompanied by rain.

**Stand-on Vessel.** The vessel or boat with the right-of-way.

**Standing Rigging.** The fixed wires and associated fittings used to support the mast.

**Starboard.** The right side of a boat (when looking forward).

**Stays.** Wires which support the mast fore and aft.

**Stern.** The back end of a boat.

**Stowing.** Putting away and securing sails and equipment.

## ▶ T

**Tack.** 1. To turn the bow of a sailboat through the wind or no-go zone so that the sails fill on the opposite side. Syn. *Come About.* 2. When the wind is blowing on a side of a sailboat on any of the points of sail (does not include the no-go zone), i.e., starboard tack, port tack. 3. The forward lower corner of a sail.

**Tacking.** 1. The maneuver of turning a sailboat through the no-go zone so the sails fill on the opposite tack. Syn. *Coming About.* 2. A command made by the helmsman when the tiller is moved to leeward to tack the boat. Syn. *"Coming About," "Hard a-Lee," "Helm's a-Lee."*

**Telltales.** 1. Short pieces of yarn, ribbon, thread, or tape attached to the sail which are used to show the air flow over the sail. 2. Short pieces of yarn, ribbon, thread, or tape attached to the shrouds to indicate the apparent wind direction. Syn. *Fly*.

**Tidal Current.** The horizontal movement of water caused by tides.

**Tide.** The vertical rise and fall of water caused by the gravitational forces of the moon and sun.

**Tiller.** The stick or tube which is attached to the top of a rudder that is used to turn it.

**Tiller Extension.** A stick or tube which is attached to the tiller that allows the helmsman to sit further out on the side of the boat. Syn. *Hiking Stick*.

**To Weather.** See **Upwind.**

**Topsides.** The sides of the hull above the waterline.

**Towing.** Pulling a boat with a another boat.

**Transom.** The back end of a boat which is vertical to the water.

**Traveler.** A track or bridle that controls sideways (athwartships) movement of the boom and mainsail.

**Trim.** To adjust a sail by using the sheet. Syn. *Sheet, Set*.

**Trimaran.** A boat with three parallel hulls, the center hull usually being the longest.

**True Wind.** The actual speed and direction of the wind felt when standing still.

**Turnbuckle.** A fitting used to adjust the length and tension of a shroud or stay.

**Turtling.** A capsize position with the boat turned upside down with the mast pointing down to the sea bottom.

## ▶ U

**Unrig.** Removing and/or stowing sails as well as securing halyards and sheets.

**Upwind.** In the direction of the wind source or where the wind is blowing from. Syn. *Windward, To Weather.*

**Upwind Sailing.** Sailing toward the wind source, or against the wind, with the sails pulled in. Syn. *Close-Hauled, Close Reach, On the Wind, Sailing to Weather, Sailing to Windward.*

**Upwind Side.** See **Windward Side.**

## ▶ V

**Vang.** See **Boom Vang.**

## ▶ W

**Walkover Recovery Method.** A capsize recovery method where the helmsman climbs over the windward gunwale when re-righting the boat.

**Water Reading.** Observing and assessing the wind blowing on the water surface.

**Waterline.** The line where the water surface meets the hull when the boat is floating at rest.

**Weather Helm.** The natural tendency of a sailboat to turn toward the wind (to weather), which the helmsman feels as the tiller tries to turn to leeward.

**Weather Side.** See **Windward Side.**

**Winch.** A deck-mounted drum with a handle offering mechanical advantage used to trim sheets or halyards.

**Wind Sensing.** Determining wind direction and velocity using feel, sight, and hearing.

**Windward.** In the direction toward the wind source, or where the wind is blowing from. Syn. *To Weather, Upwind.*

**Windward Side.** The side of the sailboat or sail toward the wind source. Syn. *High Side, Weather Side, Upwind Side.*

**Wing and Wing.** Sailing directly downwind with the jib and mainsail set on opposite sides of the boat to capture more wind.

**With the Wind.** See **Run**.

## Land Drills for Tacking and Jibing

It can be very helpful for a helmsman to practice his or her hand exchange and movements for tacking and jibing onshore before trying them out on the water. To practice onshore, three stools, a broom handle and length of rope can represent the boat as shown in the first figure of both drills show below.

### Tacking Drill

❶ Push tiller away from you. Facing forward, step across boat, crouch to avoid boom, shift body to opposite side.

❷ Trapping main sheet in sheet hand, reach sheet hand behind you to grab tiller.

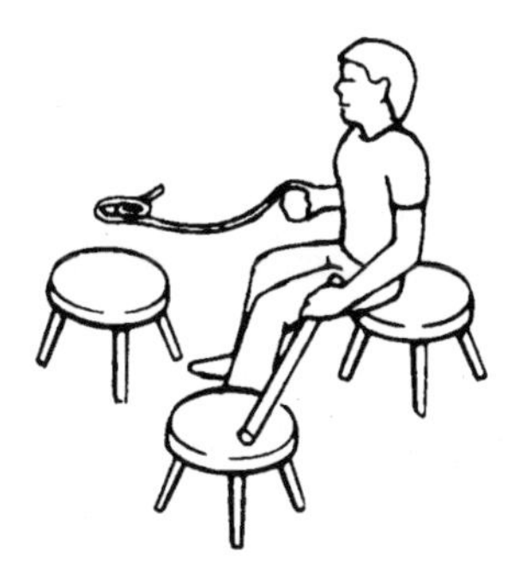

❸ Sit down on opposite side. Front hand reaches across chest to pick up sheet from tiller hand.

### Jibing Drill

❶ Preparing to jibe, grab main sheet parts, pull tiller toward you, step across boat and crouch to avoid boom as you guide it across.

❷ As boat shifts, center yourself and, facing forward, reach sheet arm behind and grasp tiller and sheet — freeing other hand.

❸ Sit down on opposite side. With new front arm, reach across chest to take sheet. Adjust sheet to retain speed on new course.

## The Nautical Chart

The nautical chart is the sailor's road map. A chart shows not only channels and buoys, but also shorelines, water depth (*soundings*), obstructions, shoals (shallow areas), positions of underwater wrecks and characteristics of the bottom. A chart also describes land references such as lighthouses, towers, other visible landmarks, and much more.

At the edge of any chart is an important note: Either "Soundings in Feet," "Soundings in Meters," or "Soundings in Fathoms," which tell you how the water depth is measured on the chart. A meter is a little over three feet, while a fathom is precisely six feet. Always check which measurement is used to indicate water depths (*soundings*) on your chart.

You will also notice the face of a compass — called a *compass rose* — printed on the chart at several locations. This allows sailors to determine, or *plot*, a compass course between locations on the chart. Most small boat sailors are close enough to land, however, that they can sail by visual references instead of compass headings.

It's great fun to study a chart of your sailing area. You'll not only learn a lot, it will help you sail with more confidence when you are out on the water.

Charts are available at most marine stores, along with numerous cruising and sailing guides to popular sailing areas that often contain charts and extra information useful to sailors.

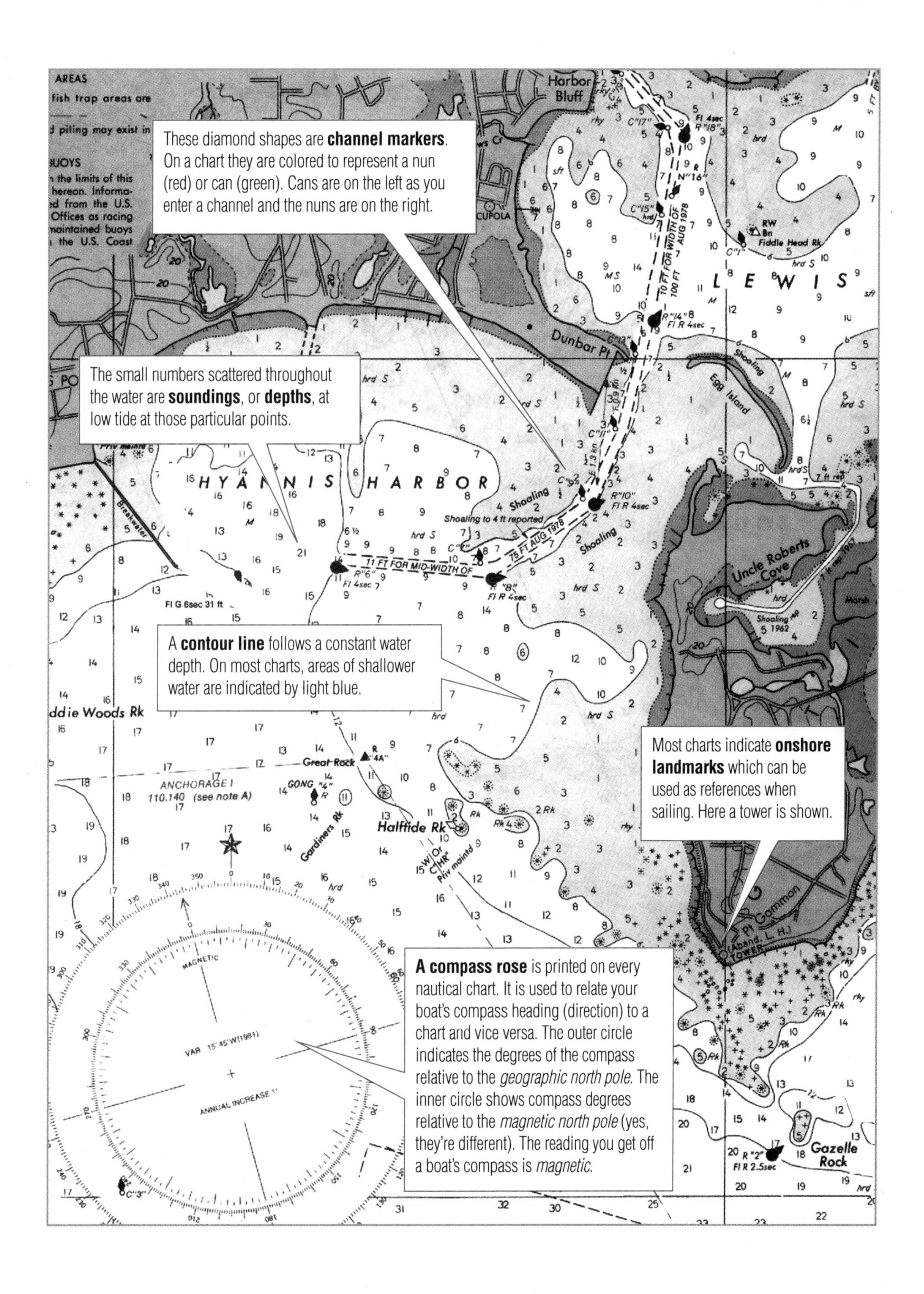
These diamond shapes are channel markers. On a chart they are colored to represent a nun (red) or can (green). Cans are on the left as you enter a channel and the nuns are on the right.
The small numbers scattered throughout the water are soundings, or depths, at low tide at those particular points.
A contour line follows a constant water depth. On most charts, areas of shallower water are indicated by light blue.
Most charts indicate onshore landmarks which can be used as references when sailing. Here a tower is shown.
A compass rose is printed on every nautical chart. It is used to relate your boat's compass heading (direction) to a chart and vice versa. The outer circle indicates the degrees of the compass relative to the geographic north pole. The inner circle shows compass degrees relative to the magnetic north pole (yes, they're different). The reading you get off a boat's compass is magnetic.
HYANNIS HARBOR
LEWIS
Harbor Bluff
Dunbar Pt
Egg Island
Uncle Roberts Cove
Great Rock
Halftide Rk
Gardiners Rk
Gazelle Rock
Fiddle Head Rk
ANCHORAGE I
CUPOLA
TOWER
MAGNETIC
VAR 15°45'W(1981)
ANNUAL INCREASE 1'

## US SAILING Certification

On the opposite page is a checklist of 19 sailing skills required for US SAILING SMALL BOAT CERTIFICATION at three different wind ranges. Using US SAILING's PROGRESSIVE SKILLS RECOGNITION SYSTEM (PSRS), you may begin earning immediate credit for the skills you have already learned. The system is self-pacing — you do not have to demonstrate all the listed skills at once.

Any currently certified US SAILING Small Boat Sailing Instructor may witness and verify listed skills by filling out and signing the appropriate wind range boxes. The verifying instructor must be US SAILING certified and *personally* observe the skill as it is performed.

You may certify at any or all three wind speed ranges:
- ▶ Light Air (5-9 mph)
- ▶ Medium Air (10-15 mph)
- ▶ Heavy Air (16+ mph)

You must satisfactorily pass all 19 skills in a wind range to be certified at that level. You receive credit automatically for any skill at a lower wind speed range by completing that skill requirement at a higher wind range. Once you have completed all of the skill requirements in any wind range, you are eligible for certification at that level. You may upgrade to a higher wind speed certification at any time by demonstrating sailing skills at the desired wind speed. Some skills have no wind speed requirement (for instance KNOTS/LINES) and need not be repeated for upgrades.

Each skill is separately evaluated on a simple pass/fail basis. Each boathandling maneuver must be performed satisfactorily in at least two out of three consecutive attempts. Every element in multi-part skills must be satisfied in order to pass that skill (no partial credits). Skills may be retested at any time, as many times as necessary. No coaching or assistance is permitted during testing.

When you have completed all of the skills in a given wind range and you are ready to apply for certification, fill out a certification application form (available from your US SAILING certified instructor) and mail it with this record to US SAILING. US SAILING membership is required to obtain certification, but not for skill verification. If you are not already a US SAILING member, you may join when applying for certification.

*All are welcome!*

The US SAILING
<u>*SAILOR CERTIFICATION SYSTEM*</u>

**SMALL BOAT SAILOR**

for dinghies, keel and centerboard daysailers and catamarans

*CERTIFICATION LEVELS:*

- ▶ ***Light Air*** (5-9 mph)
- ▶ ***Medium Air*** (10-15 mph)
- ▶ ***Heavy Air*** (16+ mph)

**KEELBOAT SAILOR**

for larger sailboats with keels

*CERTIFICATION LEVELS:*

▶ ***Basic Keelboat***
18-30 ft. sloops with tiller steering (no prerequisite)

▶ ***Basic Cruising***
23-35 ft. sloops with auxiliary power (prerequisite: *Basic Keelboat*)

▶ ***Bareboat Cruising***
30-45 ft. auxiliary sloops with wheel steering
(prerequisite: *Basic Cruising*)

▶ ***Coastal Navigation***
(no prerequisite)

▶ ***Coastal Passage Making***
30-50 ft.+ auxiliary sailboats
(prerequisites: *Bareboat Cruising* and *Coastal Navigation*)

▶ ***Celestial Navigation***
(prerequisite: *Coastal Navigation*)

▶ ***Offshore Passage Making***
35 ft.+ auxiliary sailboats
(prerequisites: *Coastal Passage Making and Celestial Navigation*)

| Skill | Standard |
|---|---|
| **1 Wind Direction** | |
| Identify 3 wind indicators | |
| Identify wind direction | *within a few degrees* |
| **2 Rigging** | |
| Drain Plugs | *installed tightly and securely* |
| Rudder, centerboard/daggerboard | *properly rigged* |
| Rig sails | *secure at all attachment points, adequate out-haul tension* |
| Raise sails | *bow into wind, fully raised, halyards secure* |
| **3 Knots / Lines** | |
| Cleat hitch | *using standard deck cleat* |
| Coiling | *as for halyards, secured* |
| Figure-8 | *correctly formed, close to end of line* |
| Bowline | *correctly formed around post, ring or rail* |
| 2 half hitches | *correctly formed around post, ring or rail* |
| **4 Departure** | |
| Describe strategy | *a safe and reasonable plan for the circumstances allowing for wind direction, point of sail, current, obstructions, etc.* |
| Execution | *successfully carry out above plan* |
| **5 Steering** | |
| Straight course | *holding a steady course for at least one full minute toward a designated target.* |
| Proper tiller grasp | *constant contact, never let go* |
| Seating placement | *windward side, ahead of tiller, inboard/outboard as appropriate for heel* |
| **6 Stopping / Starting** | |
| Full luff | *entire sail luffing* |
| Complete stop | *exhausting all momentum* |
| Trim in until full and by | *full sails and steerage way* |
| **7 Tacking** | |
| Steering | *smooth, steady turn, appropriate speed, without pause or hesitation, ending on a new course* |
| Switch sides | *windward to windward, appropriate timing* |
| Hand exchange | *behind back, constant contact* |
| **8 Sail Trim** | |
| Appropriate sheeting for: | |
| Beating | *close-hauled* |
| Reaching | *verge of a luff* |
| Running | *out all-the-way* |
| **9 Safety Position** | |
| Demonstrate safety position | *close reach, full luff: all sails including leeches* |
| | *full stop* |
| **10 Points of Sail** | |
| Demonstrate: | |
| Beating | |
| Close reach | *correct heading for each, on either tack* |
| Beam reach | *on command* |
| Broad reach | |
| Running | |

| Skill | Standard |
|---|---|
| **11 Jibing** | |
| Commands | *"Prepare to jibe," "Jibe ho," or equivalent* |
| Controlled jibe | *pre-trimmed mainsail, not a flying jibe* |
| Appropriate turn | *no pauses or round-ups* |
| Switch sides | *on windward side as soon as sail fills* |
| Sail trim | *retrim promptly to verge of a luff* |
| **12 Capsize Recovery** | |
| Scoop method (doublehanded) requiring a partner and a self-rescuing boat | *scoop partner, then be scooped* |
| Solo righting (singlehanded) | *traditional or stepover acceptable, unassisted* |
| Catamaran righting (if applicable) | *successful demonstration* |
| **13 Overboard Recovery** | |
| Appropriate turn | *jibe in light air, tack in stronger wind* |
| Approach to safety position for pick-up | *close reach, full luff, correct approach angle* |
| Close proximity | *within reach, full stop* |
| Boarding assistance (simulated) | *retrieve "victim" (float or fender)* |
| **14 Landing** | |
| Land at a dock or beach | *within a boatlength of a prescribed spot* |
| | *appropriate approach angle for conditions* |
| | *decelerate with control to a full luff* |
| | *glide to a gentle stop, no artificial braking, main backing or grabbing onto dock* |
| **15 Getting Out of Irons** | |
| Prescribe tack | *select starboard or port before beginning* |
| Back sails | *jib to desired windward side, main to leeward* |
| Tiller position | *toward desired new heading when backing* |
| **16 Weight Placement / Hull Trim** | |
| Appropriate seating | *proper fore and aft hull trim* |
| | *inboard or outboard for suitable trim* |
| **17 Unrig / Shipshape** | |
| Lower, flake / furl sails | *neat, even folds, seams parallel, secured* |
| Secure lines, rigging, gear | *running rigging taut and secure, neat, everything in place, all gear stowed* |
| Drain / bail all water | *hull empty, cockpit dry* |
| Clean | *as clean or cleaner than you found it* |
| **18 Navigation Rules** | |
| Describe right-of-way on opposite tacks, same tack, overtaking: | *starboard, leeward, overtaken are stand-on* |
| Sail vs. power | *boats under sail stand-on* |
| (exception) | *large ships in narrow channels* |
| Sail vs. muscle power | *yield to rowing or paddling vessels* |
| **19 Upwind Sailing** | |
| Demonstrate: | |
| Consistent helmsmanship without excessive luffing or falling off | |
| Finding a layline without excessive overstanding or pinching | |
| Sail trim: close-hauled | |
| Hull trim: moderate heel, balanced fore / aft | |

# Learning more...

## From US SAILING

Since 1897 the United States Sailing Association (US SAILING) has provided support for American sailors at all levels of sailing — in all kinds of sailboats. The primary objective of its Training Program is to provide a national standard of quality instruction for all people learning to sail. The US SAILING Certification System includes a series of coursebooks including *Start Sailing Right!* (see right), a program of student certifications and an extensive educational and training program for instructors. It's one of the world's most highly developed and effective national training systems for students and sailing instructors, and is recognized nationally and internationally.

US SAILING is a non-profit organization and the official National Governing Body of Sailing as designated by the U.S. Congress in the Amateur Sports Act. It has national Training Programs for sailors in dinghies, windsurfers, multihulls and keelboats. It is also the official representative to the International Sailing Federation (ISAF). The US SAILING Certification System is designed to develop safe, responsible and confident sailors who meet specific performance and knowledge standards.

For more information on membership, training programs or course materials (see right) contact:

US SAILING
P.O. Box 1260
15 Maritime Drive
Portsmouth, RI 02871-6015
401-683-0800 Fax: 683-0840
URL: http:/www.olyc.com.ussailing

## From the American Red Cross

For more help and information from the American Red Cross on swimming and water safety, lifeguarding, small craft safety, first aid, CPR, HIV/AIDS, and caregiving contact:

American Red Cross - National Headquarters
Health and Safety Services
8111 Gatehouse Rd., 6th floor
Falls Church, VA 22042
(703) 206-7180 URL: http://www.redcross.org

### Basic Keelboat

A highly visual, intuitive approach using proven methods to get new sailors sailing fast! Covers basic sailing concepts, boathandling, docking, anchoring, safety, basic navigation and more. 100p.

### Basic Cruising

An introduction to sailing larger boats. Covers cruising systems, maneuvering under power, anchoring, basic piloting, weather, safety & emergency procedures, radio communication and more. 130p.

### Bareboat Cruising

Prepares sailors for the rewards of charter cruising. Covers planning, provisioning, cruising systems, protocols and customs, navigation, health & emergencies and much more. A must for those considering their first charter. 120p.

### Coastal Navigation

A breakthrough learning tool that will help you develop sound coastal navigation skills clearly and quickly. Covers basic piloting, electronics, dead reckoning, tides & currents and passage making. 120p.